Swimming Against the Tide

Lisa Milner

Swimming Against the Tide
A Biography of Freda Brown

G
P

Swimming Against the Tide: A Biography of Freda Brown
ISBN 978 1 76041 338 5
Copyright © Lisa Milner 2017

First published 2017 by
GINNINDERRA PRESS
PO Box 3461 Port Adelaide 5015
www.ginninderrapress.com.au

Contents

Abbreviations

ACTU	Australian Council of Trade Unions
ACU	Association for Communist Unity
AICD	Association for International Cooperation and Disarmament
AJA	Australian Journalists' Association
ALLY	Australian Labor League of Youth
ALP	Australian Labor Party
APC	Australian Peace Council
ASIO	Australian Security and Intelligence Organisation
BPP	Black Panther Party
BWIU	Building Workers' Industrial Union
CARP	Campaign Against Rising Prices
CC	Central Council of the Communist Party of Australia
CFMEU	Construction, Forestry, Mining and Energy Union
CPA	Communist Party of Australia
CPGB	Communist Party of Great Britain
CPSU	Communist Party of the Soviet Union
DFD	Democratic Women's League of Germany
DPRK	Democratic People's Republic of Korea
ECOSOC	United Nations Economic and Social Council
EYL	Eureka Youth League
GDR	German Democratic Republic
ICW	International Council of Women
ICY	International Co-operation Year, 1975
IWD	International Women's Day, 8 March
IWW	Industrial Workers of the World
IWY	International Women's Year, 1975

IYP	International Year of Peace, 1986
IYC	International Year of the Child, 1979
NGO	Non-governmental organisation
NHA	New Housewives' Association
NT	New Theatre League
PLO	Palestine Liberation Organisation
SOS	Save Our Sons movement
SPA	Socialist Party of Australia
TLC	Trades and Labor Council
TUERC	Trade Union Education and Research Centre
UAW	Union of Australian Women
UN	United Nations
UNAA	United Nations Association of Australia
UNESCO	United Nations Educational, Scientific and Cultural Organisation
UWM	Unemployed Workers' Movement
WAC	Workers' Arts Club
WEA	Workers' Educational Association
WEL	Women's Electoral Lobby
WFTU	World Federation of Trade Unions
WIDF	Women's International Democratic Federation
WILPF	Women's International League for Peace and Freedom
WIR	Workers' International Relief
WPC	World Peace Council
WREE	Women for Racial and Economic Equality
WSP	Women Strike for Peace
YSL	Young Socialist League

Introduction

Some years ago I came across some of the work that a long-term Bondi resident, Freda Brown, had done within women's and left-wing organisations, and learnt about the trajectory of her life story, from Sydney to the world stage. As a labour historian and political activist two generations after Freda's, I was drawn to investigating Freda's story, which is fascinating. As a communist, and in particular as an Australian feminist working before the second wave of more well-known women like Germaine Greer, like many others Freda has been written out of history – although she was the subject of a half-hour television program, *Australian Biography*, which began my journey to unearth her life story.

I discovered Freda's story a couple of years after she had died, and contacted her daughter, Senator Lee Rhiannon. With the generous cooperation of Lee and her family, I spent the next years working within and outside Australia, tracing Freda's activism, interviewing colleagues, and writing her story. I learnt how much Freda's story deserved to be told, to provoke awareness of the value of her work within Australia and throughout the world.

Freda Brown was a political activist in the women's, peace, and anti-apartheid movements, both in Australia and overseas. A passionate believer in equality, she occupied her busy life with action and organisation. While some of her greatest achievements can be seen in her work in helping to establish and lead pioneering women's organisations, she travelled widely also in the service of political, peace and anti-racism causes. She was a widely respected activist and led an absorbing and very busy life with her political work both in Australia and overseas. She also worked as a journalist, political party organiser and theatre director. I wrote this biography to honour Freda's life as a feminist organiser and activist as well as wife and mother: around her political activity, she raised a daughter, cared for grandchildren and great-grandchildren, and nursed her husband through years of Alzheimer's disease.

Freda never had the inclination to write her memoirs, unlike some prominent Australian communists, and although some histories (in particular, some biographies of her comrades) briefly mention her, there is no detailed work on her life. Her work was generally unacknowledged, and during the time of my research and writing, I found very few people outside Freda's family who had known of her achievements – as a communist, and in particular as a woman communist, like others she has been written out of history.

Right from her beginning, all of the periods of Freda's life were connected through the thread of political activism. She was born into a working-class family in inner city Sydney in 1919. The family were poor during the Depression, and Freda's earliest memories are those of poverty and want. She didn't feel envious of rich people, but she 'felt more resentful of a society that puts us in this position'. The Lewises weren't, in fact, 'an ordinary working-class family', as Freda suggested in an interview many decades later. Her father was an organiser for the Industrial Workers of the World, a 'Wobbly', and led an active political life. During Freda's childhood, he was in and out of jail for his political activity, speaking at the Sydney Domain in defence of other activists, and as a conscientious objector. Freda remembered her father as an important model for her life in politics: she said, 'he always encouraged me as a woman to feel that I can do everything' a man could. She grew up in a very close and loving family.

The trajectory of Freda's life changed overnight when, at seventeen, she went to a performance of Clifford Odets' anti-Nazi resistance play *Till the Day I Die* at Sydney's left-wing New Theatre. The ideas in that play – as well as the censorship the Australian government applied to it – sparked her whole interest in this life of ideas and action, of often fighting against a tide of apathy and, during the Cold War, anti-communism. As well as dedicating herself to organisational and publicity work with the New Theatre, she worked there acting, producing and directing over her years with the group. One of the most important legacies that this part of her life gave her was a great flair for public speaking.

This led her into a second, connected, life: she soon joined the Communist Party of Australia (CPA), at a time when only about 200 of the 4,000 party members throughout the country were women, saying it was the impact of the theatre that led her to join the party. Freda served on the CPA's Central Committee for nearly 30 years, and for a number of years also worked full-time for the party. She had a prolific speaking career, travelling far and wide across Australia, to sell war bonds, to speak for the Yes vote for the referendum on post-war reconstruction and democratic rights, and to support the party's policies and election candidates. She was described as 'young, brilliant and enthusiastic', and 'one of the most talented of Australia's Communist women leaders', and she stood as a CPA candidate in two elections.

During her time in the New Theatre, she met Bill Brown, then an electrician. In their growing relationship, Freda opened up a political world to Bill that he'd not encountered before, and soon she recruited him into the CPA. They married in 1943, and were together until Bill's death in 1992. Freda encouraged Bill to follow his dream of writing, and he became a journalist and author as well as a full-time functionary for the party. Freda and Bill constantly supported each other in their work. In 1951, their daughter Lee was born. Family was always very important to Freda, and she took great joy from Lee, and her grandchildren and great-grandchildren.

At the end of the war, Freda had joined the New Housewives' Association, then the significant popular party group for women. There she joined forces with other women to combat grassroots post-war issues including ever-increasing prices, black-marketing, and attacks on women's wages. She rose from an ordinary member to become the national secretary in 1950, when Menzies' Communist Party Dissolution Act banned the association.

The succeeding group, the Union of Australian Women (UAW), was to embrace much of Freda's Australian work for the next four decades, when she served as national secretary and national president, and later, in honorary executive roles. The UAW campaigned on issues that affected women in Australia as well as internationally: peace, equal pay, opposition to conscription, children's and indigenous rights, and solidarity with women all over the world. Freda said, 'I think it played a very valuable role in organising women, in contributing to the peace struggle and in getting women out on the streets, because we were the first ones to get women out on to the streets. It wasn't easy in those days; we were the only women demonstrating.' The UAW's role in pioneering mid-century feminist political action cannot be overestimated, particularly during the Cold War 1950s when Australian women (particularly those on the left) took up very little political space. Along with her UAW comrades, Freda could be seen protesting throughout Sydney on diverse issues from lower meat prices to international peace campaigns. Along with this work, her rise through the CPA as a full-time functionary and well-known speaker was expanding her ambitions. Her work in this period runs counter to the stereotypical view of Australian women of the times, when post-war conservatism still defined women's roles in very traditional ways.

Because her work with the CPA had started taking her overseas, she began working with the Women's International Democratic Federation (WIDF) in Berlin as a UAW representative. Francisca de Haan, the leading scholar on the organisation, has described WIDF as 'the largest and definitely one of the most influential international women's organisations of the post-1945 era' and, through its national affiliate organisations, it had 200 million members in 1963, when WIDF executives elected Freda to the bureau as national secretary. Her passion for politics, for working tirelessly for equality and peace, had led her far from the streets of Erskineville to the world stage.

Freda rose through the ranks very quickly. By the next year, the WIDF executive elected her as a vice-president, and by 1975, she became president, a role she held until 1990. She worked as a tireless activist of an older generation during a period when second-wave feminism was beginning to flourish, and when the organisation's newer work, on women in Asia and Africa and anti-racism issues, stood along with more enduring campaigns around peace, women's and children's rights. Freda remembered her work with WIDF as 'the richest experience' of her life. During this time, she was overseas in many trips every year, when she worked at the WIDF headquarters in Berlin, organised and attended conferences at the United Nations, and toured and met members of the organisation on every continent. She worked in Korea, Vietnam, Cambodia and Nicaragua at the height of those countries' conflicts, Cuba, Brazil and Mexico, and just about every country in Europe and Asia, including north of the Arctic Circle. She worked in newly emerging independent African nations, and travelled to the Sabra and Shatila Palestine refugee camps just days after the 1982 slaughter. She worked with Indira Gandhi, Hortensia Allende, Fidel Castro, Angela Davis, Nikita Khrushchev, the Dalai Lama and other world leaders and activists, particularly campaigners for women's rights and world peace.

As WIDF president, Freda was instrumental in lobbying the United Nations on women's issues. Most importantly, she was successful in instigating the UN to establish 1975 as International Women's Year, an achievement that had long-lasting effects in many nations. She was president of the World Congress for International Women's Year and president of the UN Decade for Women Committee. She also travelled widely as vice-president of the WPC. She received the Lenin Peace Prize (the Soviet Union's equivalent to the Nobel Peace Prize), the Clara Zetkin Medal, the Anna Betancourt Medal, and the Order of Friendship.

By 1988, Bill's health was failing and doctors diagnosed him with Alzheimer's disease. Freda, at 70, gave up her overseas work and travel commitments to care for him, and she retired as WIDF president in

1991. Bill died in 1992 but Freda was never the retiring type, and said, 'I have my own personal campaign at the moment, and that is to change the image of "old".' As well as having more time to spend with her family, she continued to work with the UAW, alongside Australian organisations supporting older people. In addition, she was still speaking at protest rallies. Freda died in 2009, and her death certificate lists her usual occupation as political activist.

I never met Freda, but began to uncover her achievements a few years after her death. An ASIO operative who worked alongside Freda for years wrote that, alongside her dedication to her work and her unswerving adherence to the broader principles of communism, Freda was 'a devoted wife and mother'. She spent her life balancing her two passions, as a politically astute global activist completely dedicated to her causes, and a loving wife, mother and grandmother whose life partner supported her unconditionally in her work. Her story highlights the work that Freda did to promote equality and human rights for women all over the world. It shows the importance of networking within political and activist organisations; of being true to yourself; and of staying grounded within your family.

This biography is a long-overdue acknowledgement of the pioneering role Freda played at a time when second-generation feminism was decades away. At a time when women were not supposed to want anything more than being a wife and mother, Freda combined career and family successfully for decades, believed passionately in equality and peace, and fought for the rights of people all over the world. She was a leading member of the CPA long after many had left it, and remained a socialist all her life, preferring to hold her personal values rather than be fashionable. Behind Freda's story lie much bigger cultural, social and political ones: the flowering of alternative political ideas, the development of second-wave feminism, the sexual revolution and the changing nature of reproductive rights, and the blossoming of decolonisation and globalisation. Her legacy underlines the lives of many of us in the 21st century.

In constructing this version of Freda's life, I've fictionalised a few key points amongst the biographical detail, chronologically arranged, and included some extra material such as poems written by Freda and Bill. The afterword provides some context of my quest to find Freda.

1

Beginnings, the Theatre and the Party: 1919–1944

Face masks and jam jars

1919, the year of Freda's birth, was a time of hesitant recovery from World War I, poor living conditions for many Australians, and instability. In many ways, it was a sad year. Prime Minister Billy Hughes had gone to the Paris Peace Conference to take part in the Versailles Treaty discussions, securing the German colony of New Guinea; on his homecoming from Paris, returned soldiers carried the Little Digger down Sydney's George Street on their shoulders. Unlike their prime minister, though, soldiers returned from Europe with a different legacy: injuries, shell shock and a horrific influenza pandemic. The Spanish flu infected around two-fifths of Australians and brought 15,000 deaths. The NSW government proclaimed an official infection on 28 January 1919, and through that year public life came to a standstill as schools, libraries, hotels, racecourses and cinemas closed. The awful threat of the flu throughout Sydney even cancelled that year's Royal Easter Show. Protective face masks and inoculations were important for everyone then. In that cold month of June, when Freda was born, more than a thousand flu cases a week were being admitted to Sydney hospitals.

For ordinary people, even if you survived the flu, 1919 wasn't a hopeful time to be born in Australia. The economy was faltering into a recession, with high inflation fuelled by wartime scarcity. In March, the Red Flag Riot saw pitched battles of 8,000 people, socialists and

Russian immigrants clashing with returned soldiers and mounted police on the streets of Brisbane. Industrial action in the immediate post-war period was high, with strikes in the mining and maritime industries. Left-led trade unions, taking inspiration from the Russian Revolution of 1917, led a massive wave of post-war industrial strikes. The defeat of the strikes saw 100,000 Australians out of work – including many of the men who had survived the Great War. Amidst this economic uncertainty, political fervour and industrial turmoil, the following year saw the formation of the Communist Party of Australia (CPA), an organisation dedicated to political and social change. Many Australians believed that communism offered a solution to the problems of Australia and the world, and this shiny optimism would be very much at the heart of Freda's life.

Australian culture during this period had few highlights. The White Australia policy was still working to keep the country predominantly white and British. Early closing in pubs, introduced as a temporary wartime measure in 1916, had been made permanent in 1919, and the six o'clock swill was to stay as a part of Australian life for decades. Local life was immortalised as Raymond Longford's evocative film *The Sentimental Bloke* appeared on Australian cinema screens in September. As well as describing the hard times and romantic dreams of the larrikin Bill and his sweetheart Doreen, the film documents the conditions of working-class life in inner-city Sydney. Doreen worked at the Henry Jones IXL jam and preserves factory in Golden Grove, sticking labels on jars of pickles. Sharing Golden Grove's dark lanes and shady characters a few miles away, Erskineville regarded itself as part of the inner city. In 1919, the densely populated suburb housed 7,750 people in just 1,650 houses. Its mayor regarded it as 'the most congested suburb in NSW, probably in the whole of Australia'.[1] It was very much a slum area and, with only seven miles of paved streets for the 166-acre suburb, was undeveloped. Life in Erskineville was busy and cramped: large families in modest homes close to their neighbours, fringed with dank alleys and the soot of the railway line fallout in the air; SP bookies at the Imperial Hotel, teaching the locals how to gamble; stern black-garbed nuns up at St Patrick's school; the rabbitoh and the coal man; lighting the copper for a hot bath; the burning smell of the Newman Street tannery and the chlorine of the pottery kilns and the brickworks; cricket and billy carts in the lanes; a furious spitting bonfire on cracker night.

The great bond of the family

Erskineville had a majority of left-wing working-class voters, and the most incandescent political group in the area was the Industrial Workers of the World (IWW), also known as the Wobblies. The Australian chapter of this international movement had begun in 1907, but by December 1916, Prime Minister Billy Hughes had succeeded in having the Wobblies declared illegal; however, a great number of its members continued their activities and protests, including Freda's father, Ben Lewis.

By the time Freda was born in Erskineville, in the family home at 46 Erskineville Road, Benjamin Montague Centennial Lewis (1877–1947) was a confirmed and active Wobbly. The fourth in a family of nine children, Ben was born in Narrabri to Maurice and Miriam (née Audet) Lewis in a Jewish (English and Polish) family.[2] Maurice ran the Narrabri newsagency for a time, and later the family moved to Sydney. When he was 14, Ben apprenticed himself to a signwriter, and with his trade worked for a circus, and then later set up his own business in Erskineville. When the Lewises moved to inner-city Sydney, Ben loved the life knocking about, and was known as the king of the kids in his teenage years.[3]

Handsome Ben was tall and slim. A family photo shows him in a fine three-piece suit and bowler hat, his head confidently cocked to one side; proud, smiling, sceptical. He was a skilled orator and witty conversationalist, and he had developed his political beliefs growing up in Sydney through the hard times of the *fin de siècle*. Realising that the only way to fight against misery and inequality was to organise,

Ben campaigned fiercely against many things: police violence, discrimination against the unemployed, and the government's moves to introduce conscription. As a conscientious objector in World War I, he did jail time for his beliefs. Ben fought against the capitalist system and inequality more generally, whether it was by class or gender. Sydney police prosecuted him for 'using abusive language' with a 'seditious' and 'revolutionary tone' as a Domain Sunday speaker, when he had dared to talk of the 'overthrow of the present system of the capitalist class'.[4] His views drew him to the Wobblies' causes, and Ben became secretary of the IWW's Release and Defence Committee, and organisations of the International Industrial Unions. The cut and thrust of activist organisations suited him, and he took on other roles, as secretary of the Social Democratic League, treasurer of the Anti-Conscription League, and member of the Free Speech Committee of NSW.

In the year before Freda was born, Ben and his dissident comrades had called for the release of 12 IWW men who were in jail for seditious conspiracy. Following the Royal Commission, Ben had published a report of the commissioner's accusation of sedition, which Ben termed 'a vile capitalist conspiracy'.[5] In response to the campaign, the NSW Labor government ordered a second Royal Commission. As a result of this second commission, the IWW Twelve were eventually released.

Freda remembered her father as 'very much a rebel. He always encouraged me as a woman to feel that I can do everything' a man could,[6] and taught her 'that a woman should regard herself as equal with men'.[7] He used to say to her, 'you can do anything'. Perhaps because she was the first child in the family, perhaps because she was a girl, Freda thought she was 'the apple of his eye'.[8]

Freda's mother, Florence Mary Munroe (1889–24 August 1971), was a milliner before her marriage to Ben on 19 June 1918, and it was opposites attracting, Flo's quiet strength balancing Ben's articulate passions. Freda once said she thought her mother was 'very typical of what a woman was supposed to be', not a revolutionary in any sense, and Freda didn't think she took after Flo at all. Flo was always very well dressed, a proper lady, her sad eyes occasionally twinkling. Flo gave up her millinery work as soon as she and Ben married, and got the family through the tough times of the Depression. Rae, Freda's brother, said of Flo, 'I have forever been surrounded by very strong women, starting with my mother, who was strong in a quiet way. She got everything done but in a quiet way. For example, if my father or brother or I went out to play cricket, we would be home on the dot at five o'clock because that's when dinner would be on the table.'[9] Freda remembers Flo as a typical housewife, solid as a rock, 'very shy, very retiring', who wasn't keen on Ben's fervent activism; Freda believed that she resented it, as it meant that 'Dad was always out at meetings'.[10] She didn't take part in the political discussions that filled the Erskineville home, didn't go to Ben's meetings, didn't support the Wobblies.

Almost a year after Ben and Flo married, Freda was born, on 9 June 1919. Her Yiddish middle name, Yetta, comes from that of an aunt, one of Ben's older sisters. Freda was mostly a happy girl growing up in Erskineville. Although they never had much food, she thrived in the warmth of Ben's love of life and knowledge, and, despite the miseries of the Depression, in her mother's care at home. A dog-eared photo shows Freda, about two, with blonde ringlet curls and a pin-tucked dress, looking very seriously at the camera. Another, later pose shows that throughout her youth Flo had Freda's hair cut in a straight bob that emphasised her serious expression.

There were two more children born into the Lewis family. Leon (1923–1984) started his working life with his father as a signwriter, and became, like Ben, a socialist. Later, as a wharfie, he was active in the Sydney branch of the Waterside Workers Federation. He contributed artwork on banners and posters, particularly for May Day floats and displays, and more than a few old lefties remember him for his May Day skits (a talent for public performance runs in the family).

Rae (b. 1925) was the youngest of the family and became a wharfie alongside Leon. Rae took after his dad, with a handsome smile, strong physique, and curly hair. The family were very close; Freda recalls the 'great bond' of the family: 'we were together, we fought and played and loved each other, and there's a tremendous…bond'.[11] They spent so much time at the beaches on Sydney's southern coast: Bondi, Coogee, and Clovelly. Wiley's Baths at Coogee was a favourite swimming place. Everyone in the family loved being on the beach and swimming, and would often cross town on the trams to Bondi and Bronte; when times were tough they often used to walk the six miles to the beach from Erskineville. The cleansing surf of Bondi washed away the inner-city grime and class-ridden poverty of home: everyone was equal in the breakers, and on the baking blonde sands of Bondi.

Freda described the Lewises as 'an ordinary working-class family'.[12] This was a time when Erskineville was solidly working-class, very different to the gentrified district it became a hundred years later. The area was safe, however, and the family never felt the need to lock the house. Like most homes in Erskineville in those times, there was no running water indoors, and the NSW government had earmarked the suburb to be the first in a planned series of slum clearances. Ben had won the state lottery, and used his £5,000 prize to set up a signwriting business, close by at King Street in Newtown. He also did building and renovating work, advertising his skills as painting, paperhanging, signwriting, decorative work and house repairing. The brass plate on the house, and the ads that Ben placed in the *Sydney Morning Herald* (*SMH*), proclaimed 'No job too large, none too small, none too far away'.[13]

From around 1929, however, with the effects of the Wall Street crash reaching Sydney, like many other Depression breadwinners Ben was unable to find secure work – he didn't have a steady job for around 10 years. He had to swallow his pride and go on the dole. He also joined the communist-led Unemployed Workers' Movement (UWM) when it formed in 1930 and became an active member, organising, writing pamphlets, giving speeches and entertaining other unemployed people. Freda remembered Ben as a reader, a 'very erudite' man, self-taught and hungry for knowledge.[14] He would spend hours talking with his children, explaining the world to them, and loved to read his beloved encyclopaedias: a family joke repeated the stories of Ben taking his *Encyclopaedia Britannica* into the toilet with him to read. His outgoing nature and easy way of talking was passed down to Freda and the boys. Their house had one bedroom upstairs, with a veranda. Freda and the two boys slept on the veranda, and Ben and Flo slept in the bedroom. The kids would lie in bed at night listening to Ben recite Shakespeare and poetry to Flo inside. Although Christmas and Cracker Night were still the big events for kids in Erskineville, the Lewises celebrated other special days too: the anniversary of the Russian Revolution, and International Women's Day. With these interests, they certainly were not an 'ordinary working-class family'.

One of their neighbours, Grace Schwebel, was three years older than Freda. Grace recalls the Lewis family:

> There was a well-known family around there, the Lewis family – they were printers and signwriters and that – and my young cousins they used to play with the kids in there…still now I respect them and I respected them then but I wasn't very aware of the significance of what they were doing. My cousins played with the boy Lewises, Rae and Leon Lewis, and then the daughter was called Freda Brown – Freda, she eventually became well known as Freda Brown. You might have heard of Freda Brown talked about. Freda Brown was well known, eventually well known as a militant Communist and that. So my cousins, we would all go around there to sing in the Lewis' house. They lived in this beautiful big freestanding house in Erskineville Road just around the corner from where my auntie lived and while a lot of people were going off to church and all the rest of it we would go over there and they would have these songs and workers' songs and you'd go in there singing 'The Workers of the World Unite' and 'Red Flag' and the 'Internationale' and all that sort of stuff… I just went there because I was involved with my cousins and that's where I first met Freda Brown who was Freda Lewis for many, many years as her maiden name.[15]

Like many people their age, growing up through the Depression had a big impact on Freda and the boys; in 1932, at the height of national unemployment at 30 per cent, things were so bad that Ben had to sell his beloved *Encyclopaedia Britannica* set.[16] Like many people living through the Depression, Ben felt a great sense of shame about having no work, and a loss of pride about going on the dole. Freda said that 'because we were very poor, everything was a struggle – to get a uniform, to get books'.[17] Later, Freda said that she didn't feel envious of rich people, but she 'felt more resentful of a society that puts us in this position'.[18] There were times when food was scarce and the Lewises were hungry. Ben's parents would visit every month or so and bring some fruit. Freda remembers being sent up to the shops to ask for very cheap vegetables. This period of Freda's young life was to be formative in the development of her political outlook. She said that 'when I was very young the idea of war, or that people were hungry and suffering, really stirred me up'.[19]

One memory she had from her childhood stayed with her for many years:

> …this was very vivid in my mind, I preferred to go in rags to wear [my old] clothing, because [if you wore the clothing issued] everyone then knew you were on the dole. And I had these horrible shoes, which Dad had got, which didn't fit me and hurt me, so I wouldn't wear them. But I was outside once and my shoes had holes in them, ordinary shoes and I'd cut out paper soles, which I stuck in – and I had them upside down, putting blacking on the bottom, you see. And Dad came out, he said 'What are you doing?' And I said to him, 'I've got holes in my shoes and I put cut out paper' and I went into the kitchen and – I can see this vividly – that he was sitting there with tears in his eyes, explaining it to my mother. And you know it hadn't occurred to me, the emotion in your parent for the first time was something that I realised, that it was a pain to him to see what I was going through. But it was just that I needed these shoes, I preferred them to the others. It was a new emotion for me, the experience.

Freda's childhood, then, was not a carefree one. Her early experiences of poverty, explained by her father to her and the boys as the outcomes of rampant capitalism, clearly shaped her political views for her whole life. The Lewises weren't, in fact, 'an ordinary working-class family': number 46 was a home of non-stop political conversations. Ben held meetings of the UWM at home, and talked with his children about the war, about conscription, about politics. Freda soaked up Ben's political convictions, his activism, and his belief that women could do anything they chose. Ben's active and enquiring approach to life, and particularly to politics, had 'had a very, very big impact' on Freda, she believed, and it was absolutely an early model for Freda.[20] She took up the internationalism of her father's IWW work, as well as his anti-conscription stance.[21] He would sometimes take his young daughter with him to demonstrations in the Depression days, and took her on the Sydney May Day march when she was just six.[22] Freda remembered an unemployed people's demonstration that swept into Martin Place. Ben showed her the large Sydney sandstone buildings housing the financial rulers of the country, and said to her, 'remember, the walls of this bank are not made of bricks and cement, but out of the bones and blood of workers'.[23] And when she was 16, Ben introduced her to the possibilities that women in the 20th century could look to; he took her to an International Women's Day luncheon at the Progressive Housewives' Association.[24] It was at this gathering that leading communist figure Jean Devanny made a stirring speech and argued that 'women had the right to enjoy sex as much as men did', shocking most of her audience.[25] Perhaps anticipating the later work of Freda, Devanny wrote that

> it is by getting together, by discussion and collective decision, that the units of any force are enabled to convert energy and desire into organisation, which alone gets us anywhere... International Women's Day is one of the roots of the tree which, full grown, will put an end to the world in which the majority of women are victims of fear.[26]

Where other parents passed on silver teapots and cuckoo clocks to the next generation, Ben bequeathed the values of equality and peace to his three children, as well as the passions to keep fighting for them. Freda said that it was 'fairly natural' that 'the rise of fascism had a deep impact on me'.[27] In particular, she remembered that her father 'raised us to have a very deep respect for the Soviet Union…he also instilled in us a realisation that war was the most terrible thing that could happen to a people. It brought not only suffering and pain but terrible types of degradation.'[28] Before he became disillusioned with the Australian Labor Party, Ben supported the work of NSW Premier Jack Lang. In 1932, after Lang had been controversially dismissed from his position, Ben took 13-year old Freda to an immense demonstration at Moore Park marching behind the 'Lang is Right' slogan that the UWM people had taken up.[29]

Freda remembered the anti-eviction movement of the Depression that the UWM launched. One day, the Lewis kids couldn't go home from school: it was too dangerous. It was the day of the infamous Battle of Union Street eviction riot of 1931. A house at 143 Union Street, just around the corner from the Lewis home, was the site of this ferocious encounter between 40 police officers and 18 UWM members and supporters in the fray. The *SMH* described it as 'the most sensational eviction battle Sydney has ever known'.[30] Vivid memories of events like this led Freda to her long-held ideals of social justice; and she passionately remembered the struggles of the UWM and the Wobblies until her last days.

Flo and Ben sent Freda to Newtown Public School just around the corner. Freda enjoyed school, but she got 'just medium' grades.[31] She went to Ashfield Girls Intermediate High School, and, spurred on by Ben's love of public speaking, in 1931 passed her Trinity elocution examination.[32] She transferred to Sydney Girls' High School in 1935, where she was a prefect in 1936. She took a part in the school's play at the end of that year: in her first work on stage, she played Wei, the Tiger General, in *Lady Precious Stream*, a traditional 14th-century Chinese play. However, Freda's schooling was cut short. She got sick with an eye infection at the end of the fifth year, and went back to repeat part of a year in 1937, after not receiving any certificates (either Intermediate or Leaving) and not having a scholarship to attend a university.[33] She left that last school in May 1937, and although she did not extend her formal education, other events in her young life began to open her to new opportunities.

Unemployment levels had dropped somewhat since their height in 1932, but the effects of the Depression were still evident, with a 12 per cent unemployment rate, and job were still scarce in Sydney. After she left school, Freda was on the dole for a short time, looking for work in those scarce times, walking the streets of Sydney and getting up the courage to ask for work at shops, factories, anywhere. One refusal came from the Darrell Lea milk bar in the Haymarket. She finally got a job closer to home, at the Henry Jones IXL jam factory on 12 Golden Grove Street at Darlington, just next to Erskineville, 'standing in water peeling peaches and cutting myself'.[34] The factory employed workers for the big fruit seasons over the summer, when casuals like Freda and her neighbour Grace Schwebel could get work. Freda earned the equivalent of 94 cents a week, with overtime and work on Saturday morning, and no sick leave.[35] Freda had seen the factory before, on the big screen: the character Doreen in *The Sentimental Bloke* had worked in this factory, pasting labels on pickle jars.

Freda later joined her father in his signwriting business at Newtown when his work picked up again. This was the first time that Freda's choice of work came to public attention because a woman signwriter was an oddity in those days: a photographer from a local newspaper snapped her sitting on a ladder painting signs on a building, with the caption 'First Woman Signwriter', working 'with a deft stroke of the wrist'.[36] It was quite an unusual job for a young woman, and a telling start to Freda's working life, taking on a traditional male occupation. For a time, the signwriting business did well, and on the strength of that, Ben and Flo bought a car; family excursions to Coogee and Bondi in the car became regular affairs, much more salubrious than walking the six miles to the coast.

The New Theatre

Freda's turn as a Tiger General in high school stayed with her, and encouraged by Ben's love of Shakespeare and his UWM work in staging plays, along with her elocution certificate, she found that theatre was still an interest after she left school. 'By pure chance', Freda learned about the New Theatre, a small left-wing organisation which had begun its work just a few years before, and had rooms down at the Circular Quay end of Pitt Street in the city.[37] In 1936, when she had just turned 17, Freda first attended the New Theatre, for a performance of Clifford Odets' anti-Nazi play *Till the Day I Die*.

The play revolved around the experiences of a member of the underground opposition movement in Germany who, after torture by Nazi officials during a brutal interrogation, committed suicide. This well-known progressive play had 'caused keen discussion in other countries' before the New Theatre took it up that year.[38] The Lyons government banned it at the request of the German consul-general, Rudolf Asmis. Vic Arnold, the New Theatre's secretary, presented the play on 22 July contrary to its censorship.[39] While fighting the ban, the New Theatre staged the play every Wednesday night at the New Theatre's regular rooms at 36 Pitt Street for years. Through 1940, NSW chief secretary Alwyn Uren Tonking continued the ban, on the grounds that it would have a degrading effect on audiences. In 1941, when the New Theatre was still struggling to have the ban lifted, Freda – now with a role onstage in the play, as well as the Theatre League's secretary – confirmed 'the League believed the play had been banned for its political implications'.[40] Later, she said that 'the Government's decision to lift the ban showed the correctness of the theatre's policy in presenting the play for two years whilst the ban was in operation'.[41]

The New Theatre is one of the country's oldest continuously performing theatres. It began life with inspiration from the British early radical theatre groups and the US New Theatre. The Sydney New Theatre began in 1932, as part of the Workers Arts Club (WAC). As in many of the groups that Freda was to be a part of, women took on a variety of roles in the WAC. Jean Devanny, who claimed that she named the Workers Arts Club, was one of its founders. She was the national secretary of the Workers International Relief (WIR) in

Australia, and had just returned from its international conference in Berlin and then a visit to the Soviet Union in 1931, and was brimming with enthusiasm to establish an art and theatre section in the Australian WIR. She remembered that she had 'no difficulty in collecting around me a sufficient number of suitable types: the artistic fraternity, equally with the industrial workers, were sunk in the doldrums of the crises of that time'.[42] The club's object was 'bringing within the reach of the working classes various advantages in the way of lectures, musical recitals, art classes, and exhibitions of pictures' at their rooms at 273 Pitt Street. With the need for more space, they soon relocated to 36 Pitt Street, down near Circular Quay, with the official opening by Dame Sybil Thorndike. Art exhibitions, film screenings, concerts and dances were scheduled at their rooms as well as other sites in Sydney.

It was the drama group that proved most popular, however, with the socialist activist Nelle Rickie, one of its directors. Nelle, leader of the Theatrical Employees Union, actor and socialist, had been writing and performing plays in Melbourne and Sydney through the Socialist Party's Repertory Theatre Company and Friends of the Soviet Union, as well as broadcasting on the NSW Trades and Labor Council's (NSW TLC) Radio 2KY. In 1933, at Jean's invitation, Nelle joined the WAC to lead the drama group, and wrote and acted in a number of works as well as producing and directing. In 1936 the group changed its name to the New Theatre League, adopting the label used by the American group from which it took much inspiration.

The New Theatre was perhaps the most well-known Australian artistic organisation that constituted a formation of left cultural activists in the mid-20th century. Like Ben and his Wobbly mates, people with strongly held opinions on the nature of social justice, and faith in the utility of collective action, drove the fledgling theatre group. They mobilised their own creative resources to establish and sustain it, relied on formal as well as informal networks of communication, and often aimed to provide not just artistic but political training. While their program included classical and experimental theatre, their inspiration more often came from current political and industrial conflicts, whether local or global.

With her introduction to the New Theatre in 1936, young Freda's mind lit up with new possibilities. After the sad life growing up in the Depression, here was a life that could give her hope, through the theatre's political and artistic direction. She said that she 'was so taken with [the theatre], I went home to Dad and said I would like to leave' school, and to leave her work with him as a signwriter and throw her lot in with the theatre.[43] Her career with the New Theatre began. She said that 'my whole interest was in the New Theatre for some years'.[44] As was the case with other New Theatre members, she took on a number of roles at the theatre's rooms. She began with selling tickets, went on to be secretary in 1937, and then later on produced and performed in a number of plays, from 1937 to 1942. In 1940, she was the publicity officer and assistant secretary. In 1941, she was secretary again, and the role suited her well: she did organise things very well, and her photograph appeared on pamphlets inviting audiences to performances. She regularly took her brothers Leon and Rae along with her to the theatre to watch the plays; and later they did volunteer work for the New Theatre themselves. Rae spent a lot of time doing chalk-up publicity for various productions; he also did a little acting, in one of the theatre's many revues and later in the Frank Hardy play *Black Diamonds*.

As well as dedicating herself to organisational and publicity work with the New Theatre, Freda became very interested in the performances, and soon she was busy both acting and directing as well. Just a few examples are presented here – as the New Theatre generally didn't name the cast or crew of their productions in the early decades, a complete listing is not possible. She made her stage debut in *Behind the Scenes (Stage Door)* in 1937. In 1938 and then again in 1940, she performed in *Where's That Bomb?* written by Bob Buckland and Herbert Hodge, members of the New Theatre's British sister group, the Unity Theatre. The play 'bravely sets out to debunk anti-worker, anti-Marxist propaganda'. However, for its Australian production on 23 February 1938 with Freda, the *SMH* described it controversially as 'a comedy which was banned in the UK'.[45] This had been the case for a short time, until the Unity Theatre's writers excised a reference to toilet paper.[46]

Freda soon found her feet and went on to much more work on stage. She took a role in the anti-war play *Bury the Dead* by Irwin Shaw, written for the US New Theatre League. When it played in New York it was reviewed as 'one hell of a powerful theatre piece…the important thing is that Mr Shaw makes you want to go out and take the world in your two hands and set it right side up, and that's what a play's for.'[47] The London Unity Theatre billed it as 'the greatest peace play yet written'.[48] A local reviewer found Freda's Sydney performance 'a notable success' which 'excited a good deal of discussion'.[49]

She played Manuela, the civilian sniper, in *Remember Pedrocito* (written by US New Theatre League playwright John Loftus, although Freda billed it as 'a play recently received from Spain'[50]) that had a season from 17 April 1938.[51] She directed the skit on Hitlerism in America, *The Home of the Brave* (attributed to Albert Maltz and George Sklar), 'a burlesque on American fascism', which opened on 7 August 1938. She had a part in *The Brave and the Blind*, a play about the Spanish Civil War by Michael Blankfort. She took an acting role in *Trumpets of Wrath*, a one-act anti-war play by American playwright William Kozlenko, which opened on 28 August 1938, under the auspices of the Spanish Relief Committee.[52]

In 1939, she performed in *The Rehearsal* (by Albert Maltz) on 25 June, as Vera, reportedly being good in a difficult role. She performed in *Renegade* (by J.H. Pollock). The theatre staged this play, about problems faced by Jewish people in America, along with *Where's That Bomb?* on 10 March 1940, when she played a hire purchase collector. In 1942 she directed *Distant Point* on 20 September. This play by Russian writer Aleksandr Afinogenov deals with 'the need for recognition of people who live in a remote, forgotten whistle-stop'.[53] The play dramatises life in the Soviet Union after the revolution during the Second Five Year Plan, about the hopes and struggles of people thrown together by chance on a small eastern Siberian railway station.

Also in 1940 she took the role of wife to coal miner Jock Levy in *No Armistice*. On 9 and 16 June 1940, Freda performed as Gwevril in *New Way Wins* by Montagu Slater. In 1941, she performed in the revue *I'd Rather be Left*, written by Jim McAuley, who became one of Australia's most respected poets. Freda directed and produced *Fountains Beyond*, a work on indigenous land rights and racial prejudice, by Brisbane playwright George Landen Dann.

Throughout this time, Freda along with other New Theatre players would perform 'contact' or 'mobile' work, playing for free, standing on street corners or on the back of a truck.[54] They took this sort of street theatre further afield, out to the working-class areas in Wollongong and Cessnock. On 10 August 1942, for instance, Freda's mobile group staged *According to Plan* (written by Geoffrey Parsons) before a dance at the Richmond Cinema in support of the Russian Medical Aid Fund. Freda and the four actors travelled by train to Richmond for the evening performance, and received only travel expenses.

As an amateur theatre, the New Theatre primarily relied on volunteers both front and back of stage, with few paid roles. For decades, it provided opportunities for its members on a number of levels. Firstly, it provided opportunities for personal development and a heightened sense of personal identity. Secondly it was a place of creative and political activism for like-minded people. Thirdly, it provided a sense of belonging to an organisation, that provided 'affective bonds that grow out of shared ideals and aims, affirmed through years of cooperative activities'.[55] And perhaps most importantly for the women who took on compound roles such as Freda, it represented an organisational focus – one that was to provide Freda with valuable skills for her future career on the public stage.

For 14 years, the New Theatre took up much of Freda's world, with these activities in front of and behind the curtain. Her confidence and abilities grew quickly within this group that nurtured young energetic people like Freda. She won the first prize for elocution at the 1938 Sydney Eisteddfod with a New Theatre performance. Photographs from the theatre show her rehearsing her own roles as well as directing her comrades; at work on a big typewriter on a makeshift table; constructing sets or applying makeup to other actors – she was happy to take on any job that needed doing, not just to be happy with performing on stage. The smiles that had been absent in her childhood had returned – Freda loved the work, she loved involving herself in something that was much bigger than her. The many different acting, directing, producing jobs that the New Theatre gave her provided an entry into a whole set of new spheres, as she learnt more about different lives in Australia as well as other political and industrial troubles across the world. After the horrors of the Depression, her eyes were shining brightly, and she bathed in the warmth of the footlights.

One of the most important skills that her New Theatre work gave Freda, though, was a talent for public speaking, which carried her through to all her succeeding public roles. Carrying on her dad's love of extrapolation and explanation, she spoke at many performances and events, discussing the plays and the context behind the work of the New Theatre League, connecting its themes to current events, inviting recruits, collecting donations. In 1940, she went to the establishment of the Wollongong Trades Hall, for instance, to give her general support to union causes down south of Sydney, and to start her plans to establish a South Coast branch of the theatre.[56]

She also gave public lectures on topics such as 'theatre and the war'.[57] She often spoke in the Domain, the public park in the centre of Sydney where speakers had been airing their opinions since 1878. In 1940, Freda organised and chaired a meeting to open the Domain for open-air performances. This was ultimately to encourage Australian drama, at a time when it had been forbidden by law for the New Theatre to perform there. Freda fought for attention against a huge spring thunderstorm – alongside Tom Wright of the Sheet Metal Workers Union, Sam Lewis (Freda's cousin and the VP of the

Teachers Federation), left-wing journalist Rupert Lockwood and Ernie Thornton from the Federated Ironworkers Association.[58]

The attentions of law enforcers attending these type of events opened Freda's Australian Security and Intelligence Organisation (ASIO) file. ASIO operatives began recording her movements, tapping her phone, and organising for informants to be alongside Freda. The earliest document is dated 1943, when she was the New Theatre secretary, and she wrote to a Moscow-based theatre organisation asking for Soviet plays for the Sydney New Theatre to perform.[59] Freda's ASIO file has at least 38 volumes, tens of thousands of pages of documents and photographs. The government's surveillance of her work in various organisations lasts until 1987 at least. Freda 'has an extensive and adverse security record', so the ASIO director-general wrote to his London counterpart in 1964.[60] The many volumes of Freda's file, along with those of her family and others on the left, continue to demonstrate the state's obsessive paranoia of the times.

One of the New Theatre's aims was to develop a 'native drama', and to this end Freda quickly became active in the advancement of its indigenous writing.[61] In preparation for the New Theatre's scriptwriting competition in 1937, she wrote that 'the adjudicators will give preference to those plays with an Australian background, and which have some social significance in conformity with the ideals of the New Theatre'.[62] This was at a time when Australian works of drama were fairly rare. She thought that unions which had been assisted by the New Theatre, such as the miners, had realised what the theatre could mean to them, and urged the presentation of plays 'dealing specifically with local issues and adapted to the problems of each union'. She mentioned the success of the production *The Firing Line*, a drama quickly written by Freda along with Jock Hector – both members of the New Theatre Writers Group.[63] Dealing with the Port Kembla ironworkers' stoppage, the play was a series of exchanges between strikers and 'Big Business Government and Press Magnate'. Freda and Jock performed the play along with two of the strikers. They left a copy of the script down there so the ironworkers could produce the play for themselves. Through her activities in the New Theatre, Freda's political views were quickly maturing, along with her public speaking and writing skills.

As the secretary of the Sydney New Theatre, Freda was in constant contact with theatre people in other states, particularly those branches in Brisbane and Melbourne. She assisted in the training of theatrical groups outside the New Theatre, in organisations including the Australian Labor Party (ALP) and the Australian Labor League of Youth (ALLY). Through this work, she met people from vastly different backgrounds. Paul Mortier, the president of ALLY, was the New Theatre's secretary in the late 1940s, and like Freda was a popular Domain speaker. British-born communist Vic Arnold was a founding organiser of the New Theatre. Another colleague was Jean Blue, a trained nurse who found much pleasure in her New Theatre work as a talented actor, and then went on to screen roles in *The Overlanders* and *Bitter Springs*. Freda filled her time with theatre work, and she enjoyed it thoroughly. The companionship suited her gregarious nature as much as the dramatic and political work – and she was very efficient at the organisational jobs too. The social events that went along with the work of the theatre were great. At the 1940 Labor Jubilee Ball, at the Trocadero in George Street, Freda and fellow thespian Jack Barker thrilled the house with their act, which they had prepared with the ball's theme of the 'Naughty Nineties' in mind. Wearing original costumes, they rode around the spacious dance floor on a tandem bicycle to the tune of a thousand voices singing 'Daisy'.[64]

The war was a particularly vital time for Sydney communists and others on the left. Australian communists opposed the war as an imperialist war, until Germany attacked the Soviet Union in June 1941.[65] Beverly Symons writes that 'for communists world-wide, Hitler's attack on the Soviet Union and its entry into the war decisively transformed the "imperialist war" into a just "people's war" to defeat fascism'.[66] Amongst many organisations on the left, the New Theatre and the CPA spent a lot of energy in this early opposition. The writer

Oriel Gray had joined the New Theatre in 1938 soon after Freda, and worked alongside her in New Theatre adventures. She described Freda as 'earnest' and 'conscientious… I knew that Freda would literally put her arm in the lion's mouth for the party and the theatre.'[67] The photographs of Freda at her theatre work show a serious and passionate young woman, ready to do her duty for the theatre.

Oriel also wrote about the federal government's wartime banning of the CPA in June of 1940 until December 1942, under the National Security Act:

> I imagine that Marx House felt rather flattered in a way. We were so far out of the mainstream of events that we were hardly noticed in Europe or in the Soviet Union. A ban by a federal government must have earned us a paragraph or two in most of the communist newspapers in the world. It seems unlikely that Marx House or any of the 'communist front' organisations really disrupted the war effort, or troubled the dreams of Ming the Merciless.[68]

The banning of the CPA prompted one incident that was very important to Freda: the time that the federal police raided the theatre on 16 June 1940. This was part of a series of nationwide raids 'which were synchronised to begin together, so that organisations in one state could not be warned by those in another, were a sequel to the issue of a proclamation declaring Communist and Fascist organisations to be unlawful', it was reported.[69] At the time, the New Theatre was still performing *Till the Day I Die*, at this stage of the war when Menzies was supportive of fascism, and Freda was assistant secretary and publicity officer. She also had a performing role in the play, that night that police raided the theatre, when they arrested the cast and crew, and confiscated some 600 play scripts. Freda remembered that 'they took any books that had a red cover…they behaved like Fascists'.[70] After the raid, Freda made a disingenuous announcement that 'We have no communists in our organisation, and we are not connected with the Communist Party in any way.'[71]

Freda wrote to Prime Minister Menzies, asking for the scripts' return, or at least their preservation. Accordingly, police returned the scripts to her, along with other items (reports, leaflets, CPA booklets and eight stage rifle props) the next week. A box of detonators, however, went to its purported owner, NSW Railways. The accompanying letter notes the confiscated plays, which included works by Bernard Shaw and John Galsworthy, that examination 'does not reveal anything which indicate that such plays are used for and on behalf of the CPA, and, therefore, there seems no legal reason why they should not be returned'. This was despite Menzies' confident declaration the night before that 'the type of material seized fully justified the steps that have been taken'.[72] The incident resonated with communists and a significant number of other people as a censorship issue; Freda remembered that 'they were horrified at this attack on our civil liberties. Because there's always been a strong support for civil liberties in Australia.'[73] Freda describes the 'wonderful picture' of her sitting amongst the aftermath of the raid that the New Theatre used on their publicity.

The attempted proscription of the New Theatre did not stop at this raid. Billy Hughes wrote that by 1941 the New Theatre was still 'disseminating defeatist propaganda by means of stage plays at union meetings, street corner meetings of the State ALP (a lorry), and at lunch hour meetings at factories'. After quoting from Freda's letter that lists some of the New Theatre's activities, Hughes recommends, 'one way in which the New Theatre's activities could be stopped would be by declaring it an unlawful body under the National Security (Subversive Associations) regulations'.[74]

Reds in the limelight

They'd been rehearsing in secret for weeks; now they were ready for their first cues. Freda looked around and shivered as she waited to take the blankets that covered their flimsy costumes.

Like most people in the theatre that night, Freda was a victim of the Depression, but the despair of dole queues and empty bellies, of strangers sharing rooms because they had nowhere else to go, had suddenly lifted when she'd sat on the other side of the footlights a few months before. Drawn to the purposeful events that continually swept through these rooms, ideas and action swirled, making cold spaces warm.

This performance for the New Theatre was crucial if it was to succeed in becoming a critic of its times. They all knew that Clifford Odets' new plays vividly explained that although half a world away, the terrifying events in Europe needed to be understood, here, in Sydney. That it affected all of them.

As she waited for the curtains to open, Freda thought that because they had so much time to devote to their art, because they believed so strongly in the wisdom of their ideas in those politically charged times, the New Theatre family got a lot done on the cheap. The freezing July nights were hard to take; but they would have been harder still out on the street. As soon as they could raise money to pay for heating in the rooms, everything would be better.

She studied the audience from behind the second-hand curtain. The auditorium was full, with extra chairs brought from somewhere else in the building. Freda and Vic had walked for days of leafleting in the inner city streets and on the dole lines. What did those people think of what the theatre presented? Did they share that sense?

Finally the first play began. Jock, Eddie, Vic, Jean and the others handed her the blankets and became their characters. Freda was glad that she had refused to take on the role of Tillie – she was still new to the game, and found that the behind-the-scenes jobs suited her much better. At 18 she was still fighting to suppress her nervousness; but her organising skills were put to good use here, with so much to do. And anyway, Jean, three months pregnant, was a fabulous Tilly, who reveals in the play – both to the father and to the audience – that she is expecting, so it was a perfect fit for her. Freda had thrown herself into organising the rehearsals and performances. She was pleased with her program notes written for the season, proud to see the roneoed program stating that the plays were anti-fascist works containing a spirit of beauty that worked to fight oppression and poverty.

When she'd stayed behind after that first performance, Vic had talked about theatre work behind the scenes. He began explaining the ideas behind the New Theatre, the job they'd taken to show how the world was to ordinary *people here in Sydney, and to combat capitalism with social justice. Within a month, Vic had persuaded her to volunteer as secretary. Soon it was another home for her; making friends down at Pitt Street was as important as putting on plays. There were meetings, rehearsals, different events every night. She was even writing her own drama, and rehearsing another, as Vic's director-in-training. Her mother had asked her at first if it was the boys she kept going back for.*

The audience seemed to be enjoying the first play's conclusion, and the atmosphere was electric. Everyone was aware that the performance was going on to the second, very controversial, play, despite the minister banning its performance. Freda took a deep breath as the applause began to die away, and she stepped on to the stage.

'Friends, I'm one of the volunteers for the New Theatre. It seems like you've enjoyed our first presentation tonight.' She paused, her arms folded tightly before her.

'Its message is important, and we need to fight against this horror of fascism. And we think this theatre's work is important in presenting these plays, and anyone can join. I hope you might want to help in our fight for social justice.'

She realised, as she scanned the faces, that her talk had found resonance: she had connected. Her fists unclenched, her voice grew a little louder.

'Our work to make the theatre a critic of our times goes on, but we need your help. As long as you support our theatre, we'll use it to examine and criticise our society.'

She looked over to Vic, who passed the hat around the audience.

He recognised some faces in the back row; but he was an old hand at dealing with threats from the law. He put his deep theatre voice on, hearty and reassuring, his thumbs tucked into his tight braces, and strode back up on to the stage. 'Now, ladies and gentlemen, we've been prohibited from presenting our second play tonight. I cannot think how this play can offend against good manners and decorum. You might be able to follow the devious ways of the ministerial mind, but we think that it is an intrusion on democratic principles.' Vic continued, throwing his remarks to the back of the hall: in order to comply with the ridiculous ban, another play would be substituted, 'one that, I'm sure, will be in accordance with the law'.

Freda stared at him, searching his face. They hadn't prepared another play. Jock and Jean beckoned her back into the wings.

After a few meaningful looks between Vic and Jock, a play began. It was the play they'd planned – Vic was simply putting off the plain-clothes detectives he'd spotted. But the officers soon realised they'd been had, and there was a change in the atmosphere in the hall, voices from the back rising. Freda pulled at the unravelling hem of her cardigan, stepped further back into the wings, tripped over the pile of blankets.

Most people ran out as soon as the police stood up, but a few moved towards the stage to try and support the actors. Freda picked herself up off the floor, and, as the officers blustered up on the stage, ran on to the stage as well, to protect Jean from the oversized sergeant who had launched himself on her. Quite a few people were hurt in the confusion. Vic tried to stop things early on, but the police didn't listen, just rushing to restrain everyone.

Police arrested the actors along with the crew. The detectives moved to the back rooms, smashing the flimsy stage props on the way. Held back by two coppers, accusing them of violence and twisting to find escape, Freda watched her office destroyed, scripts, books, paper all over the floor. The detectives soon found what they were looking for.

As she was taken through the open curtains and outside to the watch house with the others, Freda was already planning her protests, her letters to the government, her work against this injustice. She had a cause, a burning hot reason for fighting, and didn't notice how cold the outdoors had become.

'I went in the other direction': the Communist Party of Australia

In 1936 when she was 17 and had just thrown in her lot with the New Theatre, Freda also joined the CPA. This was a time when only about 200 of the 4,000 party members were women, and soon after a major turning point for the party, in 1935, with the call for a united front. She soon became a talented and articulate activist for the party. Later, she was 'very proud' to be elected Central Committee member of the CPA, and secretary of the CC Women's Committee, and she was to be a party member until 1971.[75] Her experiences of poverty and injustice in her early life, as well as her father's influence, had led to her decision to join the party. She knew hardship from her childhood, and from her father's stories of his militant struggles, and like many people of that time, it formed her politics from an early age. She said,

> if there is misery, people latch on to it to make money out of it, and in those days the unemployed were very much exploited…these kind of things stirred me up. And the threat of war, that was a big thing in our youth – the horror of the First World War and the threat of the Second World War. That had an enormous effect on me.[76]

Australians on the far left were, in the mid-1930s, the only ones in the country fighting against fascism, which was rapidly emerging as a colossal threat; and it was no coincidence that Freda and many others took up the communists' cause when the CPA adopted the Popular Front at its Eleventh Congress in December 1935. Ostensibly non-party organisations like the New Theatre, along with many others in Australia and elsewhere, attracted artists, writers and others interested in creative left-wing work outside the dour formalities of the party meeting. Additionally, the youth arm of the CPA, the Young Communist League, also pursued popular front objectives with the establishment of clubs, sporting groups, camps and other activities.

Freda said it was the 'impact of the theatre' that led her to join the party, 'because it was when I joined the theatre that I talked to other people who were communists. At that stage, I was arguing against them. Using Dad's arguments. But their arguments were such that they convinced me. And that's where eventually I joined.'[77] Later she convinced her father to join the CPA, but it took a lot of debate. Freda recalls that 'for the first time I was looking to somebody else for leadership, and not to Dad. And looking back on it I think that was probably a bit hurtful [for Dad].'[78] This was an important turning point for Freda: on the verge of womanhood, moving out into the world from her close and loving family, and with her influences – particularly her political influences – rapidly expanding beyond her father's. She had had Ben's inspiration throughout her childhood, with his relentless political activity: she remembered that 'Dad was always out at meetings, but that was my model from an early age'.[79] She had always been shown what a big and varied place her world was, and now the New Theatre and the party gave more inspiration for her world view.

At the New Theatre, Freda had made many friends, who were all left sympathisers or communists; however, it was Jack Fegan who was instrumental in Freda joining the party.[80] Fegan, a committed Irish communist and IRA hard man, had, upon his emigration to Australia, been a very active (some would say belligerent) member of the UWM alongside Freda's father Ben. Fegan was a leader of the Workers Defence Corps, a paramilitary group established in 1929 in a number of Australian cities. He had joined the theatre a few months before Freda did, and played a Nazi storm trooper in the 1936 performance of *Till the Day I Die* that police raided.[81] Simon Bracegirdle, another actor in that evening's performance, recalled that Jack 'took the lead in the crisis' that night, which was Freda's first encounter with the radical theatre group.[82] Like Jean Blue, Jack's acting career propelled him onto the big screen in a number of popular mid-century Australian films.[83] His best-known role was on television, as Inspector Jack Connolly in the long-running police series *Homicide*. However, while Fegan, Blue and many others stayed with theatre and performance, eventually, Freda said, 'I went in the other direction' – to the Communist Party.[84] With all of her new-found experience at the New Theatre, Freda realised that her future lay in political action.

Through the early 1940s, party membership had rapidly increased, from under 4,000 to over 20,000. After the start of the war, with more women entering the workforce (an estimated 100,000 women moved into industry), more women joined the party. Although women were members from the establishment of the CPA in 1920, through the foundation of the party's Militant Women's Group in 1926, wartime saw a mobilisation of efforts to recruit women.[85] The party worked during the war period 'to involve them in a range of organisational and political activities, and to consistently agitate for equal pay and better conditions for women workers in industry'.[86] Throughout the end of the war period and through the 40s, the work and recognition of women in the party was gradually changing. Griffiths writes that 'in 1942 alone, some 1,900 women joined the Party and the proportion of women briefly touched 25%'.[87] A 1942 report in the *Party Builder* noted that

> a recent Women's Conference has revealed that the narrow conception of "work amongst women" is being swept out of the Party. Our greatest successes have been recorded when the organising of women has been the task for the local or factory group, and has been given attention to all Party organisations.[88]

By 1944, the CPA's assistant secretary Richard Dixon wrote that

> the Communist Party believes that just as victory over Fascism has been made possible only by the widest participation of women in the struggle, so it will be possible to win the peace only with the fullest and most active participation of women. Our post-war planning must embrace this viewpoint.[89]

By the time of the 14th National Congress in 1945, there were 16 women delegates. Freda joined them as the 'well-known Communist speaker and organiser'.[90] Leading organiser of women in the party, Betty Reilly, reported to the 1948 CPA congress that 'a broad people's movement must include all progressive sections of women, particularly working class housewives and women from industry'.[91]

It was during the period of the late 1930s, when Freda joined, that the party also reached out to the trade union movement. From around 1940 to 1945, Freda was the Actors' Equity delegate on the NSW Trades and Labor Council (TLC), and in that capacity, she promoted the New Theatre on the NSW TLC's radio station 2KY as well as more generally in public. This was just after 1939, when Hal Alexander and other trade union activists took over the management of Equity. Hal, who was the general secretary of Actors' Equity from 1939 to 1971, became a close friend and colleague for years; they had worked together in the New Theatre as well as the CPA (which Hal joined in 1941 when he was 17) and Actors' Equity. For a number of years the CPA promoted Freda as the 'first woman on the Executive of the NSW TLC'. Markey notes that from 1945, communist group representatives on the NSW TLC executive grew to a substantial minority, including Tom Wright, federal president of the Sheet Metal Workers Union, Jack Hughes, NSW secretary of the Federated Clerks Union, Edgar Ross from the Miners Federation, and Tom Nelson of the Waterside Workers Federation.[92] Through union networking, as can be seen on the TLC, Freda began to work closely with union leaders and political activists in a wider circle.

She supported close connections between the theatre and the trade union movement: in a letter, she stated that 'unions which had been assisted by the New Theatre League, such as the miners, had realised what the theatre could mean to them'.[93] In particular, she began working with women comrades who were on the state Women's Executive, including Phyllis Johnson, another member of the New Theatre and a close friend of Freda. An important part of the Women's Committee work during the war was to keep in contact with striking workers, and Freda went out to various strikes with the committee during this period, connecting her theatre and party work with picket-line meetings and public discussions. Fellow CPA member Dorothy Hewett recognised, as Freda did, the differences of opinion about women party members, and men's attitudes towards them: there were 'awful attitudes towards women, and yet the sort of women who were attracted into the Communist Party were strong, passionate and revolutionary…it was possible within the Party for women to act with more force than in any other political area'.[94] Freda avidly pursued her political training in the party, at a time when it was one of the few avenues for adult education.

A perfect marriage

It was while Freda was working at the New Theatre that she met Bill Brown. Like Freda, Bill (Wilton John Brown, 1917–1992) was a child of the Depression, and growing up in Chippendale he knew the hard conditions of working-class inner-city Sydney, and had knocked around with a gang. Bill left school at 14 and completed his electrical apprenticeship at the Emmco (Electricity Meter Manufacturing Company) factory in Waterloo. His father was John Frederick Brown, a milkman, who died when Bill was very young; his mother, Mary Jane Matilda Brown (née Miles), brought him up as a single parent. While he spent most of his time in the inner-city streets, from an early age Bill loved surfing, and learnt to surf at Bondi. Later he taught Freda to surf there, as well as their daughter Lee, and for years, he was a keen member of the Sydney League Swimming Club, and an activist for surf life-saving clubs more generally.

Coming to the New Theatre, and meeting Freda, both changed the direction of Bill's life. He reflected on his time there, when he had first met people who had wider interests than just themselves. Freda said of their initial attraction, 'I think I was sort of a bit different to the average women that he'd met and gone out with before.' She already had four years' experience as a very active and outspoken member of the New Theatre when they first met. She was playing parts in performances, and was going up on stage when not performing to make an appeal to the audience, with a growing body of public speaking behind her.

Freda and Bill instantly made a connection. Bill was 'very handsome', and was a wonderful listener, Freda believed, and a 'very humane person'. Like Freda, Bill's ASIO file is extensive. An ASIO operative wrote that he is 'a voluminous writer and speaker and has a wide knowledge of many topics that would indicate that he is fairly well educated. He is a quick worker, a patient listener with a stranger providing the person is speaking along the lines of his own ideology, very curt when one crosses his path, and a good arguer who tends to make sure of his facts before raising a matter. He will admit an error and endeavour to right it.'[95] Freda saw in Bill the possibility of a partnership that her parents hadn't, perhaps, enjoyed, one in which her political and cultural interests intersected closely with her husband's. And this was realised in their lifelong partnership.

Soon after meeting Freda and becoming part of the New Theatre, Bill joined a jazz band in Newtown, and joined ALLY. At the New Theatre, he began assisting as an electrician. As Freda and many others found, working at the theatre gave Bill an entry into another type of life, however, and he soon gave away the electrical work for a new passion. He did try his hand at acting, but he found he could write better than pursue an acting career. So then Bill mainly wrote plays, including *Headlines Today*, *Boys in the Rear*, and *The Follies Bourgeois*; and in 1942 Freda directed a season of Bill's play *Men Who Speak for Freedom*. He adapted the Lawson piece *While the Billy Boils* for performance. Bill also had short stories and poems published, and radio scripts performed on Sydney and Melbourne radio stations.

Bill's one-act play *Action Speaks Louder* took up the issue of conscription. Bill set it in 'an imaginary period when the conscription legislation threatening Australia at the time of this writing has actually become law. The play is written in the hope that it can help ensure that such a period never becomes reality. It is further hoped that the play can prove of some small assistance in the Australian people's part in the great world movement for lasting peace'. The play includes a scene inspired by Union Street's 'Battle of Erskineville', with the heartless eviction of Ma Lane and her family; 'throwing a war widow with two kids out of their home, that's crazy'.[96]

Bill was quickly drawn into the life of the Lewis family home, playing cricket with Freda, the boys and Ben, and making the regular trips to the beach, surfing with the family, and playing handball with Rae and Leon, at the court next to the Icebergs swimming pool. He found his place in this new extended family. After they started going out, Bill often stayed with Freda at her family home in Erskineville before they were married. Ben at least (perhaps not Flo) was broad-minded about such things: 'when Ben walked in on Freda and Bill in bed, he walked out again, without a word'.[97] They were unconventional in other ways too: growing up through the Depression, and entering the world of communist ideas, Freda and Bill believed they were living through the end of capitalism, and were very well prepared to marry the idea of communism as well as each other for life. Both partnerships did last their lifetimes.

Soon after they met at the New Theatre, Freda recruited Bill to the CPA, where he quickly accepted various roles as full-time writer, and eventually became one of the leading historians of the party. When asked about his commitment, Bill replied,

> Born in Australia of Australian-born parents, I am but one of the overwhelming majority of Australian Communists who have joined the Communist Party with one purpose – the building of a better land in which those who work for it can enjoy a full share in the wealth they win.[98]

An ASIO operative described Bill as 'friendly, has a quiet personality, but is very determined. He is devoted to his wife and child.'[99] Their daughter Lee wrote that he joined the CPA 'for the reasons that were to be the driving force throughout his life – his desire to see and work for a better world, where all forms of discrimination were banished and no individual could exploit or oppress another'.[100]

Bill wrote poetry throughout his life, and his methodical and analytical way of approaching his world sometimes found itself integrated with his growing love for Freda:

Dialectical Love Song

You're slightly Leninic
Speaking scientifically
Slightly Marxetic
Meaning dialectically
In life's evolution
You brought Revolution to me.

Though it sounds wrong in lyrics
Speaking empirically
Your source of attraction
Is far from reactionary
You negate my negation
By having relations with me.

Taking an objective view
In analysing I find
Basically attraction of you
Is just a matter of mind
Your charms almost mystic
Attraction is physic
So unmetaphysical
As old Hegel showed
You wind up at a node
and it's ME!

Their relationship quickly developed; and like many at the time, the onset of the war seemed to hasten events. Bill and Freda married on 20 March 1943, at St Stephens Presbyterian Church in Macquarie Street Sydney. The site of Sydney's most prestigious society weddings may seem like a surprising choice for these young radicals. But there were many aspects of their partnership that were unconventional. Freda, who was just 23 years old at their marriage, explained:

We were living in Sydney and Bill decided he wanted to go down to Melbourne. And you weren't allowed to travel in those days. But he was able to travel because he was in a reserved occupation. They put something around a ship to prevent the mines. He was an electrician. And he was transferred to Melbourne. He came to me and said 'Look, I've got to go to Melbourne; you can't go unless you're my wife. What about we get married?' So we got married. And we wanted to get married in an ordinary registry office. He was working, not only every day of the week, but he also was working overtime. And so we couldn't get to the registry office. And so we decided well, we could get married in a church, and I asked someone where there was a church, because I was not religious, and they said St. Stephens. I knew nothing about St. Stephens. And so I went up to book into St. Stephens, and the minister that I saw there or whoever was in charge of booking places for weddings said 'will you want the organ?' First thing I said to him 'Now how much will it cost because we haven't got much money.' And he said whatever it was, I think it was £2. And he said, 'But you would want the organ.' I said 'I don't want an organ, I just want it as cheap as possible.' But he said, 'You would want the big red runner.' I said, 'I don't want anything, I just want to get married as cheaply as we possibly can.' And it wasn't long after that I found out that St. Stephens is the society church, and I think it even is today. And so we got married in a society church, just because we couldn't get married in a registry office. And we were in the New Theatre at the time, so we were moving from Pitt Street to Castlereagh Street, and we went and loaded a truck, rushed up and got married, and rushed back to Castlereagh Street and unloaded the truck. And then we went for a swim at Bondi.

It's typical that Freda and Bill celebrated their wedding with a swim at Bondi. For generations the beaches of Sydney's eastern suburbs have been a favourite place for the Brown and Lewis families, celebrating births, deaths and marriages on the sand there. Like many young newly weds in wartime Sydney, they had no home of their own for a long time, and lived at Erskineville for the short time before they went to Melbourne. Rae and Leon had gained another brother, and the growing Lewis family was happy. Rae later said that 'my family has produced some of the most perfect marriages. I would say that Freda and Bill's marriage was a perfect marriage.' But Rae did remember that 'when Freda got married she couldn't boil water. She couldn't cook anything at all.'

Now that they were married, Freda could travel with Bill to Melbourne, where they lived for a short time and joined the New Theatre there. Freda stayed on in Melbourne for two years after Bill went to serve with the army in October 1943. She produced the revue *Let's Be Offensive* for the Melbourne New Theatre in August 1943. This piece, written by Bill along with Oriel Gray and Harry Hurwitz, 'pillories public and political personages with merciless intent and makes the audience like it', according to *Radio Times* critic Locksley

Shaw (the president of the Australian Theatre Movement), who found it the 'best to date' of the Melbourne New Theatre's work.[101]

It also was during her time in Melbourne that Freda trained as a journalist at the *Radio Times*, a publication started by a Melbourne *Herald* journalist in 1936.[102] As well as publishing the Melbourne radio guide, it included very politically outspoken articles, including those supporting communism and criticising the United Australia Party; one 1943 piece on the EYL was submitted by party political leader and EYL national secretary Audrey Blake. As well as other articles, Freda wrote a number of previews and reviews of Melbourne New Theatre shows. Throughout her busy life, she would regularly list her occupation as a journalist, and was an AJA member.

A few months after they married, Bill had left his reserved occupation as an aircraft electrician to join the army. One of 4,000 CPA members to enlist (around one-fifth of the total membership),[103] Bill joined up in October 1943.[104] He served with the HQ1 Australian Corps, in Halmahera in Indonesia, and on Morotai Island, Borneo, where he was a corporal in the Australian Intelligence Corps. He also served in Queensland, NSW, and Victoria, and after his discharge on 15 July 1946 Bill was awarded the War Medal, the Pacific Star Medal and the Australian Service Medal.

When Bill joined the army, he taught himself typing and shorthand, and wrote for a number of army publications. Before enlisting and while on active service, Bill had a number of short stories and poems published, and had his radio scripts performed on Sydney and Melbourne radio stations. During Bill's army service at Morotai, 'a quite strong central branch of the Communist Party was formed. It held regular meetings and study classes.'[105] He also wrote and produced street theatre and agitprop (under the pseudonym Demos Cracy) as part of protest actions of the Australian soldiers there at the end of the war. One of those, 'Boys in the Rear', criticised the Australian army command for its double standards. He was part of the organising force for a Morotai demonstration to get boats to pick up servicemen stranded there at the end of the war in 1945.

One of Bill's comrades at Morotai was Jim Cairns, later deputy prime minister in the Whitlam government. Jim spoke of Bill as among the most honourable people, with the greatest integrity, that he had ever met. After the war, at the urging of Bill and another communist from Morotai, Bob Laurie, Jim applied to join the CPA, but they rejected his application because they suspected Jim of being a police agent.[106] On another occasion, when Bill was serving out his time in the Atherton Tablelands before demobilisation, he recruited Ian Turner, who was in the same unit as Bill, a 'bronzed smiling electrician' and 'an attractive and eager young communist'.[107] According to Turner's wife Amirah Inglis, Bill recruited Ian with his 'winning personality and Marxist teachings'.[108] Turner, who was then an acting corporal in the Australian Army Education Service, went on to become active in the Australian Peace Council, and a noted historian.

One of Bill's poems about his wartime experiences is 'Soldier, Speak!'[109] Here he recounts his overseas experiences together with what he had so recently left behind in Australia.

Soldier, Speak

Oh soldier speak!
    Spare the world no word,
    Of the things you know and hate.

Oh soldier speak!
    Of the things you've sworn,
    To yourself and your fallen mate.

Speak aloud the horror of blasted limbs,
Of bleeding, sightless eyes.

Speak of agony spasms that rack the night,
Of the wounded's dreadful cries.

Of loneliness, fear, of waiting strain,
Of mud, of sweat, and of beating rain.

Speak of the stench of unburied death,
Still rotting in sodden green.

Speak aloud the wakeful, womanless nights,
Of the things life used to mean:

> The shearing shed, the surf, the sun,
> A beer in the Saturday bar,
> The Friday pay-night, the free weekend,
> A drive in the Sunday car,

> The race broadcast, the urban show,
> A summer night walk with the wife,
> The Union meet, a vote, a voice,
> In the way of Australian life.

Speak aloud then soldier, your hate of war,
With this voice in the days to come.

Speak then with your mates of farm, of mine,
And over the factory hum,

Of happiness, hope, of drying tears,
Of love, of life, and of laughing years.

Speak then of things that might still make wars,
Of prejudice, profit and greed.

Speak aloud your demand that these things must die,
In the birth of a wider creed.

Oh soldier speak!
> Don't spare one word,
> Of these things you know and hate.

Oh soldier speak!
> Honour those vows,
> To yourself and your fallen mate.

2

Communism and the Union of Australian Women: 1945–1963

Young, brilliant and enthusiastic

In one sense, the war held great promise for Freda. She said that 'women did come into their own in that period, everywhere, because all men were away in the army'. By 1943, with Bill away on service, Freda left Melbourne to join her family in Sydney, living in the Lewis family home in Erskineville. By the time of Bill's final leave in 1944, Freda had finished her work with the New Theatre – some publicity claims that she 'gave up a promising career in the theatre'[1] – to work full-time for the CPA as a paid organiser and member of the party's Central Committee. Much of her time was now taken up with the busy work of travelling around the country and speaking to raise war bonds, to help the fight against fascism. The job of selling war bonds was a key role in the party at that time, and Freda did this solo, as well as alongside other party members like Edgar Ross. It was a time when women made great advances in the CPA, particularly through the Central Women's Committee, and Freda was amongst those being encouraged to go out to speak in the Domain, and to factories and work sites.[2] As she had begun her stellar public speaking career for the party as Freda Lewis, the party continued to use her maiden name on its publicity for a number of years.

Like Freda, Phyllis Johnson, known as 'the girl in the green hat', joined the CPA in 1936; during the late wartime period, Phyl was the secretary of the Central Women's Committee. She writes that 'in that period communist speakers did a tremendous job – a number of them women – Freda Lewis (Brown), Moira Olive, myself'.[3] Phyl appreciated Freda's proactive stance: 'as a worker for women's rights Freda Brown knew women would be goaded into action as part of the working class and people's movement for equal pay and status'.[4] Fellow communist Amirah Inglis recalled that in the immediate post-war years, 'feminism to us meant equal pay'.[5] Like Freda and Phyl, Gloria Garton had also joined the party in 1936, and promoted the party's policies at factories and other large workplaces: she recalls that 'we were all twenty to twenty-five year olds who were calculated to have some effect on all these men in the factories'.[6] Freda worked in the Women's Committee alongside Betty Reilly, very active in the party as well as the Textile Workers Union, who reminded comrades that 'a broad people's movement must include all progressive sections of women, particularly working class housewives and women from industry'.[7] Amongst her party work, Freda helped to organise a Red Army celebration dance in the Sydney Town Hall on 19 February 1944.[8] She was also one of the featured speakers at the CPA's Special Conference that year (which had been called to amalgamate the CPA and the state Labor Party), at just 25 years of age. Drawing from her father's legacy of radical Australian history and her newer studies through the party, one of her conference activities was a joint presentation, a pageant of Highlights in Australian Labour History along with Radio 2KY's Sid Jordan.

Freda's involvement in politics was an integral part of her relationship with Bill (and later with their daughter Lee as well). It came as naturally and unconsciously as breathing to her. Before they were married, as well as in his final leave from the army before his discharge, Bill accompanied Freda on her speaking trips. He would sit in on Freda's meetings, practising his shorthand by taking Freda's speeches down. When the news of the Japanese surrender came through on 14 August, just after the CPA's Fourteenth Congress, Freda was jubilant along with everyone else at the party's George Street offices in Sydney. She remembered her excitement tempered with worries for Bill, still in

Borneo: 'a band came out on the roof, and played, and people danced in the streets, and people were drinking, but I can remember leaning against the wall and thinking to myself, well, I'm going to save all my celebrations till Bill gets home'. On his demobilisation on 15 July 1946, Bill joined Freda back at Erskineville Road at the Lewis family home, and he returned to Garden Island to work as an electrician.

Bill's real wish, however, was to work full time in writing. Having taught himself typing and shorthand, a break came when in late 1947 he became a journalist at the *Daily Mirror*, a newish Sydney tabloid, slightly left-leaning. While this fulfilled much of Bill's creative talent, and he advanced quickly there, there was often conflict and the looming threat of self-censorship, as he was expected to tailor his writing to the demands of tabloid sensationalism. He then went to work for the CPA's *Tribune* in 1948, where he was the editor for two years from 1954. This meant a sizeable cut in pay. When Bill handed in his notice at the *Mirror*, the founding editor Frank McGuinness, having recognised a hard-working and talented writer, was not pleased. His shock that Bill was to work for the CPA and had taken the job at considerably less pay than he earned at the *Mirror* left him speechless. The *Tribune* reported that Bill's move to their organ was brought on when he was 'disgusted with the anti-labour distortions of the capitalist press', and was 'on the eve of promotion when he decided to quit the *Mirror* for the *Tribune*'.[9] By 1950, Bill was also a full-time functionary for the party.

Bill's support of Freda's work within, and outside, the party never wavered. They had joined the CPA at a particularly opportune time for women, when specific drives to recruit and activate women were proving successful, and Freda's four years of experience as a party activist before she talked Bill into joining gave Bill a huge stimulus. He always supported Freda's work, and they shared domestic as well as political duties. As Newcastle comrade Vera Deacon remembered, 'Men were dubbed "Backward Comrades" if they did not help with family chores and encourage their wives to participate in political and social activities.'[10]

During the last years of the war, communists were increasingly accepted in the fight against fascism, and Freda's work in public speaking for the party blossomed. She was doing regular speaking at the Sydney Domain and other public events. She also went out to contribute to the debates at workplace meetings, such as at Associated Battery Makers at Leichhardt, where she 'won strong support for the claim' of the workers at a 1949 dispute.[11] She spoke to 300 men at the Eveleigh rail yards.[12] On some occasions, Freda was the speaker with ALP anti-communist politician Arthur Calwell: he found out, 'and he said if I was speaking on the same platform he wouldn't speak on it, because he wouldn't speak with a communist'.[13]

One of her campaigns involved speaking at a 1946 Newtown CPA campaign against the government's plan to convert the Newtown Cemetery into parklands and a recreation area. Freda argued that the land should be reclassified to build flats. This campaign connected to her broader push to build schools and homes in the Newtown area, and Freda had gathered over 4,000 signatures for a petition. 'The lack of modernised housing and schools is to the eternal discredit of a succession of so-called workers' Parliamentary representatives, who have on occasion even opposed plans to provide improvements', she said; Freda's plan for improved housing had been rejected by ALP members on the Newtown council.[14] She also suggested that a pool be constructed in Enmore Park, which eventually went ahead, but not until 1962, though; 'a swimming pool in this crowded area would bring new life and vitality to youngsters, could provide swimming clubs and healthy competitive sports and also provide popular enjoyment', she argued.[15]

The end of the war heralded not just thousands of fighting men and women returning to Australia, but an increase in the housing shortage. Bill and Freda were still living with Ben, Flo and the boys in the Erskineville terrace before they could manage to find their own place. Bill loved sitting with Ben and hearing his father-in-law's stories of Wobbly battles and Depression times. Bill and Rae became close mates, and while over at Bondi having a swim – the growing family still loved to swim – Bill and Rae staged fierce handball matches at the gymnasium in the Bondi Pavilion. During this time, young Rae turned 21. Freda and Bill wrote an ode to Rae for the celebrations at Erskineville with the 'Loo' (Lewis) clan:

Ode for Rae's 21st Birthday
by WJ and FY Brown, August 1946

A birthday is a great event
The same the whole world over,
From Erskineville to Dillburyville
From Dagsburydale to Dover.
And to the life of Flo and handsome Ben
(known to most as Friendly Benny)
There came to pass a great event
As great as history's any.

A child was born! But then, you'll say
There's one born every minute.
Why, even Plebeians bear their broods
So there's really nothing in it.
But, ah! My friends, withhold your words.
This birth was one of many,
This charming child of Florence-Loo
In part of Friendly Benny.

But now you must forgive me,
I feel I've let you run ahead
And leap to wrong conclusions
In the rhymes you've so far read.
For I speak not of the youngest,
The child anointed Rae.
I speak not of the other
Well – who'd want to, anyway?

I speak, of course, about the eldest,
The charming Freda-Loo,
Upon whose birth, Ben surely said,
''Tis the best that I can do.'

But no! Ben's never satisfied,
Even with perfection's bliss.
Once more, Ben wooed fair Florence-Loo,
And sealed it with a kiss.

But man, oh man, in all his vanity
That man could be so dilly.
Much wounded pride must suffer he
Who seeks to gild the lily.
For once more there came to Ben's young life
An event of such elation:
Young Ben and Flo again were blessed
With another young relation.

Upon the birth, Ben came to Flo.
'Take a look,' says smiling Florrie.
Ben took one look. One seemed enough!
Ben said to Flo, 'I'm sorry.'
Said Flo to Ben, 'Let's call it Lee.'
Ben rose from bowed dejection.
'Ho', said Ben, 'Let's try again,
Let's improve this imperfection.'

But man, o man, in all his vanity;
On a certain August day,
The family-Loo were blessed anew,
And Ben was heard to say,
'Now, Florrie-Loo, now, what's to do?'
And Flo said, 'Ben, it's here.
Now take a look, but take it slow:
Don't scare the little dear.'

Ben looked, and shook, and turned aside,
And then began to curse.
Then, always ready with a pun:
'We've gone from bad to worse!'
Said Ben, 'Of course we'll try once more.'
But Flo said, 'Listen, Ben,
Upon our laurels let us rest.
Don't let us try again.'

But Ben became most angry,
And began to rave and shout.
But when he chanced another glance
He then began to doubt.
'Well, then, perhaps it's better –
After all, we did have fun –
After this, it's rather risky
To attempt another one.'

So now, until this very day,
In fact, this August date,
The clan of Loo – with much ado –
Rejoice and celebrate
The decision Ben was bound to take
On seeing brother Rae,
When he turned to Flo, and idly said,
'Well, let's call it a day.'

The girl comrade

Freda's responsibilities in the party increased through the late 1940s
and 1950s. She went on the council of the Eureka Youth League
(EYL), the youth branch of the CPA. The CPA had established this
youth organisation in 1942, with the merger of the Young Communist
League and ALLY. Freda was 'considered the leading spirit of the
organisation', and she worked with the EYL for a number of years.
She also worked on the Sydney Metropolitan Committee of the CPA's
Sydney branch, and was a tutor at the Marx School evening classes.
Freda took to radio broadcasts very well, and 2KY listeners knew her
as 'The Voice of the People' on Monday nights, as well as early in the
mornings.[16] This radio station was owned by the NSW ALP, and was
established in 1925 by the NSW TLC as 'the first labour radio station
in the western world'.[17] Despite the widespread popularity of these
broadcasts generally, there was some opposition to them when Central
Committee member Ernie Thornton said that 'it is my own personal
opinion that these radio talks are not worth spending money on and

particularly this early morning talk that Comrade [Adam] Ogston and the girl comrade [Freda] are running'.[18]

Freda's promotion of the rights of women set her aside from others who called themselves 'feminists', at least in the first half of the century in Australia. Joy Damousi writes about this 'equal but different' status of party women, noting,

> it is important to remember that while these women were staunch advocates of women's rights and addressed women's issues, gender was not the determining factor in their politics. Their political program was structured by the language of class, and it was through this language that they expressed their grievances and asserted their rights as working class women.[19]

Freda consistently argued for equality within a class structure. In one *Communist Review* article she wrote,

> the attack on women's wages behoves the Communist Party and the Trade Union Movement to give more attention to developing the struggle to consolidate wartime gains and extend them to establish the principal of 'equal pay' for the sexes according to the job or award classification by raising women's wages to the rates established for males in the various award classifications... The hypocrisy of the bourgeois ideology of 'women's-place-is-in-the-home' will be easily grasped as women struggle against big business attempts to prepare to unload the crisis burdens with women once again as a condition-worsening, cheap labour force.[20]

In 1947, Freda threw her hat into the parliamentary ring, and nominated as the CPA candidate for Newtown. At the party's campaign launch, she was in good company, with her comrades J.B. Miles, Stan Moran, Idris Williams (president of the Miners Federation), Ernie Thornton (general secretary of the Ironworkers Federation) and the journalist Rupert Lockwood, who at that time was the *Tribune* editor. She campaigned with these other party candidates, along with her campaign director Jack Hughes, who was the secretary of the Clerks' Union.[21] The CPA contested 15 seats in this election, and they had good support:

over 3,000 people attended one of the party's rallies at the Sydney Town Hall, where Freda discussed her campaign for improved housing and schools.[22] She received 6.81 per cent of the votes (1,367 votes), and a digger in Japan, in the occupation forces, even sent a donation to her campaign; but Lilian Fowler, the incumbent Labor member and the first woman mayor in Australia, won.[23] During that campaign, some Newtown police picked her up for putting up campaign posters, but released her when they recognised her as a local girl.

Again, in the federal election of 1949, Freda stood as a House of Representatives candidate for the CPA, in the division of Evans, which took in inner-west suburbs of Sydney. This was alongside Betty Reilly and 74 other CPA candidates, the largest number ever stood up.[24] The party promoted Freda and Betty as 'well-known to industrial workers for their unceasing work for higher wages, for equal pay for women and for a general all-round improvement in living and working conditions'.[25] The two women were amongst the earliest of the post-war party women to go out and be active speakers and recruiters.[26] Freda believed that 'only Communist policy will end the depression and war program of the Liberal and Labor parties and lead Australia along the path of peace and plenty'.[27] At an election meeting, she called for 'unity of all forces of the Labor movement to fight for socialism so that Australia could harness atomic energy for the people's security instead of their destruction'.[28] She campaigned on behalf of the 'housewives' vote', pointing out that 'both Liberal and Labor had done nothing to ease the housewives' burden and that only the Communist Party had the solution'.[29]

Travelling for the party

Ian Syson writes of the role that the CPA played in bringing new dimensions to the lives of some of its women members, as their lives 'obtained a public dimension that was not available in many other areas of Australian public life. They received training in public speaking, organisational activity and public political argument. The Party might well have imposed a structure on their lives, but it at least was a structure that enabled women to achieve a relatively high level of social prominence and impact and some sense of liberation.'[30] This was certainly the case with Freda, who at a very early age was renowned for her public speaking. The earliest reports in the mainstream press of Freda's prolific speaking career for the party date from the winter of 1944, when she travelled to Perth (to the Modern Women's Club, which had been founded by Katharine Susanna Prichard, where the Perth's New Theatre was situated, and, later, the Union of Australian Women). There she presented the party's arguments supporting the ultimately unsuccessful Curtin government's referendum on post-war reconstruction and democratic rights.[31] She was regularly billed as 'one of the youngest and most talented of Australia's Communist women leaders… She gave up a promising stage career to devote all her energies to the cause of working-class emancipation. She is recognised today as one of Australia's most brilliant woman orators.'[32]

In 1945, she spoke up in the Hunter Valley and the Riverina in the early part of the year, for the Yes case for the referendum.[33] She was only 25 then, and as well as a large number of speaking engagements in halls and civic centres in this tour, she gave live broadcasts for the Cessnock commercial radio station 2CK. Back at home in Sydney, she spoke with workers at the Garden Island Graving Dock in a lunchtime discussion group, and one builder's labourer responded to her speech, 'If that's the Communist policy, it's OK by me.'[34] From this time until 1950, she travelled widely throughout the country, speaking at communist and trade union meetings. She once did a two-hour trip by horse and gig to address a meeting of farmers at the remote town of Balldale, in the Riverina; the AWU delegate who had organised the tour, Andy Ursin, reported that 'there are few women who would put up with the discomforts Freda has endured – and without a murmur'.[35]

Her years of public speaking for the New Theatre and the party prepared her well for these trips. In Victorian Morwell, she was described as 'young, brilliant and enthusiastic'.[36] The *Tribune* reported that 'in many towns visited by Miss Lewis, there were no Communist Party members, but ALP members welcomed her, and arranged meetings'. A letter from a South Australian ALP member congratulated her on her talk at Mount Gambier: 'I think all who heard her here were electrified at the wonderful power of speech she possesses. It is indeed a great tribute to our Australian women when they can produce people of Miss Lewis's ability, and is a good omen for the future of this country.'[37] She spoke at Temora, where 'a sergeant of police asked visiting speaker Miss Freda Lewis to stand for Parliament in the next elections. And an 80-year-old countryman followed her round to every meeting in Ganmain, repeating, "I've never heard any one like her in my time."'[38]

In the autumn of 1946, she went on another nationwide speaking tour, and her itinerary shows her energy, enthusiasm and organisational strengths. On 8–12 March she spoke in Queensland at Gladstone, Rockhampton, Ogmore and Mount Morgan, where she was billed as being 'considered by the Australian Communist Party to be its most outstanding young woman speaker', and a 'brilliant young woman speaker'.[39] On 25 and 26 March she spoke at a number of Townsville meetings. On 8 April, she spoke at a public meeting on a street corner in Cairns, where she was supporting the CPA candidate for the municipal election. On 31 May, she spoke at the Town Hall in Morwell, Victoria, in support of the Federal CPA candidate, Wally Williams. The local press billed her as 'the outstanding speaker, who, on her last visit to Morwell, held her audience spell-bound'. Her earlier work in public speaking for the New Theatre had brought her much skill and acclaim throughout the country, and this carried through to government intelligence; an ASIO agent named Freda as the 'best-known CPA speaker in 1946'.[40]

While she was in Townsville, she was finally able to be with Bill, who had not yet been demobbed and was still working for the army. They hadn't seen each other for more than a few hours at a time for a few years, and they found a billet with some party members in Townsville. A family story tells that because the party had kept billing Freda under her maiden name, she was doing this Queensland tour as Freda Lewis. One of their comrades commented that, as Freda was on a speaking tour for the party, and being billed as Freda Lewis, it might be a better look if Bill changed his surname to Lewis. Bill was, reportedly, not amused.

When she travelled to speak at Grafton, the city council refused the use of the Market Square and other council buildings to hold a public meeting.[41] Freda defied the ban, and although police attended, they didn't make any arrests, and Freda spoke to an enthusiastic audience, as well as selling 45 newspapers.[42] In another dramatic journey, she braved the rural folk of Cowra. Amidst interjections, jeering, and the chairman losing control of the meeting, a motion was carried 'to the Federal Government to declare the Communist Party an illegal organisation'. It was reported that 'the meeting carried the motion by a large majority', and everyone in the hall walked out – but not before Freda bravely jumped at the chance to issue a challenge to anyone in the hall to meet her in the street the next day to debate communism with her.[43] 'Men need little courage and intelligence to join an organised body to interject against a lone woman speaker in a hall,' she said.[44]

For progress: the New Housewives' Association

Never backward in increasing her networks, Freda joined the New Housewives' Association (NHA) at its formation on 19 June 1946. With the increasing number of post-war political campaigns of all persuasions to focus on the needs of women, Freda said that the aims of the NHA 'attracted me to the women's movement and that's where I worked after that'. The NHA's slogan was 'For Progress', and its objectives were

> to organise housewives (on a state and national scale) in order to exercise their influence in the interests of the community in a non-sectarian and non-party manner;
>
> to work to maintain and improve the standard of living of the Australian people;
>
> to defend the democratic rights and independence of the Australian people;

to work for world peace and security based on international cooperation and understanding and to cooperate with progressive women of all countries to achieve this end.[45]

Progressive women established the NHA, initially in Sydney, at the instigation of the CPA. Barbara Curthoys writes that

the NHA included in leading positions women like Betty Reilly, Freda Brown, and Hetty Searle, who made no secret of the fact that they were members of the Communist Party, and considered that they had the same rights as anyone else to join and help establish an organisation. However, the fact that prominent communists were in leading positions led many to attribute to it subversive motives.[46]

The NHA worked closely with trade union committees; and amongst male supporters, attending their protests and contributing articles for the NHA's journal *The Housewife* were leading left unionists and party comrades Tom Wright and Pat Clancy, as well as Bill. The women that Freda was to work with in the NHA and its succeeding organisation were to be her closest friends for many decades. They established and maintained networks of individuals and organisations working in many fields. Zora Simic reminds us that for women activists between the waves, like Freda, 'Feminists and other women activists in this period established the space, framework, networks, tools and discourse for campaigns such as equal pay that came to fruition in the women's liberation period.'[47]

In 1946, rationing was still in place from the war, and prices of food and general goods were very high. Early and enduring campaigns for the NHA were equal pay and demonstrations against high prices. NHA members organised courageous and high-profile protests in Sydney and elsewhere over the next few years, primarily against high prices, which were a contentious issue in post-war Sydney particularly. One, in the first week of March 1948 in Sydney, led by the NHA as well as trade unions, had over 3,000 people in attendance.

Soon after its establishment, NHA branches were being formed in suburbs of Sydney as well as Melbourne. The network grew quickly:

by October 1946, there were NHA Sydney branches at Granville, Hurstville, Balmain, Ashfield and Mosman. There wasn't a Bondi or eastern suburbs branch up until around 1949, when Freda and Betty Bloch were amongst the women to establish it. Through the late 1940s, Freda continued her work in the NHA; at the 1948 IWD Domain Rally, she was one of the main speakers.[48] On 2 June 1949, the state branches convened to establish a national body, with Vena Barton as its first president and Ella Schroder as vice-president and secretary. The NHA's first national conference was held that day, at the Ironworkers Conference Hall (199 George Street), and the program included a New Theatre tableau.

In line with CPA policy, the NHA was an anti-feminist organisation: in 1948, it was battling against the conservative Housewives' Association, including 'the peddling by the Executive of Liberal Party propaganda, and their Feminist policy which divides women from men, creates confusion and helps the big monopolies'.[49] Instead, the NHA followed the CPA's concentration on class-based issues that affected women. Barbara Curthoys, leading communist activist from the 1950s, writes that 'the NHA was formed to try to combat the ever-increasing prices, black-marketing, attacks on women's wages together with all other problems besetting the community. Its main campaign was to stabilise prices by the re-introduction of price control.'

At one demonstration, Freda spoke in Sydney's Macquarie Place along with four other NHA members in front of a large crowd, and took to the Prices Commissioner a petition of 5,000 signatures against the high cost of living (particularly soaring meat prices). The high prices of food, in particular fresh fruit and vegetables, had been an issue for both the NHA and the CPA, along with a number of unions and other organisations such as the EYL. One of the police officers attending the meeting tried to censor Freda by muzzling her microphone, but he was verbally attacked by the crowd: there were indignant cries of 'Give her a go!', 'What did we fight for?' and 'Isn't there freedom of speech any more?'[50] Extra police rushed to the scene.

CPA member from Burwood, Adam Ogston (who was to become, by 1953, the publisher of the *Communist Review* and the chairman of the Sydney district of the CPA), had introduced Freda as 'one of the greatest orators in the Labour Movement'.[51] Freda, along with other women, and men, from the CPA, continued to agitate for lower prices for housewives through NSW and to support party members in local, federal and state elections.[52]

Equal pay was also a perennial concern for the NHA. One of Freda's articles concluded that 'the Liberal Party, the Labor Party, the ACTU and the right wing Labour Councils all give lip service to the principle of equal pay. Communists alone are capable of, and willing to lead the struggles of women themselves – the only way to make equal pay a reality. It is vital that we realise the urgency of this task.'[53] After women in Australia had entered new sections of the paid workforce during the war, they had won some struggles for wage equality, partly due to the efforts of the Women's Employment Board. The Curtin Labor government established this board in 1941 to encourage the entry of women into the wartime labour force; it had also helped get women's pay rates in a number of key industrial areas rise to 90 per cent of men's. After the war, employers fought back, however, and 1949 saw a test case in the High Court of Australia, which overturned the higher rates, and ordered the Commonwealth Arbitration Court to set the female basic wage at 75 per cent of the male basic wage.

The Union of Australian Women

With the establishment of the People's Republic of China in 1949, the Cold War was entering its worst period, and communists in Australia were under a lot of pressure. Robin Gollan writes of the party's fortunes during this time: 'from being a generally unpopular minority political party it became an allegedly seditious conspiracy on trial before the community and the courts'.[54] Liberal Party leader Robert Menzies won the federal election on 10 December 1949 with his divisive anti-communist platform, and the proscription of the CPA was among his early legislative measures. On 8 July 1949, police raided Marx House and took a number of items, amongst them Freda's files on her party organising, as well as some NHA documents and pamphlets. ASIO documents following this raid indicate a plan to include the NHA amongst the list of proscribed organisations in the upcoming Menzies government's Communist Party Dissolution Act.[55]

The ALP also banned women who were members of the NHA, including its president, Vena Barton.[56] Leading feminist and president of the NSW Peace Council Jessie Street had chosen to resign from the ALP rather than leave the NHA.[57] After the attempted proscription of the CPA and the heavy suspicion and surveillance on communist-related organisations, the NHA disbanded, and its members formed the Union of Australian Women (UAW) on 26 August 1950 in Sydney.[58]

Freda spoke of the formation of the UAW:

I think it was normal and natural that an organisation more concerned with working class women should come into being... You had the New Housewives (Association) which was an ordinary grass roots organisation...why have it just housewives, why not have it [as] a broader organisation?[59]

She said that

to embrace all women, in the factories, the office, and the home, is to be welcomed and encouraged by the whole Labor Movement and all sections of the working people of Australia. The CP, the trade unions, the shop committees particularly should do everything possible to help the Union grow from strength to strength. Women organised into action can play a decisive part in the struggle for a better living in an Australia at peace.[60]

With Bill's work on the *Tribune*, Freda was able to contribute a weekly column on the work of the UAW, titled 'Half Humanity'. Very soon after the formation of this organisation that was to play such a big role in Freda's life, she became pregnant for the first time.

The UAW's first office was in the Ironworkers Building at 188 George Street in Sydney, on the fifth floor.[61] It soon moved to rooms in

Trades Hall, where it shared the iconic labour building with a number of other left-wing political and cultural organisations for many years. Their use of the building as a collective base for politically active women facilitated their effectiveness for the UAW women for networking on many levels.[62]

In her history of Australian feminism, Marilyn Lake writes that the UAW's objectives, focusing in its early decades on the practical living conditions of women and children, 'placed it in the distinctive Australian tradition of labour movement feminism', but that its 'commitment to solidarity with the men of their class precluded an identification as feminist and made it wary of sex antagonism'.[63] A reading of issues of the UAW's popular journal *Our Women* indicates the broad range of issues covered. Throughout her time working with the UAW, Freda wrote very regular articles for *Our Women*, as well as her 'We Say' page, which brought together diverse pieces of information and ideas about the roles and lives of women in Australia and across the world. The UAW was following the CPA's line here, working against separatism (although Freda, throughout her life, organised and attended many women-only events). Queensland UAW and CPA activist Alice Hughes gave her opinion about the UAW:

> we really started to leave our mark on history in the women's movement because while the UAW didn't deal with the question of sexuality, the same as the women's liberation movement did and that's another story and how that all fitted in, in the 70's, well the end of the 60's but nevertheless it has a militant organisation that set out to develop women's politics within the Trade Union movement to change the attitudes within the working class. And we did that.[64]

The NHA and then the UAW were affiliate members of the Women's International Democratic Federation (WIDF). WIDF was one of a number of non-government, anti-racist and anti-imperialist organisations established in 1945 that worked towards the inclusion of members from non-Western nations and from all classes.[65] WIDF worked towards improved women's rights, always out of a context of improved human rights. Its founding, and lasting, aims were centred on anti-fascism, world peace, the advancement of women and the protection of children.

Like the UAW, through its entire existence, WIDF's progressive and inclusive stand has seen many accusations of being a communist front, because of its willingness to reach out to member organisations behind the Iron Curtain and beyond the developed world.[66] Francisca de Haan, the world's leading historian on WIDF, has described it as 'the largest and definitely one of the most influential international women's organisations of the post-1945 era'.[67] Freda said that 'WIDF was never a revolutionary organisation because it is not, and never has been, a condition of membership in our organisation (the UAW) or of the WIDF that women completely support socialism'.[68] As Leonie Coltheart remarks, about criticism that was levelled at Australian feminist and WIDF co-founder Jessie Street during her work with international women's and peace organisations, 'feminist transnationalist networks were neither homogeneous, nor so malleable as to become a Communist front'.[69]

The UAW ASIO file contains a report that concluded 'in its own sphere, its interests are along the same lines as the CPA, and it engages in organising discontent rather than constructive work'.[70] This was a view shared by other party members, particularly men. Jim Moss, the president of the South Australian branch of the CPA, said,

> the UAW is controlled by the Communist Party. The main aim of the UAW is to educate those women who for some reason or other are not in a position to join the Party. Every woman who is a member of the Party should be a member of the UAW. The woman Party members should not get the idea that the UAW should come first. The Party must come first always. Remember that the work you do in the UAW is actually for the Party, and you must work with that object in mind. The UAW has gained considerable strength over the past year or so and is thought of as an organisation which is interested in Peace, the working class and things like that.[71]

The UAW was not a communist organisation, or a 'front', however. Betty Reilly, a member of NHA and the CPA, believed that the views of the party should not be imposed upon the UAW and that the new organisation was not to be 'an offspring of the CPA and to have no socialist objective'.[72] Certainly, the organisation's constitution made this quite clear. Freda believed that the UAW 'had a greater breadth [than the NHA] because it involved women who worked as well as housewives'.[73] When asked if she thought the UAW was simply a front, she said,

no, no, it was an independent women's organisation. Progressive, very progressive, close to the unions, a working class organisation, but it certainly was not (a front) – we had many members of the Labor Party. I would think maybe a few, not many, a few Liberals. But the overwhelming majority would have been just ordinary women.[74]

One of the early and lasting achievements of the UAW was its resurrection of IWD marches and celebrations. During the 1950s and 1960s, the organisation was the only one to keep the importance of IWD alive, and it was very courageous of UAW women, as well as CPA men, to organise and march in Sydney and Melbourne each year. It was not to be until 1972 that second-wave feminists contributed to celebrating this anniversary and to broadening its popularity. The UAW also ran campaigns on the right to equal pay, and other important issues: 1951 was the year of the Anti-Communist Referendum, and Joy Damousi notes that the UAW 'undertook the major activity in appealing to women to vote No'.[75] The CPA spent £40,000 on its campaign, and all comrades and supporters were put to work on this most important issue.[76]

Both Freda and Bill were on the party payroll now; and they had just enough money to find a place of their own. In 1950 they moved to Bronte, renting flat 1, 13 Dickson Street. The block of flats was also known as Palmerston Court. Freda recalls, 'We lived at Bronte and we used to have the [CPA] branch meetings at our place, and a number of times we had police cars out the front and we used to say to people, "Don't go out the back." And sometimes you could hear the

– you knew your phone was being tapped, you could tell that.' After their move to the eastern suburbs, Freda became an active member of the Bronte UAW branch, along with her good friend and fellow communist Betty Bloch. Betty and Peter lived with their daughters Paula and Cathy in Bronte, at 10 Pacific Street, a cottage on top of a hill overlooking Bronte Beach, close to Freda and Bill. Freda said that 'To begin with I was, really, only a rank and file member. I worked in the area, in the locality and we formed branches in Bondi. And we went around and canvassed with the journal, and so I worked mostly in the local area.' Of course, it was much easier for Bill and Freda to get to the beaches, now only a short walk east. Swimming, body-surfing and walking on the beaches was an even more favourite activity now.

A growing family

With the war over, and Bill earning a modest but regular wage as a full-time CPA functionary and *Tribune* journalist, the time seemed right to start a family. In the spring of baby boom 1950, Freda became pregnant for the first time. Russian doctors had recently begun using the natural childbirth methods of psychoprophylaxis, developed by Anatoly Petrovich Nikolaev (later popularised by French obstetrician Ferdinand Lamaze), and Freda heard about these from writer Dorothy Hewett, the editor of the first edition of *Our Women* (writing as 'Toddy Flood'), who had seen women deliver naturally in the Soviet Union. Freda learnt about these special breathing techniques and exercises, an approach to labour which was not then widespread in Australia.

Freda continued her party work, including radio broadcasts, whilst she was pregnant and doing her Lamaze exercises. During her talk on Dubbo's local radio station 2DU, she drew listeners' attention to the fact that 'during the war the Federal Government said that this country had to be made fit for heroes to live in. Today, with Government and semi-government rules and regulations one had to be a hero to live in it.'[77] She also worked as one of the state councillors of the EYL.

Freda and Bill's daughter Lee was born on 30 May 1951, at

the King George V Memorial Hospital for Mothers and Babies at Camperdown. Lee was a healthy baby, and she was the third grandchild for Ben and Flo, after Rae's two boys Paul and Greg. Freda later said that 'the greatest joy of my life was when my daughter was placed in my arms'.[78] Before her birth, Freda had attended the prenatal classes at the Women's League of Health, in the city, and when her friend Audrey McDonald was pregnant with her son Daren, got her to go to the classes there as well.[79] Freda had kept up her swimming at the eastern suburbs beaches, and had no complications with Lee's birth. It was a family joke that the love of the surf had to be in Lee's blood – when Freda was heavily pregnant, Lee's nose would scrape along the sand as Freda caught a wave in to the shore. Much later, Freda talked of how proud she was of Lee, that 'she's lived up to all my expectations'.

Freda recalled how her commitment to the UAW increased when Lee arrived:

> when my daughter was born I went into the women's movement. Well, you started to be very concerned about things that concern women, and frankly, you no longer fitted. You had a child, you were feeding the child and looking after it and so you didn't fit in to the mainstream of political life. It was much more difficult then than it is now.[80]

The UAW was one of the first Australian organisations outside the CPA to campaign for child care, and recognised that so many women in Freda's generation would have gone out to work if they had access to organised child care. During this time, the UAW had a big campaign in Sydney's eastern suburbs for more childcare centres. Throughout their history, the members of the UAW have fought for better childcare services: the organisation's successes in promoting childcare were crucial for generations of Australian families (not just women) to come.

8 a.m. CPA office

Thought I'd come in early, while it's a bit quieter in here. Bill said he'd come in later, get Lee off to Betty's. Hope he remembers the extra bottle along with the nappies.

I know what you're thinking but you're wrong. Bill's wrong, too. Stay at home with the baby, he said. Everything will get on all right without you. But it won't, will it? Who else is going to keep on top of all of this? The blokes? They wouldn't know where to file anything, for a start.

So here I am, back at the office, getting through the post, Lee with the neighbour, breasts aching like you wouldn't believe. God, I hate that breast pump! I had to argue so hard with the doctors to get out of King George this early. Thank goodness for all those new Lamaze breathing exercises – no stitches, no forceps.

Betty said she'd ring through at lunchtime every day to let me know Lee's all right. I said, for heaven's sake why? Would I leave her with you if I didn't think she'd be right? Betty used to be a kindy teacher herself, back in Germany, before the war. God, what could go wrong?

Not another one – I'm sick to death of these rubbish threats. Just hysterical. Anyone'd think that communism had been invented yesterday. I know all the papers are full of Pig Iron Bob's referendum plans. But all our campaigning. I'm getting a feeling that even people who opposed you as a communist, lots of them, some of our neighbours even, are still saying people have the right to express their point of view. Even Doc Evatt is opposing this referendum. Surely they can't think the party is all that powerful. Yes, I think it will be defeated by the mass protest of people. I have to think that.

I thought it would all change in my head when Lee was born. Some of it has. All this work the union's been doing for more child care centres, for a start. Now it's really personal. Campaigning for women to be able to breast feed the babies in the child care centres. This rubbish idea of them being fed formulas. And they don't need it, most of the women, they could feed their baby, give them breast milk. But then they're being convinced by Nestlés. If we had more child care centres, a place to feed, show those Lamaze exercises. Mothers have been working much more since the war.

I know, now, how difficult it is when you've got a kid. Extremely difficult. Bill and I talked about it all for months: How were you going to get out and organise and do meetings if you had a little baby to look after? I'll organise it, I said. The women comrades will help too.

Don't get me wrong, you know how committed I am. Never changed my mind since I was 17. Joined up – and then convinced Bill to join. The party's my life. It is. But it's the bloody men! The attitude, you know – all right for men to drop everything when the leader calls, but women – stay at home and be meek and mild. Double standards, all the way.

We're encouraged to be 'normal' working-class women, proper marriage and all that stuff, while the men can sow all their wild oats, before AND after the wedding. I know what poor Jean Devanny went through up in Queensland. But some of the women who were married, and who were in key type positions, were told not to have children. Remember Winnie Mitchell? She and Norm decided that they wanted to have a child. They actually went to the Central Committee to ask if it was all right! So, things took their natural course. Three weeks later, JB told Norm that the party had changed its mind and that because there was important work for Winnie to do, that she couldn't have a child. Too late! And then nine months later, there's Caroline, the sweet little thing.

Another death threat! File in the rubbish bin. Thanks for nothing.

Nearly nine – Bill and the others'll be in soon. Best to try and get the rest of the filing done. All for the good of the party.

Four months after Lee was born, the federal government held its referendum to ban the CPA, on 22 September. The referendum, narrowly rejected at the ballot box, stands out in post-war Australian history not just for its democratic assertions, but also as a crucial turning point for women: supporters of both the Yes and No votes targeted women as independent, responsible voters. Freda, along with her comrades in the UAW and the CPA, had been working hard to promote the No vote; the CPA raised a huge fighting fund, No committees were established far and wide, and a massive leafleting and publicity campaign launched. Joy Damousi notes that

the UAW, which undertook the major activity in appealing to women to vote No, not only mobilised the key elements of the general No case such as the democratic right to freedom of expression and protest, but also appealed to women specifically by connecting these questions to the domestic arena.[81]

One of the UAW's leaflets appealed in the defence of democratic rights for all: 'we women are equally threatened as men in the face of such attacks on our liberties'.[82]

It was a hard time for the young family – both Bill and Freda working round the clock on the No campaign, and both caring for Lee as well. Their youthful energy, the support of those around them, and their strong beliefs kept them going. Freda remembered her work during this difficult time:

> I can only say for myself and the people I mixed amongst, there wasn't what you called fear, you faced what you had to face…your main concern was to get on and do the job, and try to prevent him [Menzies] being successful in bringing a change to the constitution… we split up the big [CPA] branches into very small cells, we arranged places to meet, I remember I had to go along and have a chat to some people who were sympathisers and ask them could their place be used. There were plans for the publication of the illegal *Tribune* and illegal leaflets… It was always a possibly (that we'd end up in jail)… I remember it upset my mother terribly, about looking after Lee if both Bill and I be arrested. Of course we were very, very pleased (that the referendum failed). But not overly surprised, because, because in the campaigning you did get a feeling that there, even people who opposed you as a communist, still said, No, you have the right.[83]

The second pregnancy

Freda became pregnant a second time at the beginning of 1953. However, things did not go as smoothly as with Lee. During this pregnancy, Freda developed placenta praevia, a condition where the placenta develops below the baby within the uterus, and which is still a major cause of maternal mortality in the developing world.[84] As was the normal procedure for those years, she was treated with bed rest and a caesarean delivery. Baby John only lived for a couple of days after his birth on 22 November 1953, however. Of course this was a shocking blow to the Brown family, a tragedy for Freda and Bill. Freda spoke about this:

> The second pregnancy, I had what was called a placenta praevia, which was absolutely terrible. It's the afterbirth over the womb, or it's wrongly placed. With me, it was in the worst possible place, it was over the womb. Which meant that about every week I'd have a violent haemorrhage. I spent months and months and months just laying on my back in the hospital. And then when the baby was born they took it by caesarean and they thought I was dying, got all the family in. Then they had to remove the womb to stop the bleeding. And that was devastating for some months. It took me a long time to recover morally, mentally, physically and every way. That was hard… They took the baby at just under 7 months. And it lived for a couple of days. Maybe in this day and age they would have saved it… I lost the second child and then couldn't have any more. That was a very great sadness. I would have liked more than one child.[85]

You battled on

In 1954, Bill became the editor of the *Tribune*, a position he held for two years. While within the world of the party and their Sydney comrades, it was a prestigious job, there was still not much money for the family. And this was a very important and disturbing year for the party faithful in Australia, with events including a protracted waterfront dispute and the Petrov affair on the eve of the federal election. When leading Russian spy Vladimir Petrov defected in April without consulting his wife, the scandal, and the resulting Royal Commission, rocked the party. A leading activist within the party, the story of Bill's full part in the affair in his role on the Central Committee is still to be told. Bill covered the Petrov trial for the *Tribune* in the first half of that year. He also edited a book on the affair, detailing his opinion that the 'truth of the Petrov Affair is that it was no more than a crude political conspiracy organised over a long period with the knowledge of the Prime Minister Robert Gordon Menzies'.[86]

This was a very hard time for Freda and Bill, not least around their own home. Freda remembered how their relationship with their neighbours at Bronte changed after the Petrovs' defection: 'we were getting on very well with them, but lots of them, for some weeks, wouldn't even speak to us after that happened…all the people in the flats, really, they ostracised us for a period'.[87] It was very lonely for the Browns for a while then; however, the bad feelings from their neighbours subsided after a while. Of involving herself in the passionate and wide-ranging discussions on the politics and social life of the time, she said, 'when you're young you don't feel that's difficult, you feel you're participating in life and in struggle.'

Having begun her recovery from her second pregnancy and John's death, Freda took a heightened interest in looking after her health. Lee remembered, though, that through her childhood Freda was not strong, and had fainting spells. Still, she returned to her work with the CPA's Sydney committee in 1954. She was also back to public speaking at the Domain and chairing those sessions, as well as at factory meetings and street meetings, including the big workplace, Metters stove makers, with over 3,000 workers, Containers Ltd, Australian Forge Engineering Co., Electric Car workshops at Chullora, and at the ports of Glebe Island. She said that 'at the factories you got a good reception mostly. But at street meetings, they were very, very tough and very bitter. It'd be nothing to have things thrown at you. But you battled on.' Freda developed a thick skin, and great arguments against the many anti-communists of the time. Usually she would win the arguments; but sometimes it was impossible.

In 1954, Freda first applied for a passport, for travel that was to last six months. She and Bill planned to work in China, Russia, Europe and the UK. Her application letter to the Department of Immigration stated that she would be travelling as a 'tourist'.[88] However, the government refused her application, a typical action during the height of anti-communism; since 1950, ASIO assumed all responsibility for screening passport applications. The trip was to have been, for Bill and

Freda, one of the many study trips that the party organised for its more promising members.

Her work with the Sydney committee grew; at the 1955 CPA Sydney District CPA Conference, Freda spoke on party finance. She was also very energetic in peace activity in the Sydney branch, and still speaking in the Domain on Sundays, sometimes with Rupert Lockwood and Stan Moran. They were all members of the Australian Peace Council (APC). The Reverends Alf Dickie and Frank Hartley and Victor James had founded the APC in July 1949 as the local branch of the World Peace Council (WPC), which was an 'anti-imperialist, democratic, independent and non-aligned international movement of mass action'.[89] Deery and Jordan have named the CPA as 'the driving force behind the APC', but like the UAW, while communists made up some of its membership, many of the leaders and activists were from church and other non-political organisations.[90] Freda was to work with the APC and the WPC for many years, here in Australia as well as overseas.

1956 and the secret speech

1956 was a momentous year for communists all over the world, with Khrushchev's denunciation of Stalin's crimes at the 20th Congress of the Communist Party of the Soviet Union, followed by the Soviet invasion of Hungary. The events further deepened the frozen Australian corners of the Cold War, with comrades' belief in the supremacy of the Soviet Union shaken to the core. Many left the movement, and many were 'abused by neighbours and work-mates'.[91] Bill as editor of the *Tribune* made the decision to use the 4 July edition to publish details concerning the location of abridged versions of the 'secret speech' and other key speeches made at the congress.[92] In a series of articles in the *Communist Review*, Bill made other criticisms of the impact the speech had made in Australia, and these included criticism of the way that the CPA leadership had handled the situation.[93]

Tom O'Lincoln discusses Bill's 'remarkable series of articles in the *Communist Review*.

Brown sought to build on the positive features of the Stalin revelations as he saw them, and to use them to strengthen the party within the context of official policy. This was a delicate high-wire performance, and Brown suffered a bruising at the end of it.[94]

Similarly, another analyst believes that Bill's 'lack of consideration of the legitimacy of members' concerns, disappointments and sense of betrayal upon hearing the contents of the "secret speech" makes his discussion of the events one dimensional and seriously deficient'. At the same time, he did, however, make some attempt to criticise the 'cult of the individual'.[95] In a series of articles, he examined 'ways in which the cult had expressed itself within the CPA, especially the reluctance of members to question the views of leaders and their dogmatic approach to issues that stifled discussion and creative thinking'.[96] Bill was reprimanded by party leadership, in particular Victorian State Secretary Ted Hill, but did not break ranks. He was elected as the secretary of the newly established CPA Sydney District Committee that year; both Bill and Freda received the highest number of votes of comrades elected. It was a busy time for him and the family, however; during this year Bill had to move to Concord to live for a short time with his mother, who was an invalid.[97]

Party member Bob Walshe recalls Bill's reactions to the speech. Typically, the sea was a balm for him in this troubling period:

> I recall being asked in to talk with Bill Brown who assured me the document was a 'falsification' by the CIA… [Bill told me] 'Look, I've read the document and it did upset me at first, but I took a fortnight off, spent a lot of time on the beach, tossed a ball around, and regained my class perspective. I'm a better party member for the experience, and I strongly recommend you to do the same.'[98]

Over the next few months, a few hundred people were expelled from or broke with the party; despite the revelations of 1956, and in particular the Soviet invasion of Hungary, neither Bill nor Freda resigned. As always, Freda never publicly wrote or said anything critical of the Soviet Union at the time. Decades later, however, she reflected on the events of 1956:

I think there were many mistakes made. Many mistakes. I couldn't go into all the details of it. I don't know, but I do think they made mistakes. But I think the difficulty was in trying to build socialism, one little island of socialism, surrounded by capitalism. And then I think a mistake was made then when, after the war, socialist armies went in to Hungary, Poland, etc. Well, I don't think you can impose a system on people, and I think there were some mistakes made there.[99]

Freda worked hard for unity within the CPA Central Committee during this difficult year, and wrote in a report that 'it is essential to get clear the cause of disunity, not only to restore unity in the (Sydney) Committee but to facilitate what I feel is all important – the turning out of the Sydney Committee to mass work'.[100] She had been championing a resolution calling for the implementation of the International Labor Organisation's convention on equal pay, writing that 'recently published figures show that the number of married working women has more than doubled between 1947 and 1954. This raises the need for facilities for working mothers – kindergarten[s], after school child minding centres etc.'[101]

Work among women

In spite of great difficulties within the CPA, the UAW was growing steadily, now with state organisations in Victoria, Qld, NSW, WA and SA. It became a national organisation at its first national conference in Sydney on 7–11 November 1956. By 1957, the UAW national membership was around 6,000, and it was an energetic and growing organisation. One of the major campaigns for the UAW during this period was the Mother and Child Campaign to extend child endowment and maternity allowances. Lee had begun primary school, and with more time, Freda organised this campaign alongside Barbara Purse, Ella Schroder, Noreen Hewett and Pat Elphinston. On 6 August 1958, the opening day of federal parliament, 280 Sydney UAW women travelled to Canberra to lobby parliamentarians for increased child endowment and maternity allowances, and work for coalfields unemployed.[102]

In 1958, the Bronte group of the UAW merged with Bondi and Paddington to become the Waverley group. Freda, along with Betty Bloch, led the group in campaigns on a number of fronts, taking young Lee along with her to after-school meetings and protests. Later Waverley leader Debbie Knopman notes that the 'local group were proud to go on sales canvasses to homes in the area promoting their work, and sometimes presenting a Petition for Peace while discussing social issues with householders'.[103] Freda became a leader of the UAW as national secretary and national president from 1963 to 1973, and continued developing her skills in political negotiations and organising. Loma Thompson was a Townsville UAW member; she recalled that 'having been to UAW conferences, having heard people like Freda Brown, you know, you're looking at some of the very strong, capable women'.[104]

Lee was growing quickly, but this did not hamper Freda's activism. As well as her full-time occupation at CPA headquarters and her work for the UAW, she was also a member of the Learn to Swim Campaign at Bondi, teaching free swimming classes to children alongside her brother Rae. Bill helped out at home as much as he could, and loved taking Lee to the beach, and teaching her how to surf. Wanting Lee to be able to protect herself if she had to, he also taught her some self-defence techniques. Freda's work with left-wing trade union groups also grew; for instance, a women's deputation, including Freda and Flo Davis, called upon NSW Premier Cahill in 1957, campaigning for equal pay.[105] Freda and Ella Schroder had become justices of the peace, and in 1958 they completed a term at the WEA together, studying the subject Women's Status. They suggested that all members of the UAW should register at police stations for jury work.[106]

Freda's status within the party was also growing. In April 1958, the CPA's 18th National Congress elected Freda to the CPA's Central Committee, 'to control party activity amongst women', according to an ASIO agent – surely an exaggeration, as there were other women on the Central Committee.[107] She spoke at the congress on the work of women in the party, and referred to the 'resistance to known

Communists being active in work among women'; she suggested that it was high time for the party to draw up a women's program.[108] Newcastle comrade Barbara Curthoys followed up, in the June issue of the *Communist Review*, with an article on the participation of women in the working-class struggle. Progressive organisations around the world were preparing for the 50th anniversary of International Women's Day. Freda wrote,

> In two years we will be celebrating the fiftieth anniversary of the inauguration of IWD in 1910. It would be good to set that as a goal for the solution of some [problems and] as a step in the direction of drawing women into the struggle for Peace and Socialism.[109]

One of Freda's accomplishments during this period was a speech at a gate meeting at the Eveleigh Railway Workshop, where she talked about equal pay, women and unemployment, and the upcoming ACTU Equal Pay Conference. This last event was an important one in the history of NSW working women's achievements, and Freda and other delegates vigorously represented the UAW's recommendations.[110] In her campaign to help women achieve better representation in the workplace, she commented on the conference and the NSW equal pay decision. She noted that although these had quickened interest in the equal pay campaign, it would not 'be given on a platter…women are becoming more socially and politically conscious every day, however it did not mean that women were yet on an equal footing with men'.[111] Freda stated that

> women lost their equality with the beginning of class society, their separation from the means of production placed them in a position of inferiority but with the victory of socialism in Russia, women regained their right to equality in reality as well as legality – the right to equal pay, the equality of opportunity, their right to be elected to all governing bodies was assured.[112]

In none of her public statements, her very few published articles or letters home was Freda ever substantially critical of the Soviet Union's polices, and she stuck to this all her life. She did discuss the Russian situation, and the party at home, with Bill and Lee, and other comrades, but was very discreet about airing any disagreements publicly.

History-soaked cobbles: Russia

By 1958 with the slight thawing of the Cold War, Freda and Bill finally got their passport applications approved, and travelled overseas in a CPA party to Russia and China for the first time, to 'do a school in Moscow'. Freda recalled it as 'political economy, international history, philosophy, the history of the three internationals, that sort of thing'. The Browns spent 14 months in Russia and China, often travelling by train across the vast plains.[113] Young Lee stayed with comrades Phil and Betty Thorne down in Kangaroo Valley, where Freda and Bill thought that she would enjoy living in a rural setting with animals – a good start for her later studies in zoology. There were around 13 party members on this trip, including journalist and New Theatre comrade Paul Mortier, Amalgamated Engineering Union federal executive Ted Rowe, Mary Crisp, Les Kelton, UAW comrade Gloria Garton and the first UAW president, Vena Barton and her husband Robert.

Bill and Freda visited factories and other sites during their 14-month trip, and worked alongside communist functionaries, trade union leaders, and journalists. Like many Western communists, they were given the tour the CPSU officials wanted them to have. Later, she recollected these early trips to the Soviet Union:

> There was both positive and negative. It was very, very different to here. But, what impressed me, I felt women had far greater opportunity there than they had here…there wasn't the great gap between the rich and the poor, you know, and there was full employment. You didn't see beggars on the street, but on the way over as you passed through Hong Kong, Singapore and Hong Kong, you saw beggars. Well, you know, those kind of things, you found impressive. I found the education system very, very impressive, you know, there was real, very great opportunities for kids. [But] you didn't feel an atmosphere of freedom like you had here, you know, it's hard to put your finger on that. For example, we live in an island continent and you go anywhere

and do what you want to. There you have to have an internal passport and often when you had to go to a building you had to show your passport. And to get in and out of the school where we were, well that was understandable, because there were a lot of illegal people there. But, so there were things like that, you know, that to me were restrictive in comparison to life here. But...if anything [my trips to Russia] reinforced [my belief in the communist system], and I think Bill's too... I thought there was more opportunity and more real equality.

Bill returned home declaring that

this is Communism's decade...let the millionaire press rave in wishful efforts to see the sixties as a bright, new decade for capitalism. The inescapable fact is that this is not the decade of capitalism. This is the decisive ten years when Communism will surge on to greater and greater victories that will stir the minds and hearts of mankind as never before.[114]

He had an article published in *Trud,* the Soviet newspaper of the All-Union Central Council of Trade Unions.[115] The article was mildly critical of Australian industrial arbitration systems, high unemployment, wage inequality, high prices and low pensions despite the post-war economic boom. It came to the attention of the Australian embassy in Moscow, where Trevett Cutts, the chargé d'affaires, described it as 'particularly scurrilous'.[116]

Inspired by his trip, Bill took to poetry again:[117]

Here Comes Communism!

Here comes Communism
In Seven League strides
Armed with a Seven Year Plan!
To the Moon and beyond,
What a threshold two years,
Dramatic,
Decisive for man
Stand here on these history-soaked cobbles.
Look up from Moscow's Red Square.

From the heart of Communism
To the Cosmos –
Hurrah!
This triumph for all men to share.
Here comes Communism!
Let the Red Square resound
So Lenin, at rest, may hear.
Stir Stalin, Krupskaya, Zetkin, Kirov –
All you great in the Kemlin's wall.
See!
Fruit of your labours
High in the sky.
New vistas for man laid bare.
Man '…storming the heavens'.
The words ring anew.
'Oh, if Marx and Engels were here.'
Here comes Communism!
See the wide swinging arms
Of Moscow's countless cranes.
New homes,
New life,
Abundance here,
A people's mounting gains.
Yes,
Here comes Communism
In Seven League strides
Up out of the days of the Tsars.
Now –
Forward from Socialism!
New days shake the world!
Look –
Here it is, man's way to the stars!

They had been having 'a marvellous time' on their study trip, Freda
wrote in a letter back home to Australia. Freda was able to leave flowers
in the snow in front of the well-known German Marxist feminist Clara
Zetkin's grave on the Kremlin Wall in Moscow; and the whole party

attended classes and meetings as well as observing the National Day on 7 November. What impressed Freda was that women in Russia had much more opportunity than in Australia – 'I thought there was more opportunity and real equality'. Later in her life, Freda sometimes acted as an unofficial interpreter for Russians she met in her travels; she wrote later that she found it 'quite incredible how much (Russian) one remembers when put to it'.[118] She wrote that 'the Russian people are very much like us…they have our same easy-going attitude. They are very friendly, hospitable, and they love a joke.'[119]

The study tour wasn't all roses; Freda became ill and was a patient for 13 weeks in a Moscow hospital. She wrote of her first-class treatment by Soviet doctors, where 'the emphasis of the entire health services is on the care, comfort and welfare of the patient…hospitalisation and medical care reflects the deep concern for the welfare of the people in this mighty first land of Socialism'.[120]

Bill and Freda arrived back in Sydney on 17 December 1959, with the Bartons. 'Back in Australia', Bill wrote, 'you settle down to adjusting yourself after living in a society that has already moved on to tomorrow.'[121] A week later, the party threw a welcome home event for them at Trades Hall. Freda brought back photographs, slides, and small gifts along with her memories of the trip; she organised slide show nights and shared stories of her travels through the Soviet Union during her many months there. Over the next months, she also published reports of her trip, which she remembered very positively, even her hospital stay. One account concluded that 'my stay in Moscow gave me a real love of the Russian people. They are hard working and industrious, but also very cultured and fun loving. I came to realise what tremendous sacrifices they made during the war.'[122]

Back to Australia

Freda was on the CPA's Central Committee and State Committee through the early 1960s at least, along with Bill, whose weekly wage during this year was £16, less than the average of £21.[123] She continued her CPA speaking tours, addressing public meetings (and doing local radio broadcasts) in Tasmania in September 1960, for the CPA's 40th anniversary, talking about the proposed amendments to the Commonwealth Crimes Act, as well as world peace, and stories from her recent visits to the Soviet Union and China. She captivated the ASIO agent at the Hobart meeting: she 'generally impressed as a fluent, coherent and forceful speaker, who, for the most part, adopted a friendly tolerant attitude with the more difficult questioners'.[124]

In June 1961, Freda attended the 19th CPA Congress. She wrote an article on Work Amongst Women for the *Communist Review*. She was continually working towards the betterment of working-class women from a standpoint of class rather than gender, seeing the pre-second wave meaning of the term 'feminism' as undesirable:

> like our male comrades, our women must become vigorous spokesmen for the working class in the trade union movement. It is a particular responsibility of all our communist women to see that they learn to speak as members of the working class, speaking for the advancement of the working class as a whole in their immediate and long range aims and to see women's interests as inseparably bound to the advancement of the whole class. They must avoid putting forward sectional feminist standpoints at all times. Just as there is no future for any section of the working class without the Communist Party, it is doubly so for women. It is our Party alone that will lead women, with the whole of the working class, to their emancipation.[125]

At the May 1961 CPA School in Adelaide, an ASIO operative reported that Freda's main point was that 'the Communist Party will take over in Australia in five years. There is no doubt about that. It is part of the Seven Year Plan. The change will come overnight.'[126] In 1961, she stood as a NSW Senate candidate for the CPA in the 9 December election, and presented her policies at the 19th National Congress and other CPA and public meetings. The CPA did not win any seats, but received 78,188 first preference votes (1.62 per cent); the eastern suburbs comrades celebrated with a party at Betty Bloch's Bronte home that night. She was working at the CPA's summer school, at Minto that year, and thereafter for a number of years, teaching various subjects including political economy and Marxism.

The only women demonstrating

By 1960, Freda's work with the UAW was increasing. She was on the UAW National Committee this year, having been elected at the Second National Conference in Sydney. At this conference, an ASIO operative noted the contrast between Freda and another UAW member, her friend Queensland Secretary Alice Hughes. Hughes 'is another in the "Russian mould" as typified by Freda Brown but is without the steadying diplomacy of Freda Brown. She is a fanatic who needs watching and would go to any lengths for her beliefs.' About Freda, she wrote,

> Freda Brown appears to have a chip on her shoulder about society. She is a very good speaker who can size a situation in a split second. She can be very diplomatic when necessary; it would be described as having a hand of steel in a velvet glove. She is a very astute person who can read a person's character in one meeting.[127]

Working for peace was an increasingly important task for the UAW. At this conference, Vena Barton moved a resolution in the form of a declaration to work untiringly for total disarmament and the end of war throughout the world. Then Freda moved an addendum that voiced opposition to the rebuilding of German and Japanese militarism. This became part of the resolution, adopted unanimously.[128]

Since its inception, the UAW had also concerned itself with the problems of women living in post-colonial countries, and this work increased with world events of the late 1950s and early 1960s. During a 1961 UAW meeting, 'Freda Brown spoke on the colonial question. Australia an imperialist country, for instance New Guinea. UAW must see that New Guinea people win independence soon. Supported the idea of Solidarity Week; referred to the printing of signs on the Belgian Embassy. Newspaper reports say that the wife of the Belgian Ambassador, after seeing the signs, had said, "it is a bit late for anyone to start writing signs now". She moved that a letter be written to the Belgian Ambassador expressing hope for peace and freedom for the Congo people; also a letter of sympathy for Mrs Lumumba' after her husband Patrice Lumumba was murdered in an American-sponsored assassination soon after winning democratic elections for the newly independent Congo.[129] Other issues of activism for the UAW in 1961 included Cuba (Freda wrote a pamphlet for the UAW, 'No War Over Cuba', produced just after JFK's broadcast), and Indonesia's independence struggles: Freda was elected to a UAW deputation to work with Johanna Nasution (wife of General Abdul Nasution) expressing solidarity with Indonesia.[130]

On 23 May that year, Freda went over to Perth to be the guest speaker at the UAW's WA division. Her ASIO file notes,

Mrs Brown, an experienced speaker, mentioned the importance of Labour [sic] and disposing of the Menzies Government at the next election. Brown urged members to take a more active part in politics by getting into Parents and Citizens and Progress Associations, Municipal Councils, Hospital boards and such like which are the stepping stones to Parliament. Members whose husbands are factory workers should take an active interest in the workers' welfare by helping in canteens and social clubs. Brown said she bought the clothing she was wearing in Moscow about eighteen months ago and it was cheaper than the Australian products. Men and women of the Soviet also put their pay on their backs and look just as smart as the Australians. Housing is still short because the Soviets are concentrating on other priorities. Brown also said that the average wage earner should belong to a Union and every union worker should vote for the Labour [sic] Party which is the Socialist Party.[131]

Apparently, Russian apparel had really caught her eye – Freda had earlier written an article for the *Tribune* on this topic.[132]

Recently married and pregnant with Daren, in 1962 UAW member Audrey McDonald took on the secretaryship of the Sydney IWD Committee, which consisted mostly of UAW women.[133] Audrey had been a member of the CPA for a number of years like Freda, and was soon to take on various roles in the UAW leadership. With her husband Tom, also a CPA member and a union official in the building industry, Audrey came to work alongside Freda and Bill in various organisations over the next few decades. Audrey says that Freda became her 'main mentor' through her work in the UAW.[134] Freda's confidence and growing experience was to inspire Audrey. She remembers Freda as

a dynamic person and an extremely talented and moving orator… she had a very strong personality and – like others – I relied heavily on her views. At times during this period, there were some issues on which I doubted the wisdom of Freda's approach. But I didn't feel I was equipped to argue against her and it seemed appropriate to defer to her view. Strangely enough, in later years when I was the UAW's leader, I suspect that some of my colleagues regarded me in the same light. This was probably due both to my personality and the fact that I was trained in Freda's mould. It also perhaps had something to do with respect for 'the leadership', which was always a part of the culture of the communist movement. Although I resisted this 'leadership awe', by involving colleagues in collective work and decision-making, somehow it was always my place to make the final decisions on most matters.[135]

From this time onwards, Freda worked more closely with left-wing trade union women's committees to implement UAW aims on a national level. She worked with trade union women including Gwen George and Audrey Barnes, both CPA members and unionists. She continued working in the UAW in other areas, notably peace activity. When Pat Elphinstone resigned as national secretary, she had promoted the idea of Freda, who was working as an unpaid organiser, being elected to that position.[136] Subsequently the UAW executive elected Freda as national secretary. Reflecting on the work of the UAW during the 1950s and 1960s, Freda said,

I think it is important to look at it historically. I think it played a very important role. Before us, there was the United Associations of Women; Jessie Street originally formed it. Organisations will come into being and go out of being, it seems to me, on the basis of the demands and needs of the times and I think we [UAW] fulfilled a very valuable role in that period…trying to involve working class women in organisation, and from the very beginning, as I remember, this was always seen at our Congresses (and) in our day to day discussion – how do you involve working women in organisation – and I think it played a very, very valuable role in organising women, in contributing to the peace struggle and in getting women out on the streets, because we were the first ones to get women out on to the streets. It wasn't easy in those days, it is nothing for everybody [to march] at the drop of a hat, but in those days we were the only women demonstrating.[137]

At the Third National conference of the UAW in 1963, Freda was elected as the national secretary of the new Federal Executive of the UAW, a role she held until 1967. Barbara Curthoys asked Freda what legacies her time with the UAW left her.

It gave me a great deal of friendships, very, very deep friendships. It gave me the opportunity to work with women, which was a very, very valuable experience, and of course the opportunity to go and work at WIDF and have this international experience.[138]

It was at this 1963 UAW national conference that a split in the Victorian UAW, stemming from disagreements over CPA peace and anti-nuclear policies, became evident. In her doctoral dissertation biography of Doris MacRae, a leading Victorian UAW figure, Cheryl Griffin reports that

the outrage of the national committee at the invasion of party politics into what was supposed to be a non- political organisation is clear. Its secretary, Freda Brown, asked the Victorian delegation to 'request Margaret Arrowsmith (Cash) and Hilda Smith to carry out the policy as laid down at the Conference', threatening that if they 'continued to oppose UAW policy…there would be no place for them in the organisation'.[139]

One of the issues for the UAW in 1963 was protesting against the French nuclear tests in the Pacific. Freda described it as 'the most important issue in this day and age'.[140] She joined Lady Jessie Street and the rest of the Australian delegation at the WPC session in Warsaw in November 1963. This was her third trip abroad that year, and it was the year that she really began travelling so often – she was usually working overseas many times every year until 1990. She also attended a women's conference in East Berlin. She travelled to London (to the Breakthrough to Disarmament conference at the Islington Town Hall in London on 23 and 24 November), and then to Warsaw for the WIDF Council, with Reverend Frank Hartley of the APC and WPC. This Warsaw meeting decided to hold a congress in Sydney the following year. Freda became a secretary, and later a vice-president of the WPC, and worked with them until 1990.

Working overseas for WIDF

One of Freda's first tasks as UAW national organiser through 1961 onwards had been to organise a delegation of 13 UAW members to travel to the WIDF Congress of Women in Moscow in 1963. From this time onwards, her work with WIDF began. Freda worked at all of the interstate UAW branches, often coordinating her interstate travel with a trip overseas for WIDF meetings. UAW members of far-flung branches appreciated these trips, and published voluminous commemorations of her visits in UAW journals, news sheets and letters. A typical announcement is when Freda was on her way to a 1962 WIDF council meeting.[141]

> Visit by National Secretary. We have had a lovely surprise. Our National Secretary, Mrs Freda Brown, will be passing through Perth on her way to a meeting of WIDF in Berlin. It has been decided to move the Management Committee meeting from Tuesday night 27 November to Wednesday morning 28th, when Mrs Brown can attend. She leaves Perth for Berlin at lunchtime that day, so it will be necessary to start the meeting at 10:15 sharp. It will be at the rooms. Although this will make things difficult for members who work and those with children on holidays, we hope it will be possible for quite a number to come. Small gifts for Mrs Brown to take as presents to other countries or WIDF would be welcome.[142]

In 1962 and 1963, Freda worked for WIDF in China, Poland, East

Germany, Hungary, Romania and Bulgaria. She had coordinated her travel this year with Bill being sent to Bulgaria and Moscow on another study trip.[143] Bill's work included his attendance as an Australian delegate to the 8th Congress Communist Party of Bulgaria. His poem 'Spring in Autumn' came home with him from that trip:

Spring in autumn
(to the 8th Congress Communist Party of Bulgaria, Autumn 1962)

Beautiful Bulgaria,
> Softly,
> Behold and stand –
> a visitor entranced
> by this Autumn-tinted land.

Battle-steeled Bulgaria,
> Quietly,
> Think and pause –
> Valiant blood flowed unspared here
> for mankind's noblest cause.

Beautiful Bulgaria,
> Gaily,
> Build and sing –
> for here this special Autumn
> heralds your finest spring.

This pattern of travelling overseas to work in women's and peace causes was to last many years for Freda. She found the travelling tiring and boring, but it was exhilarating to arrive at an unknown city and work with women from all over the world. It was a rare type of life for an Australian woman, particularly one who believed that she was from 'just an ordinary working-class family'.

In January 1963 in Moscow, Freda and Bill met with Boris Ponomarev, secretary of the CPSU. They also talked with the Soviet leader Nikita Khrushchev and his wife Nina, along with the cosmonaut Yuri Gagarin, at a New Year's party. Freda described Khrushchev as 'a very jovial fellow', and they drank vodka together.[144] Again, as for her earlier overseas trips, she was given official tours, and wrote up her travels for the UAW journal *Our Women* and the CPA's *Tribune*; 'in the Soviet Union she was impressed by the improvements in life for the ordinary citizen notable since her last visit three years ago'.[145] She remarked on the developments there, where she had lived three years ago, and said 'that in that period of time places that were open fields now housed half a million people; the re-housing was breathtaking in its immensity'.[146] She also did some travelling around the GDR, and gave a lovely report in the 10th anniversary issue of *Our Women*.[147] Her tour included the Ravensbrück concentration camp, where the Nazi holocaust victims included around 130,000 women. She was missing the Australian climate, and wrote that 'Over in Europe, deep in winter, one loves our Australia all the more. We are so lucky with our beautiful warm sunshine, a land of abundance, untouched by the horror of war.'[148]

The Moscow Congress of Women, 1963

In May (for May Day) and June 1963, Freda again travelled to Moscow, for her first WIDF Congress of Women. These large events had been staged regularly since the 1945 foundation of WIDF, and Australian delegates had attended since that time. This Fifth Congress achieved a certain amount of notice on the world stage, not least because, as it began, the USSR's Valentina Tereshkova had just become the world's first woman astronaut, and her presence at the congress was feted as a positive image of the Soviet woman. WIDF president Eugenie Cotton connected this achievement of space travel to the WIDF's promotion of women's issues, writing that 'like many people, I am sure that if a woman ever flies into space, it will be a Soviet woman'.[149] Cotton went on to give the opening speech on 'The WIDF in the struggle for Peace, National Independence, Women's Rights and Happiness of Children'.

Over 1,500 people represented 113 countries at this Moscow congress, far more than had been originally envisaged, and included delegates from non-member nations and non-member organisations, including UNESCO, WILPF, the International Association of Students, the Conference of African Women, the International Red Cross, the International Federation of Trade Unions, WPC and the World Federation of Democratic Youth. Freda led the Australian delegation of 13 women.[150] She was thrilled with many different aspects of the congress. Firstly, that she was able to meet so many women from so many countries. One delegate she would become close friends with was Valentina Tereshkova, a modest and generous woman. For Freda, one of the highlights of the congress was when Valentina 'asked permission to introduce her mother at Congress. She was so shy as she took her place on the presidium. I'm sure every delegate appreciated, as I did, her love and gratitude to her own mother.'[151] For the next decade, Freda and Valentina would work together on the WIDF executive, and would meet regularly in European assemblies.

Freda wrote that the Australian delegation of 13 women 'were especially pleased that their propositions on the struggle of the Aborigine people, and the rights of the people of Papua and New Guinea to independence, were included in the Congress findings'.[152] This, however, had discomfited the Australian security service: the head of ASIO, Charles Spry, notes that Freda's 'activities in Moscow included showing "how Aboriginal people are discriminated against and how Australian imperialists exploit and keep in subjection the people of New Guinea".'[153] The CPA had been critical of Australian colonial practices in New Guinea ever since the 1930s, and the issue was subsequently an important one for the UAW as well.[154]

On her return, Freda addressed 40 meetings and made two television appearances. A CPA and UAW Sydney member, Beryl Jury, said earlier that 'this hasn't been announced officially, but as Freda attended the [WIDF] Council meeting in Berlin late last year, the Party thinks that continuity will be preserved if Freda goes. It is also important that Freda should go because the trouble between China and Russia will be discussed.'[155] And Beryl's prediction was correct: at the congress there was argument on the issue of the Sino-Indian boundary, with the leader of the Chinese Women's Delegation, Yang Yun-yu, at the centre of controversy.[156] Freda was not on the platform for this early conference, but she was the leader of the Australian delegation, and was a member of the WIDF Executive at this time; and the UAW elected her national organiser two years prior to this congress, in order to prepare for it. Her good friend Kapila Khandwala wrote that 'yes, I remember you putting China in her place at the Council meeting'.[157]

Freda chaired the Moscow session in which the delegates from China repeatedly rose from the floor to oppose the majority view. At a subsequent UAW meeting, she described the issue:

China delegates did not co-operate and she was very surprised and sorry when she saw the report of the Chinese delegates to the effect that the Russian women had tried to wreck the Congress. All she could say was that the Russian women were very good and didn't try to force issues at all. She was sorry that the Chinese said the Congress was not democratic, the Congress was efficient and the democratic movement of it very effective.[158]

The *Japan Times* reported that delegates 'howled down' the Chinese delegate Madame Yung Yun-yu 'at the final tempestuous session', when the entire congress, with the exception of China, Albania, North Vietnam and North Korea, approved a resolution in favour of general disarmament and coexistence.[159] Yun-yu felt that the congress 'made a very bad showing' whereas 'the Chinese women and the rest of the Chinese people will always stand united with the women and other people of all countries and struggle for the complete victory of the cause of peace, democracy, national independence and socialism'.[160]

When she was back in Australia, Freda sent a letter to the Chinese delegation, who published much criticism of the congress: 'Our experience at the Congress', Freda wrote, on behalf of the Australian delegation, 'does not allow us to agree with you. We therefore feel impelled to express our point of view.'[161] She wrote in this letter that 'it is not, and never has been, a condition of membership in our organisation or in WIDF, that women completely support socialism'. At the CPA 20th National Congress, Freda talked about the ideological characteristics of the Chinese delegation. Her ASIO file records that 'the UAW was an important women's organisation at the moment, but that it had also been involved in the ideological dispute. She said that China promoted the dispute and it had endeavoured to narrow the WIDF congress but it had been defeated.'[162] Freda wrote that

> the attitude of the Chinese delegation at the Congress did not assist its work and their subsequent statement that the Congress was undemocratic is unfounded. The Chinese spoke three times in the plenary session which was more than any other delegate. The Chinese representatives at times refused to abide by the adopted procedure at the Congress. If this had been permitted to go on and other delegations had taken the same attitude, it could have caused chaos and prevented the Congress from finalising its business. However, the Australian delegation and many others expressed the hope that the Chinese women would abide by the democratic decisions of the overwhelming majority of the women.[163]

It was at this congress that the WIDF bureau elected Freda as a vice-president for Australia, the first from her country ever to rise to the position. Freda was brought up in a time when you didn't talk about yourself too much, and modestly felt that it wasn't so much her personal qualities that saw her elected to WIDF, but more that she came from Australia, 'and therefore I could be seen as really independent and particularly getting away from Europe and yet, being English speaking was very, very valuable. In the early days it was dominated by the French, and then it shifted, because English became more the recognised language internationally. And being English speaking I think was useful.'[164] She didn't accept the post immediately:

> No, at first I was absolutely horrified at the thought. I said to them, 'Look it's too far away. You can't expect me to be travelling backwards and forwards from Australia. I've got a family'. Lee, at that stage, was still a schoolgirl, and I felt I needed to talk to Bill about it, which wasn't possible because they raised it with me at the last minute almost.

And I did have reservations, because when you go to these congresses you get these women who can speak half a dozen languages. And nearly everyone can – even from Africa, they'll speak two and three languages. Here's me able to speak only English. And they said to me, 'Not to worry, you'll always have an interpreter.' Which of course, I didn't always have. So I had very great reservations about taking it, from the point of being so far away and the problem of travel, the problem of only having one language and the problem of not really having an understanding of the international situation, which was extremely complex. So I went into it with a lot of reservations. Valentina Tereshkova convinced me. They sat up and talked to me until 3 o'clock one morning.[165]

3

Branching Out: 1964–1969

From the mid-1960s, Freda's life was one of organising action, travel and events for three organisations: as national secretary for the UAW, through the Central Committee and Women's Committee of the CPA, and as a bureau member of WIDF. In 1963, WIDF, with Eugenie Cotton as the president, had elected Freda as a vice-president. She would hold this role until her election as president in 1975. This work would take her overseas at least five or six times a year until 1990. This was, Curthoys writes, 'a source of pride for the UAW, as the UAW was comparatively quite a small organisation among those affiliated with WIDF'.[1] These three roles often crossed over, and, as through all of her life, collaborative networks were crucial to her success in the multiple roles she took on.[2] The importance of these was already quite evident in Freda's criss-crossing activities with the New Theatre and the CPA through the 1930s, 40s and 50s; now her addition of the UAW and, in particular, the WIDF helped to expand her work greatly. Her work with WIDF helped her to build networks of international connections, beneficial for the CPA, the UAW and WIDF as well as for Freda personally. It allowed her to tap into existing women's, peace and left-wing organisations in every country through diverse sets of activities, friendships and collaborations, as well as to build these up and help to establish new ones. The networks of people in these groups were at the core of Freda's activism throughout her life, and allowed and inspired her to mobilise other women to secure better human rights and living standards. The transnational and global linkage of organisations allied to WIDF allowed her to connect to these women across borders as well as around areas of global concern.

The increasingly inclusive nature of WIDF meant that the number of vice-presidents (roles for women from many parts of the world) accordingly increased over the years from its establishment, from four at its establishment in 1945 to 10 in 1953. By the time of Freda's election, she was one of 14 vice-presidents, showing the growing reach and popularity of the international organisation. In November 1964, Freda travelled to Delhi in India in her new role of WIDF vice-president, and spoke at the World Conference for Peace and International Cooperation, the conference that followed on from the earlier Sydney meeting. Following this, the UN designated 1965 as International Cooperation Year (ICY), which was a project began by American anthropologist Margaret Mead, and 'originally conceived as a project of women visiting women around the world to see the different ways in which basic tasks of caring for families and communities were carried out'. ICY was to be the precursor of International Women's Year, a global event to which Freda contributed enormously.[3] At the Delhi conference, Freda said,

> Always, since its inception, WIDF has encouraged nationally and internationally solidarity action with all people struggling against oppression and aggression...women's fight for peace has always been closely linked with the struggle for the complete abolition of colonialism, for national independence and against imperialism.[4]

This was a natural extension of her work in the CPA and the UAW.

Work at home

Freda's work continued in Australia. Following decades' work by the CPA and other groups, equal pay had been on the agenda for the UAW since its establishment. A commentator of the time reported that 'no issue affecting the status of women in Australia is more alive or more complex than the increasingly vocal demand for equal pay for equal work'.[5] UAW members, including Freda, attended an ACTU equal pay conference in Canberra in 1964, which over 100 people attended. On 8 April, Freda and other delegates put their case to the Minister for Labour, Mr McMahon.[6] This was a continuation of struggles for equal pay waged since the start of the century, particularly from the ACTU and unions and their members. Equal pay in Australia was not legislated until 1972, when the Australian Conciliation and Arbitration Commission adopted the principle of equal pay for work of equal value.

The work of the UAW continued its very broad approach. Along with equal pay, anti-racism campaigns had always been a part of the organisation's agenda. Through 1964, for instance, Freda and the UAW were campaigning against the death sentences imposed on Vuyisile Mini, Wilson Khayinga and Zinakile Mkaba, three members of the African National Congress, for their opposition to the South African government's racist laws. The UN Secretary-General U Thant also appealed for their reprieve, along with many others, including the UN Special Committee on Apartheid and the UN Security Council; however, the three were hanged in Pretoria Prison on 6 November 1964.

The dangers of nuclear war were also still on the agenda for peace activists in many walks of life, particularly after the 1962 Cuban Missile Crisis and China's nuclear test in 1964. Freda was in the march for the Hiroshima Commemoration Committee at Easter, alongside other UAW and CPA comrades. An event Freda attended in October was the Australian Congress for International Cooperation and Disarmament in Sydney, organised by Save Our Sons and a number of other organisations, including churches and left-wing trade unions, as well as the CPA. It followed on from the very successful Melbourne Peace Congress in 1959, which the UAW enthusiastically supported. One of the speakers at this congress, speaking on 'the Malaysia Issue' was Michael Kirby, later to become Justice of the High Court of Australia.[7] Ralph Summy writes that this congress 'proved to be an important watershed in expanding the base of the [peace] movement and integrating peace sentiment throughout the nation'.[8]

Freda's work for the party continued, organising meetings, writing speeches, and other duties. At the June CPA 20th National Congress of 1964, where the Central Committee re-elected both Bill and Freda, she spoke on Work amongst Women in the party. She said that 'there is a great deal of work to be done concerning women in industry', and she suggested that a challenge to the party should be to attract more women to the trade union movement, and to select factories to launch equal pay campaigns, leading to equal pay incorporation into state awards.[9]

Through the 1960s, she continued with her work on the CPA's Central Committee and its Women's Sub-Committee, and was very active in teaching, leading meetings, participating in organising and discussions. Following her rise to the WIDF executive, she was feted as the guest of honour at the 1964 Tribune Ball in August. Never confined to the Sydney party offices, later that month she travelled to Broken Hill, and then she went to Adelaide as the guest of honour at the opening of the UAW's new rooms on 23 August.

Local indigenous rights were important through the 1960s, with many organisations on the left continuing to seek racial justice. Freda and other party members had supported the 1965 journey of the Freedom Bus to Moree, Bowraville and other regional towns.[10] Modelled on the American freedom ride of that era, the protest by Sydney University students (including Barbara Curthoys' daughter Ann) was designed to draw attention to racist practices in rural Australia.[11] Freda said that 'the protest group were a courageous people with a lot of guts, because it was not an easy task to face up to open hostile opposition'.[12] Over that year's Easter weekend, Freda and Bill went to Canberra for the Eighth Annual Conference of the Federal Council for Advancement of Aborigines and Torres Strait Islanders, attending as observers.[13] The UAW had always been active in its support of equal rights for indigenous women and children. In 1964, for instance, Freda visited the Yasmar Juvenile Detention Centre in Haberfield to visit a young Roy Hickey, an indigenous boy (murdered Redfern boy T.J. Hickey's uncle) who had been gaoled at Walgett.[14]

Photos of Freda during this period, as always, show her relaxed and approachable, and always wearing clothes chosen for comfort over style, and no makeup. One ASIO file report for 1965 reports that Freda

prefaced her account of her trip abroad with a submission on the necessity to be tolerant to the customs and habits of the peoples of Asian and European countries which to a foreign visitor seem to be extremely stupid. She instanced marriage customs and bathing habits. Her point was the customs and habits were secondary to issues such as equality of sexes, equal pay, problems of women and children, and peace. When speaking of customs and habits she deplored the use of cosmetics by women.[15]

Throughout her life, Freda was opposed to the use of make-up, and apart from her early years on stage at the New Theatre, there are no photographs of her with any cosmetics. She also railed against the profit-driven fashion industry, claiming that 'changing fashions are not dictated by women's desires, comfort or climate'.[16]

Bill and Freda were part of the same ideological group in the Sydney CPA as Audrey and Tom McDonald. The links between the CPA and the UAW, although never official, were always close in these early years: Audrey calls Freda 'a godmother of the UAW', and her prominent role in both organisations boosted women's activity in both.[17] In March, the CPA reported that Freda's visit to speak at the Melbourne branch 'will be a landmark in the 1965 Party building year. Her talk should be reported back and discussed fully in each Section and Branch'. On 12 March in Melbourne, she spoke 'of the development of the work among women', and 'gave an outline of organisation and new policy for women in building a mass party'. She urged the party to 'look very closely at the policy of the UAW to see that it was the best policy'.

Audrey says of Freda's role as a negotiator between the UAW and WIDF that

Freda was a key person internationally. Because of (her roles as) vice president of the WIDF and then president of the WIDF, she knew all the things that were happening in the international women's movement and the United Nations – the programmes and so on. We were able to take advantage of that, and that raised our status (the UAW), and we became on equal terms with these organisations.

Tom recalled,

If I summarise Freda, I would say she had all the qualities to command respect by everyone: the quality of firmness, decisiveness yet flexibility, the ability to promote compromise solutions and her very strong and determined personality that commanded respect. That got her a long way in the international movement, wherever she went.[18]

Vietnam

A major concern for the left during this period was the Vietnam War, a divisive event for many countries, not least Australia, politically and culturally. Freda campaigned in pioneering actions through WIDF, the UAW and the CPA, beginning as early as 1964. Australian reaction to the conflict began when, on 10 November, Menzies introduced a conscription bill into federal parliament. Rowan Cahill writes that 'apart from trade unions, churches, and political parties, there were at least 146 organisations actively opposing conscription and the Vietnam War during the period 1964–1972'.[19] Bill was similarly involved, and in particular took the platform in a number of public debates on Australia's involvement in Vietnam. From 1965, they both worked with the Save Our Sons (SOS) group, formed in June that year, to protest the arrest of the first conscientious objector, Bill White. Freda continued to campaign against Vietnam for years, travelling there a number of times, both to North and South Vietnam. The 60,000 Australians who served in Vietnam, the 521 people killed and 2,400 people wounded were added to the estimates of one to four million Vietnamese soldiers and civilians killed.

Freda organised and took part in many Vietnam protests overseas with her WIDF work, as well as in Australia. Fifty years later, in her maiden speech to the NSW parliament, where she had been elected to the Legislative Council as a Greens Party representative, Lee said, 'Being raised in a household steeped in political campaigns leaves one with many proud moments. One of those was the night my father and Jack Mundey became the first people arrested in Australia for protesting against the Vietnam War.'[20] Bill (representing the CPA as its NSW secretary) was arrested at the Martin Place 'sit-down' anti-Vietnam rally, on 3 May 1964, along with Bruce Steele and Jack Mundey, then secretary of the Builders' Labourers Federation.[21] The ABC news reported the rally that night and Freda said it was 'a very good show'.[22] Bill was 'very pleased'[23] with the arrests, which the party had anticipated: 'of course, that was part and parcel of it', said comrade Ron Marriott, 'to get publicity. Some of the boys thought we broke it up too soon and that there should have been more arrests…the bail was only £2. Bill said they treated him with the utmost courtesy. Even when they hauled him off and put him in the van they said, 'there you are, sir, be careful". You can just imagine it.'[24]

Overseas again

In 1965, Freda worked in Greece, Pakistan, Ceylon and Afghanistan. Accompanying her on this trip was Esther Newill, who was the mother of an American GI in Vietnam, and a member of WILPF and Women Strike for Peace. Esther had visited Australia as a guest of the UAW to talk on civil rights and the Vietnam War.[25] In Greece, Freda worked with women who were considering forming a Greek branch of WIDF; she met with Maria Sbolos, secretary of the Pan Hellenic Union of Women. Freda wrote that

> Mrs Betty Ambatielos, who fought for 17 years for her husband Tony's release from Greek prison, was our interpreter. The women I met had served sentences or had been exiled for from 2 to 15 years. Some still work for the release of their husbands. Their crimes? They worked for peace and the freedom of Greece.[26]

Betty, formerly Betty Bartlett, a member of the Central Committee of the CPGB, had moved to Greece in 1945 after meeting Tony, a prominent Greek communist, in her hometown of Cardiff. In 1947 Tony had been sentenced to death as a communist guerilla of the Greek Civil War; in 1952 his sentence was commuted to life.[27] In Australia at the time, there was a significant Greek-Australian membership in the CPA, and in the left more generally, particularly after the post-war migration period.[28] A number of Greek-Australian women took leading and active roles in the UAW and the CPA, where Freda heard about their migrant experiences.

Freda's first time in Afghanistan was a revelation for her. She said that in Afghanistan during 1964, 4,000 women had learnt to read and write. 'To meet a middle-aged Moslem woman in a great thick black veil who has just learnt to read is a great experience,' she said.[29]

I was entertained Afghan style by the women's Society in Kabul (they were all wearing veils five years ago). On the way, we passed what was a women's theatre. There was segregation in any public entertainment until 5 years ago. We reclined on low couches, ate unusual food and even tried out the hubbly bubbly pipe. That day a conference of 60 volunteers had planned their work to assist women in sanitation, childcare and health and medicine. In 1964, the women's society put four thousand women through literacy classes. There is still over 90 per cent illiteracy in Afghanistan.[30]

As usual, Freda reported on her trip – she gave talks and showed her slides for UAW meetings on her return.[31] She received a higher than normal level of mainstream media publicity, including an article in the *Australian* about her travels. Freda, it was reported, 'a housewife from Waverley', 'takes an annual trip abroad in the interests of womankind'.

When she was in Moscow, she attended a wedding at one of the wedding palaces.

It was the full family wedding, with everybody there, the bride in white with a flowing veil, Mum having a little weep, the groom looking very formal – almost identical to the Australian church wedding. There was even a young family friend making a movie of the occasion. There was one major difference, however. The person officialising at the ceremony was a woman judge from the Moscow Court, who gave a couple a pep talk on one important aspect of marriage – the production of children, and their importance to the country.[32]

Freda worked in New Zealand in the winter of 1965. In Auckland, she visited the Union of New Zealand Women, and attended the 50th anniversary of the WILPF's Auckland branch. At a luncheon, Freda spoke as part of a panel on Vietnam. She also met women from the Labour Party, pacifists, peace groups, church organisations and the National Council of Women.[33] In Christchurch, she was guest speaker at the Bertrand Russell Peace Foundation, and worked at Communist Party branches in Christchurch and Dunedin. This was just a month after the expulsion of the Dunedin branch from the CPNZ, in late June 1965.[34]

She was still very active for the UAW in Sydney, and launched the union's 1965 radio and television campaign:

> Many people heard of our organisation for the first time recently when our National Secretary, Mrs Freda Brown, made a broadcast on behalf of the UAW on Radio station 2GB, Sydney. Following this broadcast, not only did we gain some new members, but Freda was invited to appear on television as a guest of the *Tonight Show* with Don Lane. Members who watched the television show were impressed with the way in which Mrs Brown presented the UAW and our international organisation WIDF. Also the respect with which Mr Lane treated Mrs Brown and the work of our organisation.[35]

During 1965, Freda also worked in Paris, for the Union of French Women's Ninth National Congress and 20th anniversary. Over 1,000 women from all over France attended this. The UAW press release for this notes that 'a delegation of North and South Vietnamese women addressed the Conference, and Mrs Brown had the opportunity of having a discussion with them'.[36]

In Germany, she worked in Leipzig and Berlin, and visited the Auschwitz concentration camp. She was surprised to see the brown shirts and black shirts still in existence, and that the Hitler Youth Movement was still very much predominant. She also visited East

Germany where, because of the needs of reconstruction, 'over eighty per cent of married women are working. In these conditions, the work of women at municipal level takes on special importance and women's organisation in the councils has developed varied and effective means of assisting married women workers. There is a paid half-day off every month to help working women do their shopping,' Freda reported.[37] She also attended the 20th anniversary of the WIDF in Salzburg. The UAW press release for this notes that 'it was decided to hold an international conference on the welfare of children, a series of seminars on the education of young women, and to present a "Eugene Cotton" prize to women every two years for outstanding contributions to international understanding and peace'.[38]

During this trip, she attended an international women's peace conference in Rome. She was included in an audience with Pope Paul VI, where 'the discussion was on a very deep theoretical and theological level'. Freda wrote that

> it is becoming more and more obvious that many very sincere people are coming to the peace movement and to peace activity and action. But they will do so in their own way. Prayers for peace are still regarded by some as the only way. Others advance the idea that while God provides the original concept, this must be developed by man and it needs courage and determination for man to do God's work for peace.[39]

She spoke with leading Catholic women at these peace talks, where the main demand was for a ceasefire in Vietnam.[40] Freda reported that

> one French woman spoke for two hours on the advantages of war. This woman explained that as it is sometimes right for two men to fight it is also right for two nations to fight. This woman upset the conference and put the time schedule behind two hours. She was regarded as an outcast from the time of her speech by the other delegates at the conference.[41]

The heated argument brought 'sharp clashes of opinion in a debate carried on in different languages. The main issues discussed were whether there could be real peace without religious belief, and whether people and nations could be strengthened by struggle.'[42] In Rome, she also worked with renowned peace activist Professor Klara Marie Fassbinder, Professor of History at Bonn University, who spoke at the conference.[43]

During 1966, Freda was re-elected national secretary of UAW, at its Fourth National Conference. A notebook from an unnamed delegate at this conference lists some of this event's concerns: most were about peace.

Freda Brown spoke on the programme for young married. Price increases. Demand a Test Ban Treaty. There should be wide spread protests on the French Nuclear tests in the Pacific which are to take place this year and the danger to Australia, New Zealand and the natives of Polynesia from fallout if wind changes occur and it drifts back over these areas. Opposition to conscription of 20 year olds for overseas service. Opposition to war in Vietnam. General and complete disarmament.

Freda's anti-Vietnam work continued. In May 1966, Freda travelled to Tasmania for the CPA, where she met with party members in Hobart. She brought with her *The Threatening Sky*, or *Le Ciel, la Terre*, a 25-minute 16mm film made by Joris Ivens along with Australian journalist Wilfred Burchett and Madeline Riffaud, a French journalist then writing for *L'Humanité*. Burchett and Ivens asked Riffaud to travel to the Vietnamese village of Updo to help make this film in 1964. The ASIO operative present at one of the Hobart film screenings reported that the film was 'completely pro-Vietcong' and 'graphically depicted the barbaric nature of the Vietcong activities and should not be allowed to circulate in Australia whilst Australian troops are serving in this campaign'.[44]

Freda's work overseas for WIDF was rapidly increasing in this time, and it brought benefits for international communications back in Australia. The UAW reported that

Since Mrs Brown has been attending WIDF council meetings we have become more aware of the frightful problems facing women in so many countries particularly where they suffer political persecution and may have already spent years in prison. Wherever possible we must do more to give these women support even if it only means writing a sympathetic letter.[45]

With her talents bringing much success to Freda's role as a vice-president, the European WIDF executives were urging Freda to take a more active role in international events.[46] The Communist Party of the Soviet Union (CPSU) took a part in WIDF's grooming of Freda for higher level work. The 23rd CPSU Congress took place in Moscow between 29 March and 8 April 1966. When CPA National President Richard Dixon was there, Valentin Mikhailov talked with him about Freda becoming general secretary of WIDF. Mikhailov, a worker with the Novosti news agency of the CPSU, which Bill also worked for, had met Freda in New Zealand the year before.[47]

> Dixon pointed out the difficulties involved domestically if she were to take this position and also expressed his personal views on the unsatisfactory condition which developed when any Australian cadres were isolated from their national movement.[48]

Despite Dixon's reluctance, the WIDF executive persisted: Freda reported that they 'discussed with her the position of General Secretary of WIDF and asked if Mrs Brown would be available to take the position. She replied that it was "quite impossible", and assured them of the honour in making this request to her. She was then asked to accept more responsibility in her capacity of Vice-President and has been asked to visit Cuba'.[49] Freda's increasingly prominent and independent work with WIDF, then, was causing concerns for some party leaders, not just within Australia, and this point marks the beginning of a schism between Freda's loyal and obedient work for the party and her need for a more independent stand.

Cuba

One of Freda's overseas trips in the middle of 1966 was to Cuba. She was travelling there for the 26 July celebrations as a vice-president of WIDF along with other WIDF VPs Cesa Nabarawi from Egypt (co-founder of the Egyptian Women's Federation, and one of the first women in Egypt to unveil herself in public) and Connie Seifert (communist founder of the UK's National Assembly of Women).[50] Freda arrived just four hours before the nation's leader Fidel Castro addressed the crowd. She said that 'Castro is a very young man, full of vitality, and who oozes personality. He spoke for three hours, saying that at one time he had been exiled but had come back to lead his people to true democracy. It was wonderful to see this tiny place taking such a stand.'[51]

Freda's daughter Lee remarked that this trip 'certainly had a big impact on her'. Freda recalled this trip with great excitement, especially her meeting with Castro:

I was indeed very, very impressed with the man. I think he really, sincerely, is interested in the well-being of his people.

He is a devastatingly wonderful human being. He had a profound effect, not only on me, but on everybody who met him. I think he is a very courageous man and extremely competent. I attended the July celebrations, that was when Cuba achieved independence, and I attended their rally in the Revolutionary Square. Such a huge rally...in those days, the people's love for him was tremendous. Because under the Americans, the situation in Cuba was horrible. You went there for drugs, to buy prostitutes. No matter how openly you could buy it in Cuba, well he changed all that. He gave the people education. And I think it's tragic that today America is still making life for them so difficult.[52]

Revolutionary Square was packed with over 800,000 people. Some had been there all night and all through the long, hot Havana day. Even at 5p.m., when Fidel started to speak, the Havana panorama still danced in the waves of heat. On the Sunday, we met Fidel... in a personal meeting his relaxed charm and interest in each person he meets gives one a glimpse of the leadership capacity that he had brought to the Cuban people.[53]

Upon Freda's return from Cuba, ASIO directed the Customs inspector on duty at Sydney Airport to target Freda for 'a thorough

Customs Inspection. It was suggested that he look for notes both personal and roneo, literature of a subversive nature, films, negatives, or any other matter which he considered would be of interest to this organisation'. The Customs officer seized all her speeches and books. Amongst them was a speech by Castro, Spanish-language pamphlets and a copy of the Second Declaration of Havana.[54] Castro had delivered this declaration on 4 February 1962, in the year following the revolution's defeat of the US-sponsored invasion at the Bay of Pigs. Freda wrote to Prime Minister Menzies complaining of this search:

> I consider that this is a violation of my rights as a human being and an Australian citizen… [there was] no reason for the Government to deface my passport and try to intimidate me.[55]

Freda had thought that getting through Customs was 'always embarrassing'.[56]

Vietnam

1966 witnessed the growing Australian protest movement to the war in Vietnam. This year was the occasion of the first visit to Australia by a US president, Lyndon Baines Johnson. Freda and Bill were at the anti-Vietnam protest on 25 October, the day that Johnson's motorcade went through Sydney; Bill was one of the organisers for the CPA's protest. At that year's UAW conference, Freda said,

> Peace or War is the issue of our times. On the question of Vietnam, there is a national division in Australia with wide opposition to the Federal Government's policy coming from the ALP, the ACTU, the Church, women, youth and academics. This was not only in Australia but also in the US where Walter Lippmann had written that there should be the formation of a government in Saigon. We want to see this done; Vietnam is an undeclared dirty war. The Digger who was killed died in vain. He did not volunteer, and his death achieved nothing. American goodwill is bought with Australian lives. When Vice-President Humphrey came to Australia, he made a deal: you supply the men, we'll supply the dollars. We must not make politics

with human lies. What are they fighting for – freedom? It seems to me that they are fighting to stop democracy. It had been said that we are fighting to stop them from coming here, and so it appears that Australia and America have the God-given right to stop them. If we go to South Vietnam, they have every right to come to Australia. We have no right to interfere. History will show that PM Holt is carrying out the same policy that Menzies did for 25 years. The only solution is a return to the Geneva Agreement.[57]

At another one of the growing anti-Vietnam protests this year, a policeman hit Freda on the side of her head when one of the first conscientious objectors Bill White was arrested outside his home in Gladesville on 22 November. Another demonstrator, Patrick George, described the event as 'savage'. The protest events of that year became increasingly violent. One notorious incident was the wild demonstration at the Rockdale Town Hall on the evening of 23 November, when a large body of activists protested against Harold Holt, who was there giving an election speech.[58] Freda, who had been at this protest with Lee, wrote about the work of the UAW and that year's Federal election results:

> while the loss of so many seats is disturbing, it is to the credit of the Australian people that, in the face of such distortion, 42% saw through the propaganda and voted against the war in Vietnam, against conscription and for an independent foreign policy…the UAW, with the peace organisations and the trade union and labour movement, will continue to work for peace in Vietnam and against Conscription, confident that life and experience will prove our policy to be in the interest of our people.[59]

The anti-Vietnam protests continued. On 26 January 1967, anti-war protesters gathered to demonstrate against the five-day visit of the prime minister of the Republic of Vietnam, Air Vice-Marshall Nguyen Cao Ky, and his wife. Along with Freda, 'most members of the anti-Vietnam War movement in Sydney that day were attending a demonstration organised by the Vietnam Action Committee. A crowd of up to 10,000 people rallied under the Harbour Bridge at

Milson's Point, where Arthur Calwell gave an address. A large number of activists then marched to Kirribilli House, the Prime Minister's Sydney residence.'[60] The vast majority of the Australian people would have still been in sympathy with the war; this is reinforced by the large number of supporters of Ky and his wife in mainstream media reports of the visit. Freda attended the Vietnam Action Committee conference (convened by Bob Gould) on 27–30 January that year. Other protests that year included a very big Peace March on 16 March that went from Rushcutters Bay to Town Hall.[61] Freda, along with a number of other CPA comrades, was a member of the Association for International Cooperation and Disarmament (AICD, later changing its name to People for Nuclear Disarmament). This group was founded in 1960, and, based in Sydney, was one of the principal anti-war groups involved in organising the Vietnam Moratoriums.

Taking on the top job at the UAW

Audrey McDonald writes that

> in 1966, the UAW's National Secretary Freda Brown asked me to become the National Publicity Officer. Freda and the Party were keen that I come and work in the UAW and capitalise on experience in the union and women's movements and travel abroad. I agreed, because it was expected of me, but I was keen to repay the Party in some way for the wonderful opportunity it had afforded me. I worked closely with Freda and found it to be difficult, but exciting.

She notes that 'Freda was good to work with very creative, enthusiastic and full of ideas'.[62] Audrey wrote about the work of the UAW in this period:

> The UAW worked around a broad range of issues from living standards and working conditions to peace and international questions. Although it campaigned for women's rights, it was ridiculed as conservative and 'old hat', partly because it didn't succumb to radical feminist approaches and confine itself to 'women's issues'. It was also belittled for its traditional methods of organisation, which it firmly

believed in and argued were more democratic. The national leadership had to face these criticisms externally, but also internally from those who supported women's liberation. These political differences brought about a disagreement and trauma in the UAW. Freda and I responded to this by stepping up our efforts around what we regarded as 'working class women's issues': child care, equal pay, rising prices, maternity allowances and child endowment, as well as international issues of peace and disarmament and solidarity with women abroad.[63]

In 1967, Freda became national president of UAW, and kept this role until 1976. She was not elected to this post but replaced Gloria Garton, who had resigned. It had been suggested that Freda step down as secretary and accept nominations for president, which would enable her to devote more time to WIDF of which she was vice-president. Audrey McDonald writes that

I was then asked by Freda and the National Committee to take the role of National Secretary…becoming the National Secretary was indeed a daunting challenge. The national leadership was a strong collective of experienced political women such as Freda, Gloria, Henrietta Searle, Noreen Hewett, Enid Hampson, Jean Emerson, Ella Schroder and others. Nearly all had been with the UAW leadership since its foundation in 1950 and I was quite in awe of most of them. But I accepted the challenge and worked closely with Freda to get to know the ropes.[64]

1967 was the year of the 21st CPA Congress. Importantly, this was the congress that the CPA adopted the Full Human Rights for Aborigines and Torres Strait Islanders. The national referendum, to alter the constitution to include Aboriginal people in the census, was won on 27 May. June 1967 was also the pinnacle of the strike of Gurindji stockmen in the Northern Territory. At this congress, Freda was re-elected on to the Central Committee and the Resolutions Committee. Bill was voted on to the National Executive. Richard Dixon was the national chairman and Laurie Aarons the national secretary. The work of women comrades was a growing point of interest within the party, with Freda's Queensland comrade Alice Hughes submitting her report on 'Women in Australian Society' to the 21st CPA National Congress in June 1967; the report noted that 'work among women is important', and she cited the UAW and WIDF as progressive women's associations.[65]

1967 was also the year that Freda, at 48, began experiencing menopause symptoms – lots of hot flushes and sleeplessness. She was not going to slow down, though: in that year she worked at a number of European destinations, including Stockholm, for the World Conference on Vietnam, which had been coordinated by Romesh Chandra and the WPC. Here she met the international delegates, including Dr Benjamin Spock; Freda was 'greatly impressed' by him as a person and as an activist for peace.[66] The 350 delegates at this conference were unanimous in demanding an end to the American bombing of North Vietnam, calling the American escalation of violence 'nothing less than genocide'.[67] This conference was convened annually until the end of Vietnam hostilities in 1975.

WIDF

It was also during 1967 that Freda began campaigning for WIDF to improve its status in the UN. She said that it was a great achievement for WIDF to be included in Status B of the UN; it was obvious that developing countries got a great deal of assistance from the UN, and in this context WIDF could apply for a financial grant and other assistance. Britain and the US had opposed the entry of WIDF into the UN. The next year, the UN did grant WIDF consultative Status B to the United Nations Economic and Social Council (ECOSOC).[68] Since its establishment in 1945, WIDF was branded as a 'Communist Front' by the US as well as by other Western organisations, not least the British and Australian governments; but by this time, the late 1960s, and with Cold War tensions easing, there was obviously a change of opinion within the UN at the very least.[69] From 1954 until 1967, WIDF had not been able to achieve consultative status with ECOSOC after four unsuccessful applications.[70] After this time, WIDF was able

117

to act as a conduit for information between the UN organisations and the WIDF affiliate organisations and members, as well as lobbying members of the UN.

The death of WIDF's first president, Madame Cotton, in 1967 was a big blow to Freda and the WIDF women. Freda had known Madame Cotton since her early years with WIDF, and believed that 'Cotton exemplified that a woman loses none of her femininity by also being a worker and active in public life. She was not only a scientist, but a charming and gracious woman.'[71] Freda wrote from Paris,

> The phone call came just as we were starting a meeting of the editing commission – of course everyone was temporarily stunned. As I was Chairman of the Commission, I adjourned the meeting and, at first, I thought it would be impossible to continue the work, however the women used their initiative and realised that Madam Cotton would wish us to continue and we met in small groups... When the Bureau met it asked Nina Popova (Soviet Women's Committee), Rosa Jasovich Pantaleon (WIDF General Secretary) and myself to leave as soon as the meeting finished to go to Paris to see the family and attend the funeral (on 23 June). So while it is lovely to see Paris in the spring, it is very sad also. Madam Cotton had asked for no speeches. Men and women from all over the world, her pupils, some now quite old, walked behind the coffin to the small cemetery; her family and those of us who had worked with her each placed a red rose on her grave.[72]

India

Later in 1967, Freda made a trip to India for the Sixth Congress of the National Federation of Indian Women, as the WIDF representative. She kept up a long friendship with Kapila Khandwala, who was a leader who she worked very closely with, and who she'd been working with in WIDF since at least 1963. Kapila was very helpful in making connections for Freda in India, Pakistan and Bangladesh.[73] The congress was held in the northern city of Lucknow, in an area formerly known as the King's Harem, which was then restricted to women. Freda wrote, the Congress ended with a public meeting in the Moslem Women's Park, where only women could attend. In the Park, the women listened to us without their veils, and then after the meeting, the young women covered their faces with their veils and their pretty dresses with black cloaks, to go home through the Lucknow streets.[74]

Freda sent a letter home to Bill and Lee from Lucknow, with her descriptions of the people, the city, the heat, and other aspects of life in India. It's the earliest of Freda's letters that survives, and it gives a sense of Freda and her relationship to travelling, and to her overseas work.

October 20, 1967

Darling Lee and Bill,

A terrible trip from Prague. Left 6 a.m. Bombay 1a.m. Sat in airport till 6a.m. Delhi 8a.m. Spent all morning getting ticket fixed. Left 4p.m. Arrive Lucknow 6p.m. However conference doesn't start till tomorrow, so can rest today. I need it – my legs are so swollen.

I don't know when I leave India. Probably next Thursday 26th. Expect to leave Moscow for home 10th or 11th. Very hot here and I only have winter clothes. I rang Air India office in Sydney and they advised it would be like winter in Australia!

The hotel in Lucknow is lovely. Very old with little turrets and fluted verandah in the front, lovely gardens at back. Terrible squalor. So many people and so much hideous poverty is so disturbing. So many servants, can't even lift a plate – they move it for you.

Will you ring the UAW, tell them I will cable when I know when I will come home. WIDF Congress will be held in Helsinki, Finland, first week in December 1968.

Conference begins today at 5p.m. Been visiting tombs! India really is fantastic. The hideous poverty and apparent chaos. Laden cars, thousands of bicycles, cows, dogs, goats, elephants, and water buffalo all vying for life and often for the narrow road. Went to the Muslem bazaar. Streets so narrow could touch each side. Tiny shops in which people sell, eat, sleep etc. A tiny room, some the size of our kitchen table.

Here they are famous for children's work, hand embroidery so fine and people hardly get enough to eat who do it! Each day I ask to go to post this letter – they say 'yes' but it never happens. Today they said they could be here 9.30 and around 11:15! Here it is largely Muslim, with strong Arab influence. In the hotel they have photos of Nehru, Queen, (Prince) Phillip, Kennedy! Remind me to tell you of the picture gallery we visited and the photos of the last of the Nabobs. We all have lizards in our rooms, the Greeks and Americans don't like it!

Oct 25th. Still not been able to get letter posted – will try again today.

I should have said the hotel was a lovely old palace. Inside it's very second-class – the food is poor and it's not very clean. One gets the impression of chaos and decay; in fact, the problems seem overwhelming. The political situation is complicated by the breakup of Congress and splits in the CP. In some states there are unstable coalition groups of breakaway-Congress, CP, left CP and others. In Calcutta with the unstable breakaways etc.

Congress began at 6p.m. Everything has to be translated Hindi-English or English-Hindi. The Governor opened it and made an extended speech on women's rights, responsibilities and peace. The hall belongs to the big landowners, at front a huge tent so colourful, but such a gap between some of the gracious cultured sari ladies and the poverty all around.

Thinking of Lee studying and Dad with journal – hope you are not finding it too difficult. Will book to leave Moscow on 10th – if that is possible. If I don't' sign this you'll know I got it away in a hurry. I carry it around hoping – then open it again each night.

End of the Prague spring

During 1968, Freda's work with the CPA, the UAW and WIDF continued, as did her participation in Vietnam and peace actions. On 20 August, Freda was with Melbourne comrade Bernie Taft at the Sydney airport, where they did a television interview about the Russian invasion of Czechoslovakia.[76] This was the day that the Soviet Union led troops in an invasion of Czechoslovakia, to crack down on reformist trends in Prague. Two days before, the Party's Central Committee had met to discuss the alarming situation, and Freda and Bill were at that meeting. By July 1969 the next year, Freda and Bill were amongst a list of CPA National Committee members who supported Jim Mitchell 'with regard to the Russian invasion of Czechoslovakia and the CPA National Committee statement released following the invasion'.[77] At the CPA's Sydney District Conference on 25–27 October 1968, Bill spoke in support of the National Committee decision on Czechoslovakia.[78] The major differences in the party over the Czech invasion – a modern democratic base with decision-making powers or a bureaucratic movement run from the top – were to have lasting ramifications, and were in essence the facilitator of the forthcoming split. The CPA was the 'first communist party to publicly condemn' the invasion.[79] Bill's article at the time, on democratic centralism, tried to tread the fine line between both camps.[80]

Of course, the Soviet invasion of Czechoslovakia was a huge issue amongst the left. In the history of the UAW, Barbara Curthoys writes,

> Not wishing to involve the UAW in the hostile argumentation taking place at the time, the national committee made only one reference to the Czechoslovakian crisis in a letter which was circulated to the state branches. Freda Brown, as national president wrote to the Soviet Women's Committee on 26 August 1968 as follows:

> Members of our organisation can understand your concern at the re-arming of West Germany and the growing strength of the fascist forces there; but we consider the invasion of Czechoslovakia a departure from your past attitude of solving international problems by patient, flexible negotiations and from the basic principle of non-interference in the internal affairs of other countries. We urge the Warsaw pact nations to withdraw their troops from Czechoslovakia and request you to convey our opinion to your Government.[81]

Freda still undertook plenty of work with the UAW, active in high-level decision-making processes as well as small tasks (like taking advertising copy to the printers).[82] This was the year that the National Committee organised the 20th anniversary of the UAW. Major issues for the busy organisation in 1968 included the conflicts in Czechoslovakia, equal pay, South Africa, AICD and work with SOS, which had risen indirectly from the UAW. In May 1968, the UAW

National Committee, amongst their resolutions, made the following one on conscription:

> The UAW condemns, and will not co-operate with, Government persecution of objectors to conscription implicit in current amendments to the National Service Act. Fully conscious of the legal risks involved, we declare our intention of giving support and encouragement to those courageous young men who obey their conscience and resist this undemocratic law even at the cost of imprisonment or heavy penalties. We ask all women who stand for peace and democracy to do likewise. We declare support for conscientious objector, Simon Townsend, and call for his immediate release from Holsworthy military prison and from the army. We congratulate those organisations and educational establishments who have already refused to make their records available. We call for requestion of the National Service Act amendments, no imprisonment of objectors and reaffirm our policy for the complete repeal of the National Service Act.

Freda spent most of June working overseas for WIDF in Berlin and in London, where she stayed with her friend Connie Seifert, host over decades to numbers of international leftists, including Paul Robeson. In London, Freda met with members of the CPGB as well as the Cuban ambassador, Alba Grinan Nunez, renewing their acquaintance from Freda's first trip to Havana.

An ASIO file records a WIDF issue of that year:

> Valentina Tereshkova, President of the CPSU Women's Committee, has replaced Nina Popova as the USSR representative to WIDF. Freda had previously disagreed with Popova that the next World Congress of Women had to be held in Helsinki in Dec 1968. This was not only for climatic reasons, but also because she disagreed with Popova's argument that the Congress would had to be held before the meeting of Communist and Workers Parties in case there were divisions which could adversely affect the holding of the Congress afterwards. Freda told Popova that they could not develop WIDF if they let it be tied to the international Communist movement. The date was changed, to June 1969, but it was still in Helsinki.[83]

Freda's work commitments and increasing travels were making for a busier professional life for her amongst all her family events of this period. At the end of 1968, Freda's mother Flo became very ill. Freda's diary notes that she collapsed on 9 October. An ASIO agent discussed this with her at a UAW meeting on 20 October, where Freda said that 'her mother was critically ill but that they are keeping her at home because the local hospitals will not take her in as she is dying'.[84] However, Flo was admitted to a convalescent home on 13 November, and later died in 1970. It was a stressful time for the family in other ways. Lee was nearing the end of her study at high school; and Bill was concerned about the family's financial situation; he felt that the family would soon need more funds, particularly if Lee went to university. Lee, now at Sydney Girls High School, helped to found an organisation called High School Students Against the Vietnam War. Growing up in the politically active Brown household was a wonderful influence. Lee said that 'whatever I took on, my parents encouraged me and believed I would succeed. There are many things for which I thank them, but this strength of belief that I can do it, no matter what "it" is, has laid the basis for my commitment to work for social change.'[85]

The 'Lady Anglers'

1969 was one of Freda's busiest years, and one in which the tensions between CPA executives and Freda began to boil over. By this year, the pressure of the forthcoming split in the CPA was apparent. John Gandini (a Perth CPA and EYL official, who later became president of the ETU and of the WA TLC) had previously called Freda 'a publicity chasing globetrotting bitch'.[86] An ASIO operative reported that 'considerable concern is being felt among CPA leaders at the activities and attitudes of Freda', who was in opposition to the Laurie Aarons faction. Audrey MacDonald writes about the party's split and its repercussions in the UAW:

In the wake of the Czechoslovakian events of 1968, the CPA

advocated a break from the international communist movement and the international bodies it influenced, such as the WIDF. Freda's followers deplored the CPA's demand that the UAW should split from the WIDF. A core group of about 20 of the UAW's CPA members in Sydney started to caucus about how to protect the UAW from interference by the Party in our affairs. Meeting as a faction was a crime in the CPA, punishable by expulsion. So we met clandestinely, at the Irish Club near Central Railway and called ourselves the "Lady Anglers". We felt uncomfortable about this factional activity, but regarded these as extraordinary circumstances. We were angered, not only by the CPA leadership's threat to cut our ties with the international progressive women's movement, but also by its criticism of the UAW's work within Australia and the Party's emerging radical feminist rhetoric which attacked male union officials as bureaucrats and chauvinists. The men from the Left unions were amongst the UAW's best supporters and some of them were our husbands. Finally, the CPA leadership called on Freda to sever connections between the UAW and the WIDF and to give up her WIDF Vice-Presidency. When Freda refused to comply with the Party's wishes, I was called into the Party headquarters and pressured to go against her. I was torn between my loyalty to Freda and the UAW and my loyalty to the Party. In the end, I decided that my first loyalty was to Freda and the UAW, and I resigned from the CPA in 1971.[87]

Here is a report from an ASIO operative who was working within the CPA, commenting on Freda's recruitment of Caroline Rook, who was a stenographer for the party:

Freda Brown has come under considerable criticism by members of the CPA National Offices for the manner in which she has been handling work among women outside the proper Party Committee, i.e. the National Committee Women's Sub-committee. Particular actions which have been brought to notice as not having been discussed on the Women's Committee are her visit to Hanoi earlier this year and the selection of the delegation to the WIDF Congress. A further criticism has been raised concerning Brown approaching comrades directly to work in WIDF without first discussing the matter with the Party, e.g. she approached Caroline Rook about working in East Berlin without there having been any prior discussion with the Party.

Her trips overseas on behalf of WIDF have not been discussed by her with the Party and, in fact, her last trip was made without the Party's knowledge. As a National Committee member she is expected to consult the Party on her activities, and to work through the proper Party committee.[88]

Change within the CPA membership in Sydney had other outcomes. On 26 February 1969, the Trade Union Education and Research Centre (TUERC) was founded, at a function at Trades Hall in Sydney. It was the first trade union education body in New South Wales. With Freda's support and practical help, Bill (who had stopped working as a full-time functionary for the CPA on 31 October 1968) was appointed as the TUERC's director, with Audrey his assistant director. Working in the Trades Hall, he and other unionists provided classes and other forms of education, and from August 1969 published the *Modern Unionist*. Audrey wrote that 'the TUERC was established by Clancy, Bill Brown and Bill Rigby of the FMWU to provide trade union training and promote a militant union perspective',[89] although there was criticism that it contained 'little that is revolutionary'.[90] The TUERC was a forerunner to TUTA, formed in 1975 under the Whitlam government. By July that year, TUERC had 21 unions affiliated, and had already held classes and seminars.[91] John Percy believed that TUERC 'functioned as an organising centre for the anti-CPA leadership forces in the trade unions'.[92]

UAW

Freda's work for the UAW continued. UAW issues for 1969, alongside the Vietnam War and conscription, included prices, preschool education, Woomera and other secret installations, penal powers, taxation, pensioner travel concessions and equal pay.[93] An important equal pay hearing was convened in Melbourne on 23 February, with Pat Clancy's coverage of the issue in the *Tribune* supporting the case for the ACTU and the UAW. Clancy wrote, 'we must think of developing a Trade Union Charter for women, as has been done in other countries, especially Britain'.[94] There was a function at the Greek Atlas League to celebrate IWD that year; Freda spoke, along with others including federal opposition leader Lionel Murphy, Charmian Clift, Dymphna Cusack, Della Elliot and Tom Uren.[95]

When Freda was overseas and unable to make the UAW's National Committee meetings, other members made arrangements on her behalf. Already, however, there were a number of times that high-level decisions had to be put off because Freda was overseas so often for WIDF. This year Rene Mahieu, the Director-General of UNESCO, recommended that WIDF should be advanced to Status A in the UN: 'his stated opinion is that, of all the organisations with which UNESCO works, WIDF has the closest associations at grass root level which enable UNESCO to establish contact with women in Latin American countries in a way they are unable to get through other organisations'.[96]

During 1969, her overseas travel increased, and there were some astounding trips for Freda. On 10 March she attended a National Committee meeting of FUDANREN, the Federation of Japanese Women's Organisations, in Tokyo. Then it was on to other WIDF and communist functions in Moscow, Berlin, Bombay and Ceylon. She was in Bombay to address a meeting of the Communist Party's Women's Organisation, on the theme of 'Women and Vietnam'. While in Ceylon, she stayed with Doreen Young, a British-born communist who was a member of parliament in Ceylon and the wife of the president of the Ceylon Communist Party, Mr Wickramasinghe. She wrote of her trip that 'altogether it was a very worthwhile visit although I got tired and couldn't eat properly. When I got home my doctor said I had had pneumonia.'[97]

North of the Arctic Circle

Arriving home from this trip on 19 April, on 1 June Freda departed for her next trip, which took in Germany, Finland, Lapland, France and Vietnam. She came home on 11 July. This was a remarkable working diary for the woman from Erskineville.

Some excerpts from her letters from this trip help to see how her experiences in talking with women who had come to the World Congress of Women, held in Helsinki that year, from vastly different situations made a deep impression on her:

Many women have spoken of the danger of war and the tension spots in the world. Much of this you know, but when you personally meet and listen to women from the Middle East, Greece, Vietnam, South Africa, you are impressed with the need to speak out on behalf of these women and children.

On 15 June, she recorded that the 'Congress is good – five delegates from Australia. We have been invited for a ten-day tour of Soviet – by ship down the Volga.'

At the Helsinki congress, one delegate remembers that 'there was a cheering foot stomping welcome for the Cuban and Vietnamese delegations, and the star delegate was Valentina Tereshkova, the Soviet cosmonaut and the first woman in space'.[98] Freda met two of the American delegates, 'Bettina Aptheker, gaoled for demonstrating at Berkeley, as well as Charlene Mitchell, US presidential candidate'. (Freda described her: 'a woman, a negro, a communist!'[99]) Bettina remembers that 'This is before Angela Davis was arrested, and that whole case unfolded.' She also recalled the 'large delegations of women from Vietnam, and from Cuba. I remember the conversations with the Vietnamese women vividly.'[100] Freda was the chair of the important sessions:

I just chaired a session with all our proposals – we expected difficulties, but it all went through beautifully, so I can relax. For translation we have very heavy earphones, not little light earpieces we had in Berlin – they give me a headache and earache.

As a young, Western second-generation feminist attending a WIDF event for the first time, Bettina was struck by the contrast in the congress issues to those of US feminists:

Although slated as a World Congress of Women, the Helsinki gathering was certainly not a feminist one. If anything, the congress was hostile to the feminist movements burgeoning in the United States and Western Europe...at the time, I had no feminist consciousness and no historical understanding of the struggles of women in various socialist and communist movements to gain autonomy and define their own agendas. And, of course, what was on the Congress agenda was of great significance to women. The problem was not what was on the agenda, but what was omitted from it. It obscured any definition or struggle against male domination, and the ways that women internalised their own subordination. These were the issues most animating the women's liberation movements in the West.[101]

After the Helsinki congress, Freda travelled north in Finland. Her next letter home was from Inari:

Here I am in the Arctic Circle. Have a look on the map. Plane to Oulu, Kemi Rovaniemi the capital of Lapland, then Ivalo and by bus to Inari. An incredible trip, many women in Lap national dress, the bus is post and delivery as well. Very, very cold! Saw reindeer along in the bus. Lovely antlers and reindeer skin for sale. I am thinking of buying them – I don't know how I'll get them home! Bus stopped to a great to-do and a procession of cars sped past – the King and Queen of Belgium up for the Midnight Sun Celebrations! The sun just dips at midnight and then skims the horizon. It shines all night – for six months they have darkness and never see the sun. This all day and no night gives one a feeling of obligation to keep going. There is a great deal of drunkenness here.

We had a sauna bath and are now watching the sun as it doesn't set! No one seems to go to bed. Lovely huge furs from reindeer and their antlers are very cheap... We met an old woman of Finnish origin – reasonably anti-Russian – when we said we had been to Russia she immediately said, 'Then you are Communists.' On the way back to the bus we were held up by reindeer crossing the road.

So pleased I went to Lapland – it was a wonderful experience. I keep thinking of the midnight sun scudding across the horizon. We were lucky we had days of perfect weather.[102]

Going underground: Vietnam and Korea

In June 1969, US President Nixon announced the withdrawal of

25,000 American troops from Vietnam. But the Australian men and women stayed on; and in Australia the anti-conscription protests increased, with a much broader section of Australians joining the left-wing activists and students. That year, Freda travelled to North Vietnam twice – once in July after the European meetings, and once in September. In Cambodia, where she was waiting to travel to Vietnam, she wrote that

> the plane to Hanoi did not leave today. It does not go until Friday and so have to sit it out here for two days, a curse, nothing to do and everything is so dear, so I'll cut down on meals. I bought some bananas and have a few chocolates and biscuits so I only have an evening meal.[103]

On this trip, she was still lugging around the reindeer horns and fur from Helsinki.

When she finally did arrive in Hanoi, Freda connected with Jean Maclean, the Melbourne secretary of SOS and an ALP member. Along with their SOS connections, they had met at the WIDF Helsinki Congress and the International Women's Peace Conference in Paris. The Protect Paris Committee of the AICD had been established to arrange Australian delegates' attendance of the peace conference; and both Jean and Freda had been involved in that committee since its inauguration in 1968; in forming the committee, the AICD requested the assistance of the UAW. Jean had arrived in Hanoi the day before Freda, who wrote to Bill that 'Lee has heard her speak. With her long fair hair and way-out mini-skirts the locals look at her with unconcealed astonishment.' Jean, being young and blonde (the *SMH* dubbed her 'Bombshell Jean'), got most of the publicity.[104]

Freda had accepted the invitation of the Vietnamese Women's Union 'because she wanted to find out what the situation was. Our young men were dying in Vietnam, Australia was at war with that country', and she felt very strongly that 'better understanding between both peoples could do something to bring this war to an end'.[105] Freda said that when she got there, 'I was shocked. I just hadn't realised how poor the country was and what being at war really meant.'[106] They arrived in Hanoi around 29 June and stayed for 10 days; Jean and Freda delivered $100 worth of medicine to members of the National Liberation Front. Jean said, 'We're at war with the people of North Vietnam. I went there because we should know something about them. I'm going home with a much greater understanding of their determination to fight for reunification of their country.'[107] Freda made sure that she received a receipt for the medicine to prove she did not give money to the communists.[108] However, this did contravene a section of the Defence Forces Protection Act, and on their return two detectives from the Commonwealth Police questioned Jean.

Freda came home 'with a sense of outrage that an affluent country like Australia should be taking part in a war against a poor peasant people whose only assets were their pride, their devotion to the cause of their national independence, and their capacity to organise their lives to fight the war which had been forced upon them'.[109]

Living standards were poor in North Vietnam and most people owned only one set of clothing, which generally consisted of a white top and black pants. Women hand-pumped water for irrigation as the electric hydro-power stations have been bombed. To release women for war work, older women have taken over extra tasks such as minding children and preparing meals. All the North Vietnamese have gone underground; even concerts were performed beneath the ground. Cafés, hospitals, factories were all underground. In one factory alone, 300 people were employed. At this factory, [Jean and I] found lathes, milling and grinding machines, and trucks being repaired. The spirit of the North Vietnamese is still high; they say they will not be defeated. They have been fighting for 30 years and will continue to fight.[110]

She brought back a number of photographs with her to Australia. When asked in August how she got them back in through Customs, she explained that she hid them in a packet of Modess sanitary towels, and placed the packet in a prominent position in her suitcase. 'It caused the Customs Officer a great deal of embarrassment.'[111] At a talk to the South Coast TLC, Freda said that she 'was surprised at the determination of the people of North Vietnam to gain independence despite bombings which were devastating…the continuing involvement of Australia in Vietnam was building antagonisms and hatred amongst South-East Asian countries and if not resolved, could have far reaching effects in all fields.'[112]

The *Tribune* and other left-wing media gave this trip a great deal of coverage.[113] There was also mainstream media publicity, including news bulletins on Channels 7 and 10 on 11 July, and reports in the *Australian* newspaper.[114] One report was *This Day Tonight* on ABC-TV on 11 July, where Bill Peach interviewed her. She explained to Peach that although her visa for travel was stamped 'not valid for North Vietnam', 'I decided I wanted to go, I'd been invited, I thought it was important for a woman to go there, and so I just went.' She was aware that technically, she had broken the law, and indeed, expected some trouble with Customs on her return, but this did not eventuate. She said that 'she did not expect anything to come of this fact as 1969 is an election year, and the Commonwealth would know that the publicity would not do it any good'.[115]

Freda reported on her trip in 'Qld, SA, Wollongong and Newcastle and spoke at meetings of trade unions, job meetings, TLCs in Newcastle and Wollongong, meetings of high school teachers and high school pupils, and women's organisations. There have been TV, radio and press interviews in all centres. At the lovely Brisbane City Hall the Lady Mayoress, Mrs Sylvia Jones, gave a reception attended by women from other organisations, also the Lord Mayor and Deputy Lord Mayor'.[116] Throughout the end of 1969 and for the next few years, the UAW screened the films that Freda brought back from Vietnam.

When Freda flew to North Vietnam a second time in 1969 on 4 September, she took cash with her, as a donation to the people of North Vietnam to go towards rebuilding schools and hospitals. The CPA asked her to hand over some of the money; other money had come from the UAW. She presented her trip 'as a challenge to the government; if the Government will not get out of Vietnam, people will break the law and do all they can to challenge the Government's decision'.[117]

Later in 1969 in September, Freda travelled to Korea, along with Ernie Thornton (a CPA member and general secretary of the Ironworkers back in 1947, who had worked with Freda when she was running for parliament that year). They attended the Anti-Imperialism Journalists Conference in Pyongyang (also known as the International Conference on Tasks of Journalists of the Whole World in their Fight against US Imperialist Aggression), which had been organised by the International Organisation of Journalists. Freda was attending as an observer from WIDF, who asked her to attend the conference 'at very short notice'. She described this as a 'manipulated' conference – 'manipulated by the Koreans to such an extent that they antagonised many friends. This manipulation was aimed at showing the North Koreans as the world leaders. Kim Il Sung was continually referred to as 'the outstanding Marxist leader in the world today.'[118]

Freda caused some controversy at this conference. When the 13 international organisations' observers prepared a joint statement that opened with tributes to Kim Il Sung as a great leader, she alone opposed the statement's inclusion, and when asked to read out the statement she refused, and 'suggested the Peace people should read it as the most representative group'. Publicly, though, she supported the actions of the Democratic People's Republic of Korea (DPRK). In an article, she wrote that 'today the DPRK is eager to open up relations with the rest of the world…we should support the DPRK proposals for reunification of the country'.[119]

Freda said that the conference was strangely organised and delegates' movements were tightly managed and very restricted; Freda's interpreter did not even allow her to go on a walk on her own. She did, however, have an opportunity to talk with Australian leftist journalist Wilfred Burchett, who was at the conference. He intended returning to Australia; Freda said that Burchett 'told me that he intends challenging the Australian government's refusal to grant him a passport'.[120] Burchett asked her to deliver letters to Australia, to his brother Winston and his father, George, who was dying.[121] He was seeking advice from well-known criminal defence lawyer Frank Galbally on Burchett's right to leave Australia without a passport once he had returned to Australia. Burchett also asked Freda to tell Winston that he had decided to make the trip back to Melbourne to see his dying father. However, Freda's letters arrived too late, and Burchett was unable to travel to Australia at this time, although the federal government allowed him to fly in to Australia on a private plane the following year.

Burchett spoke at the journalists' conference in Pyongyang. Freda wrote, however, that 'the most spectacular and probably the most controversial speech made was by Eldridge Cleaver, US Negro leader, author of *Soul on Fire* and Minister of Information of the Black Panther Party (BPP), who is under a jail sentence of fifteen years and who escaped to Cuba and is now living in exile in Algeria'. The BPP and Il Sung's regime had come together during the late 1960s, in a period where 'the American radical left regarded Pyongyang as an important alternative from Moscow and Beijing'.[122] Cleaver was at this conference along with the BPP's Deputy Minister of Defence Byron Booth. Cleaver's 22 September speech was robust:

In our era of class war and revolution against capitalism, racism, imperialism, colonialism and neo-colonialism, we are able to zero in on the very geographical location of the hiding places of the enemy. Standing dead-centre on the bulb eye, we find the United States of America – US fascism and imperialism – to be the No. 1 enemy of all humanity, the arsenal and banker of exploitation and oppression, and chief purveyor of death and destruction all over the planet earth. The United States of America is not a democratic country. It is a cruel fascist country. It is a democracy for the bloodsucking capitalist vultures and the bloodletting warmongers who control the U.S. government and benefit from its barbaric policies. It is a prison for everyone else and President Nixon is nothing but a warden of the prison. Indeed, US imperialism seeks to turn the entire world into a huge prison under its bloody thumb and under the boots of its troops and puppets.[123]

On the way home from one of her trips this year, Freda spent a day in Delhi and attended the Gandhi centenary celebrations. Honoured guests included Indira Gandhi and the Dalai Lama. Freda wrote that 'the permanent memorial and the meeting was most impressive. Friends in India told me the recent nationalisation of the banks and other moves have resulted in an enthusiasm and hope for progress that has not been felt in India for many years'.[124] She writes of her visit to the Indian Congress,

The public meeting last night was quite fantastic! In Muslim Women's Park, only women can enter. A huge meeting with many women in bright colours with silver tinsel and some children dressed in gold. At the end, many women covered themselves with a black cloak and black veil. Outside in the little narrow streets life SWARMS – children squat on the end of the gutter and use it for a toilet – the noise and smell is beyond my power of description…did I mention the kidnapping and mutilation of children for use as beggars? A decision of Congress was to refuse to give or take dowries and boycott weddings where dowries are given. Every day Congress got a good press.

Benjamin Montague Centennial Lewis
(1877–1947), Freda's father,
a committed Wobbly, 'very much a
rebel', Freda recalled.

Florence Mary Munroe (1876–1971),
Freda's mother, 'very typical of what a
woman was supposed to be'.

The family home at Erskineville, and Ben's signwriting office.

Freda aged three or four.

Aged seven, looking very serious despite the thrill of a pony ride.

Aged 10.

Freda loved the beach all her life...

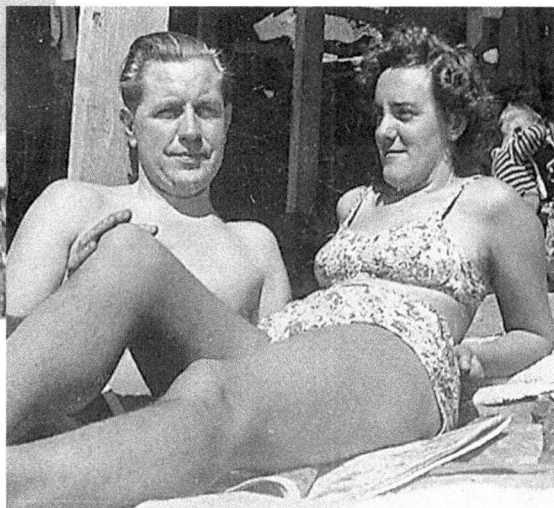

...and so did Bill.

Leon, Freda and
Rae strike a pose at
the beach.

'The Girl Comrade': presenting the party line at a Newcastle factory gate meeting.

TS' SCRIP" WOMAN SIGNWRITER

WITH A DEFT STROKE of the wrist, Miss Freda Lewis, of Erskineville, p a finishing touch to a sign. She is a member of the staff of Lewis Sig

The mainstream media takes an interest in Freda's signwriting work.
(Daily Telegraph, 22 May 1937, p. 5.)

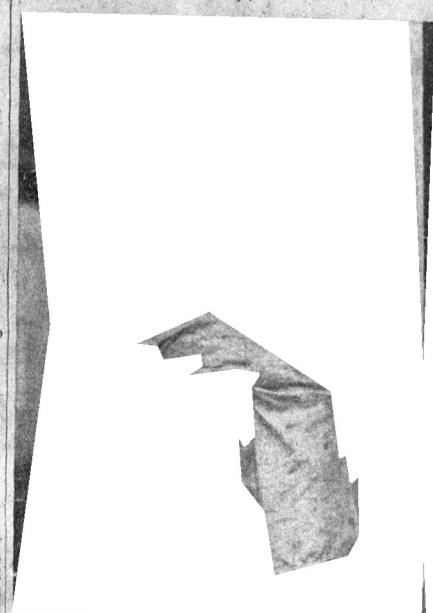

Freda refashioned her high school uniform after leaving school in 1937.
(New Theatre Archive, State Library of NSW, reproduced with permission.)

Freda Brown, Vic Arnold and Charles Kitchener in a publicity shot for the New Theatre's performance of Remember Pedrocito *in 1938. (New Theatre Archive, State Library of NSW, reproduced with permission.)*

The happy couple, Melbourne, soon after their marriage.

THIS
IS
YOUR
VICTORY

The Federal Government has returned the property of the New Theatre League, seized by the police on June 15th!

This, Mr. and Mrs. General Public, is your victory. You supported our protest rallies, signed our petitions, poured resolutions in to the Government.

You have found that repression will retreat if it is faced by determined public opinion.

Our work—to make the Theatre a critic of our times— **New Theatre's** goes on.

So long as you support our Theatre we will use it to examine and criticise the society in which we live. **Work Goes On**

We have faith that you will help us carry on that work.

Every Sunday Night Performances are given at the League's Rooms, 36 PITT ST. (NEAR QUAY), every Sunday Night.

You and Your Friends will be Welcome.

The Worker Trustees, 238-240 Castlereagh St., Sydney.—40-Hour Week.

The raid on the New Theatre's office in 1940…

...but Freda, Jock Levy and others keep the show going.

Smashed Fingers—Musician's Reward

SEE **The Big Scenes from**
A BANNED PLAY

Still under the ban of the Chief Secretary, Clifford Odet's drama, "Till The Day I Die," is strong anti-Nazi propaganda. It has been performed once in Australia in defiance of the ban and PIX was present. Get your copy and see the highlights of a show the whole world is discussing.

In **PIX**

6ᵈ *at all newsagents*

Freda and Bill at the Sydney Town Hall, May Day 1940.

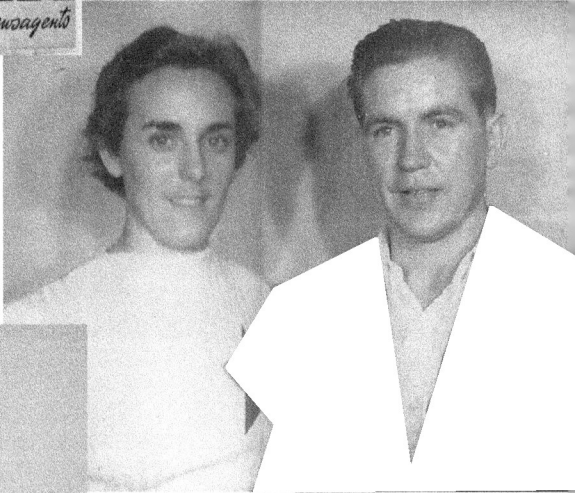

Roll No. is
Your official
. . . .

HOW TO VOTE

BROWN

COMMUNIST

[1] **Brown, Freda** (Mrs.)

[3] Fowler, L. (Mrs.)

[2] Greenup, A. E.

You must vote in order of preference

Authorised by J. R. Hughes, Campaign Director, 3 Gardiner's Chambers; King Street, Newtown.

Newsletter Printery, 21 Ross St., Forest Lodge.

Vote One Freda Brown.

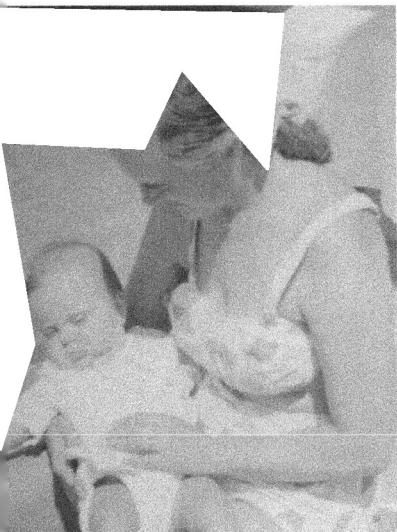
Baby Lee and mum in the sun at Bronte, summer 1951.

A family picnic.

Learning to read with mum.

Camping holiday.

Bill, Freda and other CPA delegates in Leningrad. Freda's young interpreter, Nina, in the centre.

Freda with members of the Australian Delegation waiting to place a wreath on the Lenin Mausoleum in Moscow.

Freda and Indira Gandhi.

At the 1962 WIDF Council meeting in Berlin, with the delegates from Laos and British Guinea.

Giving a speech at the CPA's 20th Congress, 1964.

Outside NSW Parliament House, to present the UAW's 1968 petition against price increases. From left: Janet Copley, Freda, Audrey McDonald, Janet Mundie.

Katherine Susannah Prichard and Freda, 1969. (Photograph by John Gilchrist; courtesy of the State Library of Western Australia.)

A PINEAPPLE OF DEATH...

Quizzed by C'wlth cops

JUST BACK from Hanoi, Mrs. Freda Brown, National President of the Union of Australian Women (left), is pictured with Mrs. Jean McLean, of the Save Our Sons Movement, at

Kingsford Smith airport, Sydney, last Friday. Mrs. Brown is holding a "pineapple" anti-personnel bomb used by the US in its bombing of North Vietnam which was presented to the visitors by the Union of Vietnamese Women.

Commonwealth police visited Mrs. McLean's Melbourne home at the weekend to quiz her about the handing-over of $100 worth of antibiotics to the Hanoi representative of the Provisional Revolutionary Government of South Vietnam. (See story, p. 3.)

Freda and Jean McLean return from North Vietnam with a cluster bomb. Tribune, 16 July 1969. (Photograph reproduced courtesy of the Search Foundation.)

One of the UAW campaigns for 1970.

Lee, UAW and SOS member Noreen Hewitt, and Freda at a UAW event.

Freda, Nell Johns and Betty Olle at a UAW demonstration.

Working in China.

Hard at work at the UAW office in Sydney.

Leading the WIDF.

Solidarity with Bangladesh activists Maleka Begum, Motia Chowdhury and hunger strikers at the US Embassy, March 1971.

1973, and Fidel Castro and Freda share a joke.

A WIDF Council meeting in Berlin, with delegates from Angola and South Africa.

Freda presenting her keynote speech on the opening day of the World Congress of Women in Berlin, 20 October 1975, for International Women's Year.

Leading the way for International Women's Year.

Happy International Women's Day: Freda with the UAW card, March 1978.

Bill and Freda with their first grandchild, Rory, 1978.

Leading the 1979 congress.

Freda and Mikhail Gorbachev open the Moscow World Congress of Women in 1987.

A leader of women in the world.

Friends at a WIDF conference.

Commemorating Hiroshima Day 1979, with the UAW poster designed by Ralph Sawyer

Hiroshima Day 1980, with granddaughter Kilty.

With delegates at the CPSU 26th Congress, Moscow 1981.

A journalist at work in war-torn Beirut, 1982.

Children of Lebanon, 1982.

Fidel Castro awards Freda with the Anna Betancourt Medal, 1985.

With Raul Castro, his wife Vilma Espin, and Fidel Castro in Cuba, 1985.

At the 1985 Nairobi World Congress of Women, with Angela Davis and other delegates.

With young admirers at the 1987 12th DFD Congress, Berlin. (Bundesarchiv, Bild 183-1987-0306-113 / photographer: Peer Grimm / Licence CC-BY-SA 3.0.)

Time with the grandkids at Copa.

Rory, Freda, Lee and Bill in June 1990.

Freda in 1992, helping the fight to save Erskineville's park, on the site of her old family home.
(Image by Conrad Walters, reproduced with permission.)

1994, at her beloved Bondi Beach.
(Image by Belinda Morgan Pratten,
reproduced with permission.)

Four generations.

Bondi Beach was always a popular place for the family.

4

Living in the Seventies: 1970–1974

WIDF in the 70s

Lee finished school at the end of 1969 and, with her promise of a university education, it was a time for great celebration in the Brown family. Freda was able to fit this in before beginning the next year's work. WIDF then asked Freda to deliver a paper at a seminar in Khartoum, Sudan, 31 January to 9 February 1970. The seminar was organised by the Union of Sudanese Women and the Sudanese government, with the assistance of WIDF and UNESCO. Representatives from 30 African and Arab countries attended the seminar. Reports provided news on the fight against illiteracy among women, particularly in African and Arab countries, and one of the responsibilities of the seminar was to plan literacy programs for African countries. Reporting on the seminar, Freda wrote that delegates 'spoke of the oppression in their countries and how illiteracy is greatest where people are hungry. Hunger, disease and ignorance go together, and how the elimination of illiteracy and economic and social development is linked with national independence'.[1] Freda later described how the nomadic lives of many Sudanese makes it harder to give people an education, outlining that the strengths of the Union of Sudanese Women were in spite of the illiteracy, and how they managed to publish a magazine. For their work in improving literacy amongst Sudanese women, they were awarded the UNESCO Nadezhda K. Krupskaya Literacy Prize.

Freda's work with the Sudanese women, in particular with WIDF executive member Fatma Ahmed İbrahim, was important to her. She wrote that 'problems left by colonialism are not easily overcome after independence. The countries face monumental problems of under-development. Poverty and technological backwardness mean limited material and financial facilities and this can assume a vicious circle.' She also wrote about the issues left by colonial authorities:

> African delegates expressed the opinion that in the period of slavery and feudalism, illiteracy was not as inhuman and unjust as under colonialism. With the industrial revolution and technological advancement, the illiterate were reduced to pawns manipulated by the colonialists and working at starvation wages.[2]

In this trip, she also visited Nairobi, and then Mauritius, where WIDF asked her to contact women's organisations. One of the most important things that struck her about her experience in Mauritius was how well women were informed on family planning.

A major project for WIDF in 1970, together with UAW and other women's organisations, was the funding of a research centre for mothers and children to be built in Hanoi at a cost of 35 or 40 million dollars.[3] The year before, Freda had brought home Vietnam badges, scarves, rings and ornaments made from planes that had been shot down, as well as four films (two from the North and two from the South). The UAW used these in the campaign to raise money for the research centre, a five-storey hospital with 100 beds, now called the Hanoi Obstetrics and Gynaecology Hospital. Freda opened the hospital at a ceremony on 20 November 1974. Throughout the fundraising and construction period, Fanny Edelman (as WIDF general secretary) sent progress reports, with detailed technical information on the ongoing plans and construction, to the national women's organisations including UAW to help intensify the fundraising campaigns, and to build solidarity with Vietnamese women. As well as collecting very large sums of money (for example US$125,000 from the German Democratic Women's Union), WIDF organised other ways of raising funds; they produced tens of thousands of Vietnam badges and distributed them to the national organisations for sale.[4]

The CPA split

1970 was a very busy year for political dissidents in Australia, with much for ASIO to cover. Activist and journalist Wendy Bacon writes that for her and her brother Jim, 'our files, and many others, also document the intensity of life in 1970, a year of huge moratoriums against the Vietnam War, anti-apartheid protests, land rights marches, student occupations and growing women's and gay liberation movements'.[5] All of these ferments were taking place alongside, and inextricably enmeshed with, continuing dissension in the CPA and a continuing process of de-Stalinisation, leading to the split between pro-Moscow Stalinist sympathisers and Trotskyites. When Freda was in Adelaide in February, she went to CPA meetings, discussing the impending confrontation. At a CPA meeting on 20 March, Freda 'was the only speaker to date to really attack Trotskyism and other Left groups. She said that the current Party aims are those of Rex Mortimer who has recently left the Party…she left the rostrum in dead silence.'[6] Freda and Laurie Aarons were on different sides of the split. Freda said, in an Adelaide meeting, that Aarons 'was now ruling with an iron hand – if he did not have your full support, he would destroy you…if you were called to his office, he would sit you opposite him with the light from the window right in your face, and he would really browbeat you'.[7] For his part, Laurie had begun referring to Freda as 'that old gorgon-face'.[8]

It was at the March CPA 22nd Congress on 27–30 March that the split came to a head, when the congress voted out a number of the party's National Committee members: Tom Wright, Vic Elliott, Edgar Ross, Geoff Curthoys, Robin Gibson, Judah Waten, Bill and Freda Brown, and Jim Mitchell. Pat Clancy was dropped from the party's 12-member National Executive to become one of the ordinary National Committee members. Bill got 20 votes, Freda 17, Alf Watt 12 and Edgar Ross 16. E.V. Elliott got less than 20. Pat Clancy's vote was just enough to enable him to scrape in.[9] The split was widely publicised in Australian mainstream and leftist newspapers.[10]

In one of her addresses to the congress, Freda 'found it very disturbing that the CPA had moved to accept Trotskyist ideas', and urged the party to base its strategy on the 'United Front', and said it had neglected the interests of people in the country.[11][12] Some viewed the congress as a move to polarise the party.[13] Bill Brown was on the anti-Aarons faction that also included Sam Lewis, Eddie Maher and Edgar Ross. Ross notes that 'there were opposition groups of women, led by Freda Brown'. Freda brought up some of her issues at the congress in her speech:

> Since our last Congress we have moved to adopt alien ideas – alien to Marxism-Leninism...most disturbing is the move to embrace Trotskyist ideas. Not only is the fifty-year history of Trotskyism that of disruption and worse, but the estimation of other communist parties today – [especially] France, Britain and Japan – is that the Trotskyists are continuing to disrupt especially the student youth movement... of course we must welcome the new and the revolutionary. But revolution is a complex question. A revolution attempted too soon can disarm and destroy the Communist Party and the people can suffer terribly...calls for violence, and the use of revolutionary phrases that take no account of objective conditions have and can lead to tragedy as the provocation to which the Communist Party of Indonesia fell victim... Sectarianism is still a danger and is today being injected in the youth, trade union and women's movements in both policy and methods.[14]

Women and the split

In a letter to Carol Rooke, now working at the WIDF in Berlin, Freda listed the problems she believed were at the heart of the split. These included her attitude to younger feminists:

> I no longer consider we have a Communist Party in Australia, it is, in fact, a pro-Trotskyist clique. Dennis Freney is now on Tribune and writes articles on the in-fight in the Trotskyite grouping between himself, Bob Gould and the Percys. The policy pursued in the trade unions is very adventurist and divisive. Most of the women activists in the UAW have in fact boycotted all the party meetings on women,

we are of the opinion that they are divisive and we are not willing to submit ourselves to these wrangles; we intend getting on with the positive work. The party is all out in support of Women's Liberation, seems more concerned with abortion, the right to use filthy language etc., than basic questions of prices etc. In fact, we were told the UAW is not only reformist but a reactionary organisation (Pat Healy – Aarons) and we don't need to be concerned with prices, we need to really challenge capitalism.[15]

These increasing tensions affected the views and position of women party members. On 1 June, there was a CPA Women's faction meeting, to which Freda was not invited. She also advised other UAW women not to go. However, Audrey and Barbara were going to go along, and would 'just be listening'.[16] In a letter to Barbara Kaufman, editor of WIDF's journal *Women of the Whole World*, Freda wrote,

The Party is still doing everything possible to undermine our work. In fact, it was said that since I lead the UAW, the party must undermine it and establish some other women's organisation. They are working very hard to push Women's Liberation – mostly it only has a base in the university, but the party is sending women out to try and set up branches in all the cities, so far with no great success. However the situation is not easy for us, in the objective situation in Australia building a women's organisation like the UAW is not easy of course, and so you can imagine with the party working against us it is extremely difficult. However this new organisation, Campaign Against Rising Prices (CARP) is doing well, and had a deputation of 50 women to Canberra for the opening session.[17]

The rise of the Women's Liberation movement in Australia meant that some of the younger women activists viewed the UAW's approach as increasingly irrelevant and out of date, particularly for trying to include men in their protests, and for understanding issues as part of a class struggle and not a gender struggle. Marilyn Lake characterises this schism:

to the extent that Women's Liberationists were aware of their hard-working predecessors, they were usually considered an embarrassing legacy to be overcome, rather than a tradition with which to connect. Whereas earlier feminists had acted as exemplary citizens, Women's Liberationists were self-styled revolutionaries, scornful of the politics of reform and the respectability of reformers.[18]

In 1970 Freda had said that the burgeoning Women's Liberation organisation 'had some good ideas, but they thought that men were the enemy instead of the class structure. She did not feel that this was a good approach.'[19] She was not alone in her opinion: many of the older members of the UAW were not in agreement with the aims, and the actions, of younger feminists.

Margaret Penson comments that 'the impact of the women's movement came at a time when the relatively new 1960s Communist Party leadership, particularly under the influence of Laurie and Eric Aarons, was attempting to reverse a situation where Party membership was declining and the influence of the Party within Australian labour movement politics was much less than it had been in the previous thirty years' and as a result, 'some UAW members could not accept either the changes which the Party was making to its political programs nor the Party's positive response to the women's movement'.[20] Another area of disagreement was the younger women's alacrity to adopt strong language and explicit imagery. Audrey McDonald writes,

During the late 1960s, the Women's Liberation Movement emerged. The UAW women disagreed with the feminists' concentration on sexual and 'women only' issues. While the UAW supported feminist policies, it was uncomfortable with 'wayout' actions, which it regarded as offensive and responsible for driving many women away from the movement. I can recall in one march in the 1970s when women's liberationists were distributing rubber penises and feeling shock and horror when I trod on one. It was never clear to me what message this sort of action was intended to convey. People watching the marches on the sidelines turned against us when the women's movement needed their support. Our women were embarrassed and it got to a stage in the UAW, particularly amongst our young members, that they refused to participate in the International Women's Day marches.

The UAW was at odds with the women's liberationists over a number of issues, in particular their anti-male and anti-union attitudes. The UAW worked closely with the unions and it was from them we got our strongest support. We also disagreed with feminist approaches to organisation, which favoured informal collectives instead of executives, and rotating chairpersons instead of elected presidents and secretaries. We were accustomed to traditional, formal structures and procedures and continued to see them as the most democratic method of organisation. It concerned us that informal approaches became leaderless and lacked clear direction in decision making. We were also opposed to men being barred from International Women's Day marches, functions and meetings. To confront this, the UAW organised men supporters to march side by side with us in 1975. It was not very comfortable for the men, who were booed and ridiculed for joining the march, but we were determined to make our point. Still, the Women's Liberation Movement did play a critical, positive role through its confrontational approach in forcing society to face up to the issues confronting women.

The UAW worked around a broad range of issues from living standards and working conditions to peace and international questions. Although it campaigned for women's rights, it was ridiculed as conservative and 'old hat', partly because it didn't succumb to radical feminist approaches and confine itself to 'women's issues'. It was also belittled for its traditional methods of organisation, which it firmly believed in and argued were more democratic. The national leadership had to face these criticisms externally, but also internally from those who supported women's liberation. These political differences brought about a disagreement and trauma in the UAW. Freda and I responded to this by stepping up our efforts around what we regarded as 'working class women's issues': child care, equal pay, rising prices, maternity allowances and child endowment, as well as international issues of peace and disarmament and solidarity with women abroad.[21]

Around the political tensions of party life, the UAW continued its work through 1970, including the participation and organisation of Vietnam Moratorium activities, and Freda attended a number of the other interstate moratoriums during this period. Freda spoke at the

Adelaide 8 May moratorium alongside the SA Leader of the Opposition Don Dunstan.[22] Freda was later vilified in parliament by the Speaker, John McLeay, who described the protesters as 'human trash littering the steps of Parliament House', and who deplored the ALP's involvement in the Vietnam Moratorium Campaign: 'What more obvious unity ticket is there than this Red Moratorium committee?'[23]

Freda was re-elected national president of the UAW at its Fifth National Conference in 1970, also the UAW's 20th anniversary.[24] Freda was the opening speaker on the subject of peace and friendship. She ended her talk by saying that

UAW is not feminist; it recognises that women alone could not win their demands, this would only be done in unity with men and that was why co-operation with the trade union movement was so important. UAW is part of a world movement of women, part of a bigger movement for the whole of man and womankind for peace and progress.

Of course, the UAW also devoted its attention to other issues. During this year, Freda made a trip to New Zealand as UAW president to talk with the CARP group. Freda was very impressed with this New Zealand women's initiative, and came home to establish branches in Australia, along with others, including Phyllis Johnson. Left-wing trade unions and labour councils supported CARP's work alongside the UAW. Freda brought Daisy Spiller from the Auckland branch of CARP to speak at UAW meetings.

During a trip in September, Freda met up with her friend Valentina Tereshkova again, at 'Space City', two hours' drive from Moscow, where Soviet cosmonauts live and train. That night Tereshkova and other Russian women (including Valentina Gagarin, widow of cosmonaut Yuri Gagarin) cooked dinner for Freda; 'we toasted each other in Georgian wine, drank Russian tea from the samovar and sang Russian songs. I was deeply touched with the modesty of all these courageous people.'[25] Freda then went to the WIDF council meeting in Budapest and then a training course in Berlin.

In May 1970, Bill and Freda moved from their Bronte flat and bought their home at 23 Frederick Street, North Bondi. They signed the agreement on 18 May and moved in on 21 May. It was when Lee, now 19, was away overseas for the first time (she had left Australia on 19 January by the Russian ship *Shota Rustaveli*, and 'spent that long voyage reading *Lord of the Rings* and socialising').[26] Lee remembers that the house cost them $18,000, and Freda scrimped and saved for it. She also borrowed a sum of money from CPA/UAW member Eve Parsons. Bill, Lee says, could have lived in a room with a typewriter, but buying their own home was a very big deal for Freda. Later, Bill was very grateful to Freda for organising the house purchase; he was very appreciative. In 2012, advertised as being 'well positioned in one of North Bondi's best streets', this home sold for $1.37 million, an indication of the changes in property values in Sydney – at the time of writing, the most expensive city in the world to live.[27] Freda said, about buying their own home,

> We'd never had much so we didn't expect much. You knew how to get by and your expectations weren't high. Only one thing really did worry me. The possibility of not having anywhere to live. And it was the one thing Bill and I had a difference of opinion about, because Bill always used to say 'Look, Freda, if I've got a room and a typewriter, I'm happy.' And I used to say 'Yes, Bill, but I'm not. I'd like…' But, really, I had to push him. But eventually I did, and we were able to buy a house, based on the fact that we could pay it off as, that you got a War Loan. It was only 3% and that's how we got a house.[28]

Comrades no more

A life-changing event for Freda in 1971 was her resignation from the CPA, along with Bill and a number of other comrades.[29] On 24 February Bill had laid charges against Laurie Aarons on issues that stemmed from Laurie's reactions to the 1968 Czech events – which were ultimately unsuccessful and, according to Greg Mallory, 'deepened Party divisions'.[30] Bill spoke for around three hours at one of the hearing sessions, which itself lasted for seven hours, and was attended by around 200 members.[31] Amongst those called as witnesses were Jean Curthoys and Denis Freney. Bill had written to the CC, in December the previous year, that their plans to expel him were not caused by any 'alleged technical breach of the rules', but was the outcome of an 'ideological struggle between petit-bourgeois radical trends that have penetrated the Party and those who adhere to a sound Marxist standpoint for unity in the international communist movement'.[32] Laurie Aarons called the charges against Bill 'completely unfounded'.[33] Bill wrote a scathing analysis of this event and the ensuing destruction of the old party.[34] On 22 May at the CPA's National Committee meeting, a vote was taken to expel Bill, with 27 votes to nil, and one abstention.

After Bill's expulsion, Freda resigned from the CPA on 31 May 1971, tendering her letter of resignation to the Bondi branch. Her resignation was newsworthy enough for the *SMH*.[35] Ted Docker had tried to talk her out of resigning, but she had made up her mind. In the same period, Joyce Clark, Audrey McDonald and Audrey Grant resigned as well, along with Tom McDonald, Stan Sharkey, W. Gould, Ray Clarke, Len Grant, Paula Sharkey, Bonnie Jago, E. Hokin and Eve Parsons.[36] When Laurie told Eric Aarons that Freda had resigned, Eric commented that that was 'two down and two to go', and agreed that it was very good.[37] Audrey and Tom MacDonald were members of the split group. Audrey recalls, 'Whilst Pat Clancy was recognised within Australia and abroad as the leader of the communist grouping to which Freda, Bill, Tom and I belonged, behind the scenes Bill was the common link that held us all together even though Clancy would have felt this was due to his leadership.'[38] Paul Rafael interviewed Freda on the ABC's *PM* radio program about her decision to leave the party. An extended excerpt from Freda's letter of resignation lists Freda's reasons:

> I have found myself increasingly in disagreement with the policies pursued by the leadership:
>> the rupture of the united front, the way, I believe, to the advancement of the Australian working class

the development of divisive policies that pose youth against age, woman against man, students against workers

the attempts to undermine the mass positions of those who disagree with the policy of the leadership

the substitution of petty bourgeois radicalism for Marxism

the increasingly anti-Soviet tone of the Tribune reflecting the attitude of the leadership, epitomised by the General Secretary Laurie Aarons speaking in praise while in the Soviet Union and returning to Australia to attack the Soviet Union.

As branch members know, I expressed my opposition at branch meetings, national committee meetings and at the National Congress and worked to change what I believed were wrong policies detrimental to the struggles of the Australian people for their immediate needs and the ultimate socialist objective. However, recent events have determined the course I now take:

the expulsion of comrades who have given a lifetime of service to the CPA. I particularly instance the expulsion of my husband, Bill Brown. This expulsion was carried out in a most unjust way before the decision of the Tribunal set up to hear charges he brought against Laurie Aarons. This reveals that the case has been prejudged before the Comrades on the investigation tribunal were given an opportunity to bring down their findings, thus laying bare the bureaucratic methods of the present leadership.

the advocacy of violence that has resulted from the adventurist sectarian impatient policies the leadership advanced in the trade union movement climaxed by physical violence recently at the Labour Council. No matter how the leaders of the CPA try to excuse it, this violence stems directly from their present line.

the handling by the printery of pornographic material of the type I attach.

It is because the leadership has succumbed to the political and moral decay of Imperialism.

These are the kind of things that have resulted in my no longer wishing to be a member of the CPA. However, I have been a Communist all my adult life, I will never cease to be a Communist, and I will actively work for it as I have always done.

Lee later said that

people often ask me what my mother thought about the upheavals in the communist movement and the collapse of the Soviet Union. She saw the divisions in the left as an enormous setback for the progressive movement. Freda often said that she believed that whatever side people ended up on they still had a deep commitment to the struggle for a more just world. The loss of life-long friendships caused by the splits gave her the greatest sadness, however.[39]

She said, in a later interview, that with the events of this year, she 'felt they were betraying what I believed in'.[40]

I haven't found any instances where Freda publicly criticised the CPA, or indeed the CPSU, and she remained a socialist all her life. Privately, however, both Freda and Bill, like some other lifelong communists, had their own criticisms. Freda, for instance, thought that if Germany had been the first country to come under socialist control rather than Russia, history would have been much better. In a late interview, she did acknowledge that

I think there were many mistakes made under socialism, but I wasn't going to attack it. I mean there was enough people all over the world attacking it, so I wasn't going to attack it. But there were problems.[41]

Freda described the time of the Split as

a very painful period…this was the period when the Communist Party took a different stand, and as far as I was concerned I then left the Communist Party…because I didn't agree with the policy that was being pursued by the Communist Party at that time, and there were rifts with women I had worked with for a long period, and that was very painful and very sad.[42]

It was this destruction of firm and long-held friendships that was the hardest for her, and the break-up of networks of collegiality that had held the left together in Sydney, and Australia, for so many decades.

After the party

During this period, Freda continued to attend as many UAW NSW and national meetings as she was in Australia for, and to report on her overseas work for WIDF. She was still doing much of the high-level organising for the UAW national conferences, including on issues like Indigenous rights. Through 1971, the UAW were still working with Hannah Middleton on the Gurindji strike, such as supporting it through letters to the Minister for Aboriginal Affairs. The previous year, At the UAW National Committee on 28 November 1970, the agenda was altered 'to allow Miss Hannah Middleton, Student at Humboldt University, East Berlin, now working and studying for thesis at Wave Hill–Gurindji'. Middleton continued her connections to politics and activism, and for a period was the head of the CPA.

The Angela Davis campaign was growing in Australia. The American activist was arrested on 13 October 1970, accused of supplying weapons to the attackers of a courthouse (she was acquitted 18 months later). Campaigns to free Angela quickly sprang up around the world in solidarity, particularly from communist parties and other left organisations. Freda had started the campaign within the UAW, who launched the 'Save Angela Davis' fund in Australia. On 22 December, Freda took part in a demonstration outside the Sydney US Consulate, about Angela Davis. Pat Clancy, Elfreda Morcom and Freda went inside the consulate, where a vice consul accepted their petition from the UAW.

This year in June, Lee came back from her 18-month overseas trip. On 7 August, she was arrested at an anti-apartheid demonstration at Moore Park, near the Springboks rugby league game (for assaulting a police officer), along with Mark Aarons, Fred Hollows and Jack Edmonds.

On 24 August, Freda's mother Flo died. It had been a very big year for her, with more to come. Freda wrote to her friend Barbara Kaufman (editor of WIDF's journal *Women of the Whole World*) in Berlin:

> Life has been a bit difficult. Of course, the political situation is complex and has taken a great deal of my time, but the two real problems were personal. My mother had another heart attack and

after some months of suffering died, although she was over 80 and had been ill for 2 years, it was a much greater blow to us than we realised it would be, and for a while, I'm afraid I just let things go. Added to that my back has deteriorated. You might remember that I had a car accident on Christmas day 1969, and over recent months, it has become very painful. I had to have a myelogram, a hideous test. It takes about 3 hours – they inject dye into the spine and then rotate you until you are finally standing on your head with your head chocked back to the spine. If you are conscious (frequently I wasn't) you can see the whole thing on TV as the iodine pours up and down the spine and they take photos. The specialist says I should have an operation – but I'm not going to.

… In December, we are having a conference of those people who oppose the line of the CP (so called) and I am sure we will decide to establish another party. It is not a decision easily taken, but the party in Australia has degenerated into a Trotskyist clique. If you could see some of the *Tribune*s, e.g. on the front page of this week's *Tribune* is the heading 'IS SEX OBSCENE?' and a photo of a small boy showing a little girl his penis. There is an obsession with sex, drugs, and semi-terrorist actions.

On 27 October, she flew to New Delhi and stayed with Kapila in New Delhi. At this time, Kapila wrote to Freda,

the Bangla Desh question is getting grimmer and grimmer, and yet there is a glorious side to it in that the freedom fighters are giving a tough time to Pakistani hordes and only if they had proper and adequate help from other countries they could come out victorious very soon. We met some of them and their organisations here and made them explain the Bangla Desh situation, especially to the Muslim world here… I am glad you are actively supporting Bangla Desh.[43]

Freda was a member of a representative delegation that visited the Calcutta refugee camps and Mukti Bahini (freedom fighters) camps with the National Federation of Indian Women. She had gone on behalf of WIDF because their secretary-general Cecile Hugel could not attend, as she was unable to receive the required vaccinations. She met and spoke with representatives from the Red Cross, Dutch Relief, Save the Children and other charity groups. Kapila Khandwala wrote to Freda about the situation,

East Bengal or Bangla Desh, where Pakistan's perfidy has massacred innocent people and systematically is killing off intellectuals and progressives has created a problem for India as well. Eight million refugees on our soil is a stupendous problem and no other power has come to the legitimate and needed help of either Bangla Desh or India.[44]

When Freda came back home she worked to raise donations for these camps. At the Mukti Bahini's camp, 'these young men are living under incredible conditions. It was pouring rain, and they had a sheet of plastic on the ground, a sheet over four corner poles, some only had a ragged bit of material round their waist, only a little food, but they are carrying on their courageous fight against the Pakistani army.'[45]

After visiting the refugee camps, Freda attended a regional seminar to combat illiteracy among women, conducted jointly by the Federation of Indian Women, the UN and WIDF, which the Indian President V.V. Giri opened. Then she spent six days with Kapila, who she accompanied on a 'shopping round and social program... Freda is better, but at times she suffers from her back aches rather painfully.'[46] By the next month, Bangladesh had been officially recognised as a country. Kapila wrote that

we are very glad that Bangla Desh has been recognised and there are jubilations everywhere. Yes, war is terrible and very destructive, but it is thrust on us and we have to wage it until our aim is achieved. Dacca of Bangla Desh is within a gunshot and will fall to us at any moment.[47]

On 15 November, Freda was in Tanganyika, Tanzania. She had received an official invitation from the Tanzanian government to attend 10th anniversary celebrations. President Julius Nyerere personally invited her, along with a number of other leaders of international organisations.

The SPA

At the end of 1971, Freda, Bill and other comrades formed a new party, the Socialist Party of Australia (SPA), also taking with it a substantial number of the trade unions and their members that had been with the CPA.[48] Increasingly at odds with the line taken by some revisionist CPA leaders, this new party has often been characterised as pro-Soviet or Moscow-sponsored.[49] The party described itself as 'a party for working class unity – for peace, international solidarity and socialism – against monopoly and imperialism'.[50] At its launch, it outlined the reasons for the establishment of the new party:

> Having considered the Australia-wide decline and disintegration of the Communist Party of Australia and its serious departure from Marxist theory and practice, we consider the immediate establishment of a political party based on scientific socialist principles, essential for the further development of the people's struggle against monopoly capitalism, for peace and advance to socialism. Conference therefore, resolves to establish a political party to be called the Socialist Party of Australia.[51]

The Socialist World Bookshop at 61 Liverpool Street, Sydney, opened in January 1972.[52] Both Freda and Bill worked to help establish the shop. Ray Clarke managed it, and Gisele Mesnage later joined the staff there. Gisele reflects on her relationship with Freda:

> I first met Freda Brown in 1973. I had joined the Young Socialist League (YSL), the youth group of SPA that year, and had become friends with her daughter, Lee. The day I met Freda, I had just lost my job at the Walton's Department Store in Liverpool, the Sydney suburb where I lived. There was a SPA function being held in the city that evening and I remember mulling over whether I should go, as I was feeling pretty down about losing my job, the sixth job I had lost since starting work after leaving school two years earlier. I decided to go. On arrival, I went straight to my friend Lee and told her about losing my job. Lee took me over to meet her mum, Freda, explaining the situation. Freda told me to just enjoy the evening and not to worry.
>
> A day or two later, Freda asked me if I would like to work at

the party's bookshop, the Socialist World Bookshop (later renamed the New Era Bookshop). She told me that she had spoken with Ray Clarke, who at the time was the bookshop's manager, and Ray had agreed to offer me the job, as they were looking for a sales assistant. Freda explained that I would be responsible for opening and closing the shop and serving customers. As I was near blind, the responsibility of looking after a bookshop on my own frightened me, and I remember saying to Freda, 'But I won't know if someone steals a book'. Freda gently replied that I need not worry about that, because 'the people who come to our shop would never do that'.

And so with that reassurance from Freda, I took on the best job I ever had in my life. Ray was a caring manager and it was the only job I ever had where my disability was not seen as a problem, the only job I managed to keep. And I owe this first and foremost to Freda Brown. Bill would often drop in to talk with me in the shop and to make sure I was okay. When I hear people making disparaging remarks about communists, I always think back to Freda, Bill, Ray and other communists who were part of my life, who were such compassionate, humane souls.[53]

By the middle of 1971, SPA's Sydney branch had over 38 members, and divided into eastern Sydney and western Sydney branches. On 1 July, the party started working towards setting up a youth group. They kept campaigning on a number of issues that had previously engaged them in the CPA; on 15 July, police arrested Pat Clancy for handing out anti-draft leaflets (along with Jack Hendry). Freda and Bill had gone to the police station to bail him out, but he had already been bailed out (Freda and Bill were friendly with Pat Clancy in the set-up of the new organisation).

Freda spoke at a NSW Trade Union Peace Committee meeting on 10 July. She said that in relation to SPA's interest in peace, the aim of the party should be to establish a broad peace movement that would embrace all sections of the community. This was the SPA's main tactical aim and the whole reason for launching themselves into trade union work. The SPA must try to re-establish this type of peace movement that was largely destroyed by the CPA, the Trotskyist and neo-Trotskyist groups working within the AICD.[54]

In October, though, Freda was thinking about resigning from the SPA, because 'of what she alleged was discrimination against women at the SPA's First National Congress'.[55] She had been talking with Barbara Curthoys and other women about this.[56] The congress was in Sydney on 29 September to 2 October, and about 120 people attended. Later Freda said to Barbara Curthoys that 'it was the worst conference she'd been to in 20 years, and she was appalled by the attitude towards women'.[57] Bill and Freda were elected on to the Central Committee, however.

The work of the SPA was very outward-looking. Bill and Freda, amongst others including Les Kelton, were working to have the ACTU call on the government to recognise the German Democratic Republic. This was good news to Sepp Fischer of the Society for Cultural Relations with Foreign Countries, in the GDR. And on 22 December, the newly elected Whitlam government did recognise the GDR, and China as well. This was also the year of the formation of the Australia-German Democratic Republic Friendship Society, and both Freda and Bill joined. During this period, Freda was also very active with the Australia–USSR Friendship Society, and the NSW Trade Union Peace Committee (Ernie Boatswain was the secretary).

December 1972 brought the federal election that saw Whitlam's ALP success. It must have been such an exciting time. Freda wrote to Lee, who was travelling in India,

it really was exciting. I sat in front of TV from 6.30 to 12.30 and enjoyed every moment...the results won't be final for about two weeks, so they can't choose a cabinet and ministers, but they have already moved decisively on conscription, equal pay, and there is a feeling of enthusiasm among people.[58]

Throughout the Whitlam era, there were many initiatives on women's issues. In the week of Whitlam's victory, Freda began petitioning him personally – and getting thoughtful responses from the busy new prime minister.

Freda continued to declare herself against those women fighting for women's rights who called themselves 'women's liberationists'. Reflecting the changing of the guard from older feminists to the second wave, Freda lists the IWD march this year in her diary as a 'women's lib march' and not 'IWD march'. Janey Stone describes it as the 'first new-wave IWD march' in Australia.[59] Even though there was a lack of understanding from both 'sides' of the divide between older feminists and the second wave, Freda showed a great deal of interest in the work of the younger generation; when Germaine Greer left Australia to investigate women's issues in Bangladesh on 23 March, Freda thought it noteworthy enough to put in her diary.

Once the 1972 federal election had brought in the new Whitlam Labor government, the UAW and the women's movement more generally received significant government support. Audrey McDonald assesses the period:

> It was not until the early 1970s with the election of the Whitlam Government and the ascendancy of the women's movement that ALP proscription of the UAW 'faded' away. This change in approach was marked by the Whitlam Government ensuring Embassy staff in New York afforded Freda Brown great assistance when she attended the UN Status of Women Commission as a WIDF representative.[60]

Indeed, Whitlam's Minister for Labour, Senator Clyde Cameron, supported the work of the UAW and believed that the group

> has a solid and enduring reputation for speaking out on issue of broad humanitarian significance. Time and time again your organisation has identified itself with some of our most urgent social causes – such as the continuing struggle for women's rights, and the opposition to the gratuitous shedding of blood in man-made wars. It isn't always my good fortune to deal with organisations having such a fine record.[61]

Throughout 1973 and 1974, Freda and the UAW pressed the Whitlam government for support and recognition of Australia's representation and actions on 1975 as IWY. This includes Freda writing to Whitlam on matters of women's organisations in Australia and the UN.[62] In his pioneering work to establish the office of Women's Adviser to the Prime Minister and many other initiatives, Whitlam perceived the focus on women's issues as part of the 'struggle for universal human rights'.[63]

In April, Freda worked in New Delhi, the US, Moscow and Berlin. She said that her meeting with the CP of India had been 'tremendous, and from our point of view (SPA), much better than could possibly be imagined'.[64] While she was in the USA during this trip, she had met Gus Hall, general secretary of the CPUSA. The WIDF Council meeting was in Varna, Bulgaria. She went to Bulgaria with Audrey McDonald, who writes about her first time at a WIDF meeting working alongside Freda,

Varna was a beautiful place with tree lined streets and arts and crafts displays in spectacular designs and Bulgarian colours of red, green and black. The council was held at a holiday complex and Freda and I shared a room. I was there for my 35th birthday and obviously through Freda, Valentina Tereshkova came to me with a present. I was overwhelmed by the visit of such a world-renowned VIP. Valentina had achieved fame as the first woman in space and was now a WIDF Vice President. She was a young, stylish Soviet woman, rather reserved, slim and attractive. She was committed to the cause of women and peace, having seen, as she told me, 'our beautiful planet from outer space'. The WIDF greatly admired her hard work for the organisation.

The Council meeting was attended by women from over 100 countries. I found it inspiring to be able to meet and hear women from all over the world. One of the main subjects under discussion was action to involve young women. I was able to speak about the UAW's 'Young Marrieds Program', which took up the needs of young couples in finding a home and starting a family. The Council was my first contact with the WIDF and I could easily see why Freda had tenaciously fought to maintain our affiliation. I could see first-hand the mammoth amount of work it did for women and its international influence, particularly as a major non-governmental organisation before the United Nations. I listened intently to women from India and Bangladesh talk of the seemingly impossible problems of poverty and overpopulation; the Latin American women talked of their fight against dictatorship; Vietnamese women pleaded for support to end the war; and the South African women urged international protest over the atrocities of apartheid. This was an emotional eye opener for me, which embedded a deep conviction in my heart about expanding the UAW's international solidarity work.[65]

One of her Bulgarian comrades had a special memory of Freda. Evgenia Kiranova was a prominent Bulgarian peace activist, and would later become the general secretary and then vice-president of the International Committee of Solidarity with Cyprus.[66] She recalled,

I have met Freda Brown at many various place. I have heard her speak from the rostrum and informally. I find it difficult to even sketch the whole of her tremendous activity, her personal contribution to the development of the women's international democratic movement. She knows down to the minutest details the situation of women in one country or another; she is familiar with their demands and the problems preoccupying them. She makes a skilful use of her knowledge to fight for complete equality for women, which is one of the principal goals of WIDF. More than once she has spoken about these problems at big international forums, the UNO included. Freda has always correlated the solution of the so-called women's problem to the solution of mankind's cardinal problem – the preservation of peace.[67]

1972 was the official beginning of the planning towards an International Women's Year. 'Together with the other NGOs present at the 1972 session of the UN Commission on the Status of Women, WIDF drafted and presented a proposal for an IWY to the Commission which it in turn presented to the UN General Assembly. The General Assembly unanimously adopted the recommendation with Resolution 3010 (XXVII) of 18 December, 1972.'[68] During 1972–1975, Freda attended the UN Status of Women Commission as the WIDF representative; there, she followed in the footsteps of Jessie Street, who, as the only woman on the Australian delegation to the USA that founded the United Nations, was instrumental alongside other women activists in the establishment of the UN Status of Women Commission. Hilkka Pietilä writes that the WIDF President Hertta Kuusinen 'brought to the March 1972 session of the Commission a proposal of the WIDF requesting the proclamation of an 'International Women's Year' in order to bring the needs and views of women to the attention of the UN System and the world'.[69]

This year Lee went travelling with a friend, and they stayed with Kapila in India while they were there. Also in 1972, Freda and Bill started looking for a holiday place on the Central Coast. However, money was tight, and in November, Freda applied to the ABS to do census work to help household funds. Her health had not been good this year, though; she had migraines and stomach and bowel pains, and began hormone tablets.

24 January 1973 marked the end of the Vietnam War. US President Nixon described it as 'Peace with Honour'.[70] So much of Freda's energies had gone into fighting against this terrible war for so many years; it was a great relief to be at the end of it. Freda and Bill's start-of-year holidays for 1973 included their Sussex Inlet break. This was to the Sydney trade union holiday homes down at St Georges Basin. Freda and Bill went there for a week, when Rae and Joyce Clark were there – Rae had just bought a speedboat, 'so you can see we are living it up rather well in affluent-ridden, Labor Government-run Australia'.[71] Freda started playing golf down there: she wrote to Lee, still in India, 'I didn't think I would ever play golf regularly but had a lovely game, especially as sometimes as many as a dozen kangaroos stood watching.'[72]

But they still wanted a bolt-hole of their own, and in 1973 Bill and Freda bought their holiday home at Copacabana, 90 kilometres north of Sydney at Gosford. It was important to have a place close to the beach, and the family loved 'Copa', their home up the coast. Freda's grandson Rory recalls that, from the 1980s when he was coming along to Copa on holidays, it 'was such a big part of their life; it was just a beautiful place, it was like a family retreat where we could escape. Nanna and Grandad could leave everything behind in the city and go up there and relax and there was a beach close and gardening.' Bill's family had come from that area, and Bill would write songs about Copa for the grandchildren. In her letters home, Freda longed for her return to Sydney, as well as a few days' holiday up north: 'my eyes are only on Copa', she wrote.[73] She never saw her constant travel as a threat to her relationships with Bill and Lee, although she missed them very much when she was overseas.

UAW

At the Sixth National UAW Conference in September 1972, Freda had been re-elected UAW national president. On 29 March 1973, Freda was the chair of the inaugural meeting of the Committee to Plan for 1975. This was a committee of 15 women's organisations and trade unions, established to work for the IWY in 1975. As UAW national president, Freda presented a list of points that could be considered on the agenda, and asked for the nomination of the chairwoman of the committee. It was unanimously agreed that Mrs Brown take the chair.[74] She also asked the Australian government to declare 8 March 1975 a public holiday for women for the IWD of IWY.[75] One of the achievements of this committee was lobbying the Whitlam government, successful this time, to issue a stamp to mark International Women's Day.

The UAW, and in particular Freda and Audrey, were instrumental in making International Women's Year in Australia such a big one. They were very proactive in organising meetings and events, contacting people from every sector and publicising the plans towards 1975. They worked with federal, state and local governments, ACTU and unions, and many other organisations. They were a part of the United National Association of Australia for this too. A UAW pamphlet claims that 'In NSW the UAW initiated a planning committee representative of a number of women's organisations, to work towards this important goal' of 1975 as IWY in Australia. Freda wrote that

> it needed a great deal of perseverance to make it understood that women's struggles for their demands could only help the general fight against social injustice, against exploitation, and for the preservation of peace in the world, and that satisfaction of these demands would release vast new forces.[76]

WIDF

In April and May, Freda had travelled to Cuba again, to attend a WIDF Bureau meeting, the first in Latin America. Vilma Espin de Castro, president of the Cuban Women's Federation (and a WIDF VP) and Fidel's wife, opened the meeting. While she was there, Freda had a long discussion with Fidel. ASIO believed that Castro

> stated the main reason for his visit to the Soviet Union last year was to counter the capitalist propaganda that there were differences of opinion between himself and the Soviet Union and this could cause a split. He claimed that if there had been any criticism it was not meant as differences in the overall relationship with the Soviet Union. He claimed that Cuba is on the best of terms with the Soviet Union and the Socialist countries, because Cuba could not exist, at present, because of the close proximity of the USA.[77]

Freda had also come to Cuba to promote the invitation the Australian trade unions had made to the Cuban trade unions, to come to Australia for the next year's May Day celebrations (Freda having joined in the May Day festivities in Cuba this year). 'Fidel Castro, in discussing the invitation with Freda Brown, suggested the delegation of trade union representatives should also include a representative of the women and youth movement in Cuba.'[78] Back in Australia, Freda said that Fidel was 'an incredibly charming man'.[79] She 'met Castro personally and along with all the other woman delegates, received an orchid sent to my hotel room by him'. She also said that she had never met a human being who had the charisma that he had, with an incredible magnetic personality. Freda also talked with Vilma and Fidel's brother Raul.

On 11 September 1973, the violent overthrow of Chile's democratically elected Allende government by the US-backed Pinochet coup, along with the subsequent murder of thousands of people, sent shock waves through the world. A WIDF open letter declared that 'American imperialism is primarily responsible for preparing and executing the horrible crimes committed in Chile'. Here the group's focus was through Mrs Hortensia Bussi de Allende, a member of

WIDF and an honorary vice-president. The US, which still considered both organisations as communist fronts, found Allende ineligible to receive a visa because of her affiliation with the WPC and WIDF.[80] WIDF swiftly organised meetings, sent letters to the Chilean military junta, the UN and other bodies, and publicised the Chilean situation. WIDF executives attended a WPC conference called Chile Is Not Alone, the International Conference in Solidarity with the Chilean People, in Helsinki, 29–30 September 1973, which was attended by 57 countries and 17 international organisations.

A letter, written on 11 October by a woman who was a member of the Chilean national organisation, was smuggled out of Chile and distributed to WIDF member organisations.[81]

> From 11 September to today there has been a series of raids of villages, towns and parts of the centre and suburbs of the cities, house by house (by dragnets, as they are so fittingly termed by the junta). Beatings, torture – thousands of dead, wounded and vanished…my youngest son was arrested at his place of work, together with all those working there. To this day, I do not know his fate and have not seen him. He is only 19 years old. They say he is in the National Stadium, a sports arena in Santiago – today we can justly call it National Concentration Stadium. About twenty thousand inmates were detained here, among them thousands of women and girls who have been beaten, tortured and raped… I am well though in great sorrow, but content to be in my land where we are able to confront everything and prepare ourselves for the future. We are going through a very bitter experience. We deeply regret it all for what it means for the rest of the people fighting for their liberation, but we will overcome in spite of everything.[82]

Hortensia's husband Salvador Allende committed suicide on 11 September 1973. Freda sent a cable on 20 September, 'Deepest condolences death of your husband strongest support restoration democracy in Chile.' WIDF held a meeting in Solidarity with Chile.[83] The meeting

> expressed disgust and indignation at the artful treason of the military junta, which took the life of the constitutional President of Chile and

let loose the most bloody repression. It denounced and condemned the US imperialists and their accomplices, the forces of internal reaction, as responsible for the destruction of the most cherished achievements of the Chilean people…the fascist escalation in Chile brings out, as Pablo Neruda said, all the savagery and infamy of the 'jackals that a jackal would despise'.

Later, a Royal Commission confirmed the Australian government's involvement in the coup. Gough Whitlam said that 'it has been written – and I cannot deny it – that when my Government took office, Australian intelligence personnel were working as proxies of the CIA in destabilising the government of Chile'.[84]

Back home during 1973, Freda and Bill celebrated their 30th wedding anniversary. On 23 August, Bill's new book *A False Philosophy Exploded* was launched at Trades Hall. Geoff Curthoys introduced the book, which Bill had written as a response to Eric Aarons' book *Philosophy for an exploding world* and which 'conveniently summarises the SPA view of the CPA'.[85] At the launch they played a recording of a radio debate that Bill and Eric had done on the Radio 2FC (which later became Radio National) program *Lateline* on 8 August.[86]

In September, Bill went to the World Peace Congress in Moscow, as an SPA delegate; there he worked alongside CPA members Bernie Taft, Mavis Robertson and Laurie Aarons, as well as Hortensia Allende and others. The SPA Women's Committee was established in February 1973; by October, Freda was urging much tighter Central Committee control over the SPA, and saying that the party must develop a 'much stronger international outlook; at the present time the Party members are far too complacent'.[87]

1974 was the year in which, for the first time in Australian history, a woman joined the bench of the Commonwealth Conciliation and Arbitration Commission, when Elizabeth Evatt became deputy president of the commission. During this year Freda, and the UAW, were campaigning for an ALP win in the upcoming election. Throughout 1974, Freda worked tirelessly at home and abroad, particularly on the planning for International Women's Year.

The UAW has been working and publicising IWY continuously since March 1973, and we have spent a great deal of time and money from our limited funds in this work. Our National President, Freda Brown, has spoken to various trade union conferences, including the NSW State Council of the AMWU, and the State Conference of the BWIU. Both have adopted resolutions actively supporting the Year. Mrs Brown recently launched the work for IWY in South Australia, at a meeting organised by UWA.[88]

Freda travelled to New York and the UN in January. For three weeks, she attended the 25th UN Status of Women Commission.[89] Freda and the other members of the WIDF delegation presented their findings on the situation in Chile after the 1973 coup to the UN Status of Women Commission (this was just before working at peace meetings in Moscow, Sofia and Berlin). The delegation stressed the necessity to restore human rights in Chile and give help to the victims of the new regime. Freda wrote,

> The agenda of the Commission embraced questions of vital concern to women: IWY; consideration of proposals concerning a new instrument of international law to eliminate discrimination against women; study on the interrelationship of the status of women and family planning; program of concerted international action to promote the advancement of women and their integration in development; protection of women and children in emergency in armed conflict in the struggle for peace, self-determination, national liberation and independence; exploitation of labour through illicit and clandestine trafficking; influence of mass communications media on the formation of a new attitude towards the role of women in present day society.[90]

This was the first time that Freda had been to New York, and she remarked on the difference between the filth, noise and high security concerns of New York with the peace, open spaces and community care she found in Moscow:

> To go from New York, the hub and epitome of the capitalist world, directly to Moscow made me see socialism through new eyes. In

contrast to the horror of capitalism – its inhumanity and pessimism – was the optimism and achievements of socialism.[91]

I'm pleased I've seen New York, but once is enough and it can come to an end as soon as possible. Sirens scream all night and the slums are unbelievable. Much worse than I imagined! It seems a joke to ask, 'Have you been mugged yet?' I admit I don't relish going out alone at night.[92]

Her later trips to the US were, similarly, 'awful'. In 1976,

The hotels were seedy, in fact dirty. In Washington there were cockroaches in the rooms and the heater was broken so I froze… New York is on an island, one end is the horror of Wall Street and the concrete jungle of skyscrapers but the other end is quite beautiful with parks and waterway.[93]

And in 1988,

New York as usual was horrifying, but there were also many interesting things. The Museum of Natural History and the film on the Grand Canyon and the Brooklyn Botanical Gardens were lovely, but the city is a nightmare of degeneracy and decay. The homeless on the streets is heartbreaking; tales of little children housed in hotels 3 or 4 families to a room, no toilet or washing facilities, crack used and sold by children 8 years or younger… I hate this place! So crowded, noisy, dirty and since I was here last, even more decayed and dangerous.[94]

While in the US, Freda travelled to Philadelphia for discussions with members of WILPF and WISP; she had lunch with Betty Friedan as well. She was missing home terribly. She wrote,

Friday night at the end of the first week (in the USA) I was thinking – two more weeks and I'll be on my way home. The phone goes! It's Valentina; she has received a cable asking me to go to Moscow to represent WIDF at follow-up committee on Conference of Peace Forces. I could have cried! However, I agreed – I could do nothing else.[95]

After returning from this trip, she reported to the Department of Foreign Affairs regarding women and their overseas activities. In a letter in March, she wrote,

I have been very busy, had radio and TV appearances, today did a 'talk back' from Adelaide. Had a very good discussion with representatives of External Affairs and we expect they might financially subsidise our pamphlet…if the government does subsidise this it will give us enormous prestige. Now I am starting to get our visit to New York in perspective, and it was a very rich experience, it is only as I speak about what became common to us that I fully realise how much we packed into those three weeks.[96]

At the beginning of February, Freda chaired the meeting of members of the Steering Committee of the World Congress of Peace Forces in Moscow. Later that month she chaired the WPC meeting in Sofia, as a member of its Presidential Board. May saw Freda working for WIDF again in Moscow and Berlin. Audrey, Phyll Keesing, Elsie Pettigrew and Patricia Lloyd (all SPA and UAW) went to the Soviet Union and Poland, meeting Freda over there. They attended a women's seminar in Moscow. Other SPA men went over to the Soviet Union also; the CPSU and SPA were on good terms. Re that August trip that she made to Geneva: this was a meeting of WINGOS (Women's International Non-Governmental Organisations) and NGO special meeting to prepare for IWY. The UN secretariat Helvi Sipila and Franklin Delano Roosevelt III were attendees. The SPA State Conference on 1 September established a Party Women's Sub-Committee, of Freda, Audrey, and Ina. Later in September, Freda worked overseas again, in India in Delhi.

On 4–5 November 1974 was the first preparatory meeting for IWY in Tihany, Hungary. Freda was the president of this group and gave the closing address.

In 1974, WIDF President Freda Brown, also President of the International Preparatory Committee Meetings for the World Congress, set up conferences in East Berlin and in Tihany Hungary. The meetings invited participants who believed 'that all forms of discrimination against women constitute a violation of human rights', and who recognised 'the equal responsibility of men and women in economic, political, social, and cultural life, in the family and in the rearing of children'; it counted on the attendance of members of a wide range of women's and youth organisations, including those from Africa, Asia and the Americas, as well as UN representatives such as Helvi Sipila, assistant UN secretary general.[97]

Among the participants were members of the WHO, the International Federation of Women in Legal Careers, WILPF, the International Alliance of Women, the World Federation of Democratic Youth and the International Union of Students. The Australian representative at this meeting was John Benson, of the NSW Trade Union Peace Committee.[98] Freda wrote that 'these organisations had widely differing aims and outlooks but worked effectively and in harmony'.[99]

> The richest experience of this meeting has been everyone's willingness to cooperate. It is so easy to talk about co-operation, but sometimes to achieve it is a painful process. It really means being willing to make concessions, and that means you, not just me; it means me, not just you. Of course, where a question of principle is involved we will all take a strong stand, but we need to be willing to be flexible, to listen to the other point of view; and if that spirit, the spirit that pervaded this meeting, continues in the preparation for and during the congress, then success is ensured.[100]

Throughout this year, Freda's business in the UAW National Executive centred more on WIDF and UN business and less on the day-to-day work of the UAW. As an example, at the meeting on 23 March 1974, she reported on her attendance of the UN Status of Women gathering, her WIDF meetings, the Moscow Steering Committee Congress of Peace Forces and the Sofia WPC. On 18 March 1974, the Finnish communist politician and WIDF President Hertta Kuusinen died, in Moscow, and this is what propelled Freda into the limelight, in her greatest role, as president of WIDF.[101]

5

A President on the Move: 1975–1990

Equality, development, peace: International Women's Year

Freda had earlier been instrumental in proposing to the UN that it constitute an International Women's Year (IWY) in 1975. The goals of IWY were 'equality, development, peace'. Freda and the UAW were lobbying the UN secretary-general since 1972, and their campaign was supported by WIDF and its president, Helvi Sipila.[1] This, then, was a huge and important year for Freda, along with women activists all around the world. The two major world conferences that year were held in Mexico in June, and Berlin in October: these had special significance being held during IWY. Freda chaired both and, at a meeting of the International Preparatory Committee, she was elected as president, and spent most of 1975 in preparation for the two congresses.

For the planning of IWD activities, the UAW (and WIDF) had contact with the United Nations Association of Australia (UNAA). This organisation was established in 1946, and was still going strong in 2014. The UNAA established the IWY Committee led by the pioneering feminist Ada Norris. In 1973, the UAW joined the UNAA. Audrey McDonald represented the UAW as a member of the UNAA National Committee for IWY, and she worked closely in conjunction with Freda over the UAW's contributions to UNAA and IWY matters. Phyll Keesing often joined Audrey at meetings as a UAW representative or an observer. The meetings were in Melbourne and so Audrey and Phyll had to raise funds through the UAW for travelling down there. On a UNAA IWY Committee meeting, Audrey reported that the UAW 'had produced tee shirts, badges and scarves which are going very well. They are conducting a survey into the participation of women in trade unions. There have also been a series of classes on discrimination and a special class on video tapes. This covered Women in the Home; and it is hoped to present this to the Human Relationships Committee.'[2]

The UAW was profoundly involved in Australia's celebration of IWY, alongside other organisations including WILPF (the Women's International League for Peace and Freedom). Since the thawing of Cold War tensions, organisations were more inclined to cooperate with the UAW; and particularly since the 1972 celebrations of IWD, newer women's liberation supporters had come on board, individually and through newly established groups such as the Women's Electoral Lobby (WEL). In 1973, Whitlam had appointed Elizabeth Reid as Women's Adviser to the Prime Minister and the IWY Secretariat. Marilyn Lake describes Reid as the 'public face of state feminism'.[3] Reid convinced the Labor government to set aside the not inconsiderable sum of $2 million for IWY grants.

The UAW worked towards a successful Australian IWY with much more than T-shirts and scarves, however; public meetings and other actions helped to make the Australian IWY a prominent celebratory time. Just one outcome spearheaded by the UAW was their production of an Australian Charter of Women Workers' Rights, which came with the contribution of TUERC from a seminar in Sydney in November 1974, and was funded by a federal government grant, one of many that Whitlam had provided for IWY. Through Freda and Audrey, as well as others, the UAW connected closely with WIDF in making the work of this year very special.

> The Council of WIDF highly appreciates the substantial efforts of the national organisations in the struggle for the rights of women and the protection of children, for peace, national independence and social progress. They are further justification of the UN decision to observe 1975 as the International Women's Year, as proposed by the WIDF in 1972.[4]

The UN singled out Australia's contribution to the preparations for IWY in a 1974 newsletter:

> Several leading women in Australia have formed a National Committee for IWY under the auspices of the UN Association of Australia. They aim to convene conferences on the rights and responsibilities of women as citizens, the advancement of women in employee organisations, and on the advancement of women in management, as well as requesting changes to be made in vocational guidance publications and school readers which reflect sex type-casting inconsistent with current social trends. They also wish to set up 'teaching units' for all age groups to give them insights into their social conditioning for sex roles.[5]

During International Women's Year in 1975, IWD was given official recognition by the United Nations and was taken up by many governments who had not previously known of its existence. Freda wrote that

> IWY gave expression to women's demands. It provoked, aroused and mobilised public opinion. It united and gave confidence to women, and it involved men…liberation of women must mean the liberation of humanity from poverty, oppression and war. The lesson of IWY is unity – of women's organisations, of men and women, of young and old.[6]

The UN General Assembly had proclaimed IWY on 18 December 1972. It was financed largely by contributions from UN member states. It was designed to be devoted to intensified action:

> to promote equality between men and women;
>
> to ensure the full integration of women in the total development effort, especially by emphasising women's responsibility and important role in economic, social and cultural development at the national, regional and international levels, particularly during the Second United Nations Development Decade;
>
> to increase the contribution of women to the development of friendly relations and co-operation among States and to the strengthening of world peace.[7]

Elise Boulding writes of this turn in international women's communications, when

a new phase in women's networking began with the establishment by the UN Economic and Social Council of the UN Committee on the Status of Women that eventually led to IWY. Through the new, less formal, non-hierarchical women-to-women contacts between continents fostered by ICY in 1965, the realisation grew that development policies imposed by the patriarchal structures of the UN Organisation and its member states were pushing Two-Thirds World societies into unprecedented poverty and dependency. Information and action networks began proliferating, linked both to traditional women's groups at the village level and to the more formally structured international non-government organisations but with a life and purpose of their own.[8]

Some of the other items on the WIDF agenda for 1975 alongside IWY were the tensions in Chile, Vietnam, and Angola, Israeli troops in South Lebanon, Portugal, Uruguay, and apartheid in South Africa: Freda worked closely with the African National Congress women's section throughout the 1970s and 1980s. However, during 1975, the IWY was paramount. In Berlin in May, the Executive Committee for the International Preparatory Committee of the World Congress for IWY met, for the second time. It reviewed the work accomplished since its first meeting in February, decided on a number of organisational matters, and laid down the basis for the preparations of the work of the Congress Commissions.

In March, Freda was in Helsinki, when, on the invitation of the WPC, she held discussions with Romesh Chandra, WPC President, along with the UN Secretary-General and members of the WPC Secretariat. Freda made a detailed report on the preparatory work for the World Congress for IWY in Berlin from 20–24 October 1975. Freda was the chairman of the Steering Committee; and some in Australia claimed her appointment as further recognition of SPA.

World Congress of Women, Mexico

The Mexico Conference, running from 19 June to 2 July, was the first world conference on the status of women, planned to coincide with IWY.[9] Freda wrote, before this conference, that

> I think things will really start to hum after Mexico, the problem is I think we will have to limit delegations. To date these are some requests: India 200, USA 150, Britain 50, Canada a number of organisations have asked for 50 each, Australia 20; that's getting up to 500 from 5 countries. It is going to be difficult to fix a principle for allotting numbers.[10]

In the end, there were 1,200 delegates, with 6,000 people attending the IWY Tribune in Mexico, which was a parallel NGO conference. In a letter home, Freda wrote that

> Many people are dissatisfied with these conferences. They are frustrating but I think they have resulted in greater interest in (the next Congress in) Berlin; now the International Council of Women and business and professional women are taking an interest. There is a very negative group of Ukrainians here – today they tried to organise a demonstration against Valentina – we will have trouble with them on Monday at our panel I am sure, but I have a plan to deal with it.[11]

Elizabeth Reid, Women's Adviser to the Prime Minister and the IWY Secretariat, was the leader of the Australian delegation. Reid believed that the conference had been 'absolutely and totally politicised. There was emphasis on the need for a new international economic order, on Zionism, on colonialism, on neo-colonialism, on racism… when you look objectively at how little was achieved in Mexico, it's horrifying. On the other hand, the little that was achieved is the only instrument women in most parts of the world have to improve their lives.'[12] Eva Bacon, a UAW leader in Queensland, was one of the 60 Australian delegates to attend. Eva said that 'participants must have gained a global view and a deepened understanding from the sessions and personal contacts. Although the most oppressed women of the world could not be there, many who did attend attempted to identify with them and speak on their behalf.'[13]

As she did in most of the countries she worked in, Freda had some hectic tourist experiences in Mexico:

> If I thought either of you were doing what I have been doing I would be worried to death. On the weekend Marta, our Mexican President, took us to Oaxaca. We left at 5 a.m., arrived as did her husband in a 3-seater plane. We got aboard and flew over the area for one and a half hours, then we visited ruins of the pre-conquest civilisation, exhibitions, arts displays, Spanish churches, markets, and then straight to a night-time display of children doing national dances. I went to sleep and fell off the chair and then finally they decided to let us sleep, after a meal, about 12.30. Then up at 5 a.m., six hours drive over mountains and the most incredible roads you have ever seen, with deep ravines and caverns. We arrived at Saltillo and straight into a helicopter. Flew to an island in the middle of the huge dam, landed and met the locals, very primitive, went to a fishing village, then to a paper factory. When I looked at the accident rate, I didn't wonder: I expected a huge roll of paper to fall on me at any moment. Then back to an open-air dinner, and singing. I fell asleep again and fell off the chair![14]

World Congress of Women, Berlin

1975 also brought the preparations for that year's second World Congress of Women, held in Berlin in October. The organisers welcomed 1947 delegates from 140 countries. Audrey led the Australian delegation of 15 women, representing various women's groups and unions, to Berlin for this gathering. UN Secretary-General Kurt Waldheim gave the opening address at this congress, and thanked WIDF for first suggesting the idea of celebrating IWY. Freda told the opening session of the congress,

> We shall never forget that there are still millions of women who can neither read nor write, who have to walk up to five kilometres daily to get some water, who have neither electricity nor heating in their

dwellings and how have to watch their children die of curable diseases, who age themselves prematurely through frequent pregnancies and know hunger in their daily lives, who even die of hunger.[15]

She suggested that the conference 'should discuss and decide the most suitable and effective ways of promoting women from the second rank into first-class citizens'.[16]

The eastern European nations, particularly Hungary and Romania, sent significantly larger delegations to this Berlin Congress than previously. Popa writes that the

delegates from east European countries, as well as representatives of international organisations, most prominently the WIDF, delivered a strong message about socialism being the only system that could ensure women's equality with men. In her report to the Congress, Freda Brown declared that 'in a number of countries the problem of women's equality had generally been solved'. She was, of course, referring to socialist countries. The same idea was repeated time and again throughout the proceedings of the Congress.[17]

A US Department of State report on the Berlin Congress reports that

It was well-organised and succeeded in securing for itself a measure of identity with the UN... Freda Brown of Australia, who was named President of the Congress and subsequently President of WIDF, played a prominent role throughout the conference, as did Mrs. Allende and Gladys Marin of Chile.[18]

Freda wrote about this Berlin congress as

an historic event. I was particularly impressed with the young, passionate, articulate women from Africa, Asia, Latin America, how they saw clearly they could not solve their problems as women without solving the problems of their countries' development. Women from Chile, South Africa, and Spain spoke movingly of their people's struggle for freedom and appealed to the women of the world for solidarity and support.[19]

Freda wrote about the importance of IWY. Here we see the importance she places on the achievement of basic human rights for women, rather than personal liberation from sexual oppression:

When the Women's International Democratic Federation first suggested the concept of an International Women's Year, there were many reservations and even outright opposition. However, when it came to the United Nations General Assembly, because of the discussion and dialogue, 1975 was unanimously proclaimed International Women's Year.

Gradually the idea caught on. Women's organizations grasped its possibilities. UN, trade union, peace, youth, and public organizations embraced the idea and developed their own programs.

International Women's Year gave expression to women's demands. It provoked, aroused, and mobilised public opinion. It united and gave confidence to women, and it involved men.

In some countries, women have made basic gains, confidently moving into new spheres of employment and political power. But there are still places where women must carry drinking water four to five kilometres; where the birth of a girl-child is regarded as a tragedy; and where mothers see their babies die of starvation and curable diseases. There the greatest achievement for IWY would be a water-tap in the house, a light that switches on, and sufficient food. Until all have these, 'equality' has little global application.

Liberation of women must mean the liberation of humanity from poverty, oppression, and war. The lesson of IWY is unity – of women's organizations, of men and women, of young and old.

In the years to come, let us take steps to continue and expand the dialogue and unity initiated in IWY – unity to inform and arouse public opinion and make it heard and heeded in the corridors of power.

International Women's Year can only become a landmark in attaining the ideals of its theme if it helps to unlock the tremendous potential existing among women to contribute to the common effort for the elimination of war and the eradication of injustice.

It is unfortunate that the IWY theme does not also focus on the work for human rights because this too is a matter of direct significance in unlocking women's potential. There are thousands of women around the world incarcerated as political prisoners and hundreds of thousands of families suffering enormous economic and political hardships and social stigmatization because their menfolk are being unjustly held in political detention.

I would urge all women's organizations to devote major attention to the human rights problem, for is it not by abrogating these rights that repressive governments endeavour to stifle the struggle of men and women alike for the attainment of equality, peace, and development? Ironically, even some repressive governments are paying lip service to IWY and expressing their support. They must be shown in no uncertain terms that IWY is aimed at developing the struggle of women against repression wherever it exists.[20]

A new WIDF president

Freda was elected WIDF president at this congress, only the third since the establishment of WIDF in 1945. She took over this role from Hertta Kuusinen of Finland, who was president from 1969 and died in 1974. About her election to the role, Freda was characteristically modest.

It was an enormous thing for someone from Australia to accept it. But I think, at that time, I was seen as sort of independent. You know, I wasn't tied to this, that or the other thing. And there was a strong feeling at that time that it was – see, it began in Europe and it felt that it was dominated from Europe. And there was some resentment from other continents. Well I was, sort of, from this little country at the end of the world, therefore there was an independence about me. I think that had something to do with my being elected.[21]

Certainly as President, I chaired all the conferences. It was the richest experience of my life. I went to the United Nations; I attended two or three peace conferences at the United Nations, the Status of Women's Commission, and ECOSOC. I presented that point of view. This was when ECOSOC always met in Geneva. Then I toured and met our organisation on every continent. I was for instance in Vietnam while the war was still raging and went right down to the border. I went down into the tunnels under the ground where they lived during the terrible bombing of Vietnam. I visited Sudan and a whole number of African countries. I attended the first World Congress in Mexico, the second one in Copenhagen and the third one in Nairobi. The simplest thing to say is that I visited and worked with women's organisations on every continent.[22]

Sylvie Jan, WIDF president from 1994 to 2002, wrote that 'Freda Brown played a big role in promoting international solidarity between women… [She] is a historical figure milestone in the history of the 20th century.'[23] One of the Australian delegates to the October congress, Pat Toms, from Newcastle UAW, wrote that 'Freda was highly respected and a wonderful chairman with the gift of diplomacy and sensitivity as well as charm'.[24]

Audrey McDonald, who was working in Berlin at the Congress, writes about Freda's appointment, which coincided with a time of political chaos back in Australia:

> I recall getting a phone call at my (Berlin) hotel in the middle of the night from Pat Clancy, who was with Freda and Valentina Tereshkova of the Soviet Women's Committee. Pat was also in Berlin for WFTU business. The call was to see whether I thought the UAW would agree with the proposal that Freda become WIDF President as she would have to spend a lot of time abroad and in Berlin and we would lose her active participation in the UAW. I weighed it up and concluded that the benefits to WIDF and to us far outweighed the losses. Freda was an outstanding candidate and it made the UAW very proud that our President now occupied such an important and influential position in the world NGO community. Her election placed us in a key position in regard to worldwide events and programs for women.
>
> On the plane home from Europe, we were shocked to learn of the dismissal of the Whitlam Government. We were devastated, not only for the Labour movement but for the Women's movement which by then, in just a few short years, had experienced open government as never seen before and saw the potential to vastly increase the opportunities for women.[25]

One of the tragedies that I have come across in the research for this biography is the lack of personal records for Freda's tremendous work in WIDF over the course of her 25 years as president. Francisca de Haan and I have conducted extensive searches throughout Europe for records. However, as Francisca writes, 'Cold War attacks on WIDF have negatively influenced the state, location, and accessibility of WIDF archives and the possibility of doing oral history.'[26] In order to write a biography of Freda that encompassed her years of international work, I began looking through the 'official' WIDF archives. What I found, in what is purported to be the main WIDF archive at the Institute of Social History in Amsterdam, is a wealth of printed programs, official documents, and impersonal letters with Freda's signature on them, but no minutes of internal bureau meetings and, importantly for my project, no personal papers. Francesca has discussed the 'overwhelming silence' about the federation in most English-language scholarship about transnational women's movements. I have tried for two years to gain access to, or even learn the whereabouts of, documents from the Cold War era, but like Francesca I've come up against walls of silence. Francesca and I agree that substantial parts of the WIDF archive are either destroyed or protected against researchers, due to censorship of communism in Europe and elsewhere, and that finding primary documents through the holdings of individuals, or other organisations, is more productive. Because the Australian reaction to worldwide communism was less rabid than in Europe, there are many WIDF documents housed in the UAW archives, and thankfully more related to Freda, than I've come across in Europe; Audrey McDonald along with Sylvia Harding and other women were very diligent about keeping these.

1976 was the first year of the UN Decade for Women, 1976–1985. This recognition was a major success of the Mexico 1975 congress. Freda wrote that 'International Women's Year gave impetus to the growing political consciousness of women and highly promoted their understanding for the close relations between the equality of women and the burning social-economic questions of today.'[27] Freda's leadership of WIDF and her continuing work in the UAW was to have great influence on the success of the Decade for Women, both in Australia and globally. The Decade for Women has been described as 'both a creature of, and creator of, the international women's movement'.[28] Helen McCarthy writes that this period 'represented a moment when women's experiences and needs became part of mainstream thinking about development, human rights and global security'.[29]

In February, Freda travelled to attend a meeting in India at the invitation of Indira Gandhi, then on to Geneva to attend the UN Women's Status Commission, and to the UK to attend the York Peace Conference'.[30] In India, Freda

> spoke at a public meeting with Mrs Gandhi, a very modest woman, and stayed behind to talk to women and have photos taken with then. I went to an exhibition to celebrate ten years of Mrs Gandhi's rule. The seminar was interesting, [and was met with] very great interest and enthusiasm. The Seminar dealt with the problems of dowries, employment; still only 17% of the women are literate. We had a lovely dinner in the grounds of the Congress Party under one of those huge colourful tents, with plates made from leaves and little earthenware dishes. We ate with our fingers.[31]

By this year, the constant travelling was beginning to wear on Freda. She wrote home that 'each time I travel I hate it more and more', and 'it gets rather a bore to continually pack and unpack', but she did not stop travelling for many years.[32] As one example, during just six weeks in March and April 1976, she worked in London, Dublin, Athens, Geneva, Luanda (Angola), Cairo, Sofia, Moscow and Sydney. That year Freda also travelled to Helsinki and India. During the early part of 1976, the WIDF executive changed her international travel schedule on short notice. 'For the first time I got annoyed: it had been agreed I return immediately after Cyprus so I would have been home in time for the UAW meeting and for Lee's birthday, however they said it was very important for WIDF to be represented "at the highest level", and while here, it is very difficult to say no.'[33] Her first passport was full by this time so she had to get another one.[34]

During this year, her travel and Bill's coincided so that they were able to spend some time together in Athens; Freda then wrote to him from Berlin at her WIDF apartment, 'it was nice to be together in Athens, but it makes me so much more lonely. I felt quite envious of you in Moscow, surrounded with people; it really is a very lonely life here.[35] It has been lovely being together for a few days', she added, from the WPC conference on development, which Freda (representing WIDF) and Bill (representing SPA) attended, along with Senator Ruth Coleman (ALP WA), representing the Parliamentary Group for Freedom and Justice, and others.[36] She often wrote of her homesickness; 'the greatest [strain] is being separated from home and from any party guidance…this isolation makes for great difficulties'.[37] Later, again from Berlin, she wrote of one difficulty in working overseas:

Work here at times is funny. I try to hurry things along. For example, I suggested that we always issue press statements on the many things we do. So to put it into practice, I knock one out, but it then has to go to the propaganda committee, then be translated, then considered by the commission concerned, so sometimes I find it is ten days after I wrote the statement that it is finally ready for typing. It is one of the difficulties of an international organisation, and being in a socialist country, as they must always check that nothing is said that will embarrass the country.[38]

Freda's increasing publicity did little to draw attention to her personal life, and she rarely discussed her family life on the public stage; however when *Women of the Whole World* interviewed Freda, she said,

I think the best way to describe us is that we are very much a political family… I must say my main interest is political – the women's movement, the peace movement etc. My main hobbies are swimming and gardening, but I do interest myself, although I have no particular ability, in art, literature or music.[39]

In March, she travelled to Angola. She wrote to Lee that 'one of the reasons for going to Angola is to arrange to hold a seminar there and then for a tour of some Angolan women to Europe'.[40] She attended the celebrations for IWD there, speaking at a number of ceremonies commemorating the work of women liberation fighters.[41] She also caught up with Australian journalist Wilfred Burchett, who was covering the end of Portuguese colonial rule.[42]

At the 13th General Assembly of NGO Conference (ECOSOC) in Geneva on 16–19 March 1976, WIDF was elected for the first time to the bureau/board of the Conference of NGOs in the UN. Freda wrote that the conference

> is interesting. It is swamped with reactionary organisations, some so small all they have is an address and a representative, but they keep out big representative organisations. Now there is a move for an all-embracing conference of public organisations whether they have consultative status or not, but this is being resisted, so it will be quite interesting to hear the arguments on both sides. Our argument is that public organisations should be playing a more important role in the UN.[43]

This was a new form of bureaucracy for Freda and other WIDF representatives to learn; Freda wrote that 'it really is another world with its own language, methods etc… [A]fter a day you get the hang of it but after Angola it's a bit repelling; however it is an important sphere of work for contact.'[44]

In 1976 when she was in Moscow, she presented the Eugenie Cotton Medal to *Soviet Woman* magazine on its 30th anniversary.

> Your magazine is the voice of the women of the Soviet Union. It is doing an excellent job in bringing the ideas of peace to the women of the world. I believe that women in many countries learned what socialism means thanks to your magazine. It is a very important task to explain to the women of capitalist countries the advantages of socialism and the need for them to participate in the fight for peace and security.[45]

Freda was spending a great proportion of each year working overseas, and something had to change. The split in her work between local and international was becoming increasingly wearing. In 1976, she stood down from all UAW positions. At a UAW National Executive conference on 11 August, she had proposed that she should resign as UAW president because of the amount of time that she was unavailable in Australia to carry on the day-to-day activities of the organisation. A proposition was discussed that in view of Freda's own opinion on the situation, that this situation be accepted, but that because of the need for international connection between WIDF and UAW it would be good if Freda held some position, such as immediate past president.[46] The UAW National Conference was in Sydney on 22–24 October. She couldn't attend this as national president, due to WIDF work. In the minutes for this conference, however, 'a letter from Freda Brown was read to delegates re her inability to nominate as President of the National Committee' because of her international commitment to WIDF.

> I believe it is desirable to have someone who can give such a position both time and creative thought as the role and tasks of an organisation such as ours is becoming more and more demanding. Let me assure you of my desire to do as much as possible for the UAW while I am in Australia and during my work overseas.[47]

Consequently, the UAW elected Betty Mawdsley to the presidency, with Audrey as secretary. However, Freda kept attending National Executive meetings when she was back home, and returned ready to deliver reports of her meetings, such as the Helsinki Conference. She also kept very active in initiating publicity and political action, revealing Freda's work on inclusiveness and delegation, as well as spreading the word.

In November, Freda was travelling again, to Ireland, Washington, New York and Berlin. She wrote of her visit to Ireland:

> It was a traumatic experience, rather depressing; women are magnificent working under the most difficult conditions of vicious sectarianism that I have ever experienced. Belfast is tense like a city under siege, barbed wire, bombed shops, houses, pubs in rubble, spot searches by the army, armoured cars and soldiers with guns at the ready.[48]

She added that 'the sectarian violence is terrible, frightening in its mindlessness; one night we missed a shootout by a few minutes'.[49]

During 1977, she had health troubles that had really started the year before, although her travelling continued at the same frantic pace. In January, Freda was in Moscow at the World Forum of Peace Forces as WIDF President, also as vice-president of the WPC and the Australian Peace Committee. In February, the International Committee on the United Nations Decade for Women was founded in Berlin, with Freda, who had inspired the establishment of the committee, chairing the meeting as president of the World Congress for International Women's Year.[50] There were representatives of 49 countries as well as the United Nations, UNESCO, UNICEF and the UN Economic Commission for Africa.

In March, a WIDF delegation travelled with Freda to Australia and NZ for the IWD celebrations. They were Eugenia Cunhal, a Portuguese office worker and chief editor of the Portuguese *Women's Journal*, Farrah Hassam from Somalia, and from Poland Barbara Moroz, a journalist.

An important family event occurred in 1977, when Lee and Paddy Gorman (1931–) were married, on 3 September, at the Wayside Chapel in Sydney's Potts Point. Paddy, born in Ireland, had been working in the labour movement for some time, often as a journalist, and had joined the YSL and the SPA. It was wonderful that Freda was able to be at home for the wedding, and not working in Europe. Two days after their marriage, Lee and Paddy, along with seven other young YSL and SPA members, took a short trip to the USSR. In the next year, Freda's first grandchild, Rory, was born, on 30 May 1978.

In October, Freda was in Prague, as the president of the UN Decade for Women Committee, to open the International Committee for the United Nations Decade for Women. She reported on the enthusiastic response by the many organisations and movements throughout the world to the proclamation by the UN of the IYC in 1979. She recalled that the decade committee at its meeting in February 1977 at Berlin had decided to organise a world NGOs conference on the problems of children. At this conference, Freda made concrete proposals for the content and the method of preparation for the world conference. She said that 'there must be an end to the arms race so that war budgets can be reduced and eventually abolished and money diverted to improve the conditions for all children'.[51]

Marie Lean was the UAW representative at this Prague conference. She also went to the WIDF conference in Berlin that month. Marie commented,

As a member of the UAW one could not help but feel very proud at the praises that were heaped on Freda Brown by delegates from all around the globe for the magnificent work she is doing in developing the work of WIDF. Once people knew you were also a member of the UAW that gave you a sort of special aura, but you also felt you had something to live up to. Many new organisations were in attendance as a result of Freda's work and particularly the various UN subsidiaries.[52]

Still during October, Freda attended a Yugoslavian conference on women and development on behalf of the UAW as well as WIDF, at Ljubljana.

Freda came home to celebrate International Women's Day for 1978, and gathered a fair amount of local media attention. She was a guest on the *Mike Walsh Show* on television.[53] Mandy Wilson, a journalist for the *Australian*, interviewed her when she was home. Wilson described 'our Freda', adopting her for the media when it suited the times. Wilson interviewed Freda when she was 'dressed in a cotton housecoat and bare feet', who 'doesn't appear to be the very important person she is'. She described her as having an 'uncut' quality.[54] Another IWD feature described Freda as heading 'the international struggle among women for equality'. Freda said,

To have economic equality, you must have social recognition of the role of motherhood. A woman should not be penalised for having a child. There is inadequate childcare for women who want to work. It's terrible that the government has cut pre-school so drastically. Too often career women opt out of having children. It's sad that a women denies herself that. The greatest joy in my life was when my daughter was placed in my arms.[55]

She attended the WFTU Congress in Prague on 17 April, and wrote that

the Congress was very impressive, 345 organisations from 140 countries, 1,100 participants, 90 of the organisations from ICFTU and social democrat unions. A great development since the last congress in 1973 in Varna where there was 183 organisations and 93 countries. I went to present the Eugene Cotton Medal to WFTU for their work on peace, equality of women and solidarity.

She met with Romesh Chandra (CPI leader and president of the WPC) there, continuing their long and close professional relationship.

In April, Freda spoke at a Women and World Disarmament seminar in Vienna, opened by UN Assistant Secretary-General Helvi Sipila. She was the only Australian there. In a letter to Audrey from Vienna, Freda wrote:,

We had an interesting reception from Frauenring (Deutscher Frauenring), an organisation of women from all the parties represented in the parliament. The woman minister for science and research was a very progressive person who expressed regret that there were no communists in the parliament. Next year there is a seminar in Manila organised by the International Council of Women and they have asked WIDF to send a delegation and help in the organisation. It's on rural women so it would be another topic to discuss with their Australian branch.

She then travelled to Angola, and Berlin, and to the WIDF Council Meeting in Moscow.

Freda's working year for 1979 began in February when she left Sydney for the Preparatory Committee of the Bebel Conference in Berlin. This International Conference of the SED Central Committee, to mark the 100th anniversary of the publication of August Bebel's book *Women and Socialism*, was on 24 February. August Bebel was a leading figure of the social democratic movement in Germany. That same month, Freda travelled to Moscow for the IYC preparatory committee. It was a busy time for her, travelling widely; Freda was in Finland on 6–8 March for the International Emergency Conference in support of Vietnam. Delegates from 102 nations attended, including Bill (as a WPC representative) and Freda (as WIDF president). Freda was then in Mongolia from 16–21 April, where she received the Order of Friendship of Peoples, then she attended the WPC in Prague.

International Year of the Child

1979 was the UN International Year of the Child (IYC), and much of Freda's time was taken up with the many meetings, conferences and celebrations for this event. Lee, by now a UAW member, was on the steering committee for the IYC events that were to be staged through the Waverley branch. The UAW, and in particular Audrey, achieved a great deal organising within Australia for this. Freda returned to Australia on her 60th birthday, 9 June. Earlier that month, she had represented WIDF and the World IYC Conference International Preparatory Committee at a seminar organised by the NSW IYC Secretariat in Moscow, and had discussed the participation of the special IYC envoy, Dr Albada Lim. Freda discussed the preparation:

> during this period a great deal has been done, from the practical organisation of children's facilities in localities to the formulation and adoption of international laws. But the most important thing is the attraction of close and interested public attention to the needs of the child. National committees for the holding of the Year of the Child are now functioning in 153 countries of the world. They focus their main attention on the urgent problems of children that demand a solution.[56]

The effects of the promotions and organising undertaken for IYC had long-lasting effects. Under the impetus of IYC, 'many countries have initiated national surveys on the situation of children, as a basis for long-term planning,' said Dr Lim.[57]

[Freda] was handed a set of documents containing a draft appeal to be issued by the conference and draft working papers prepared for three of the Conference's four working Commissions. Mrs. Brown referred to the great difficulties involved in working out a compromise on the working paper for Commission 3 – on protection of solidarity for children living in extremely unfavourable social and political conditions (e.g., armed conflicts, racist and oppressive regimes, and others). However, it was apparent that she made real effort to avoid excessive politicisation of the conference. Mrs Brown also reiterated WIDF's invitation to the Special Representative to attend the Conference.[58]

The Lenin Peace Prize

It was in the first week of May this year that Freda was awarded the Lenin Peace Prize (its full title is the International Lenin Prize for Strengthening Peace Among Peoples), the Soviet Union's equivalent to the Nobel Peace Prize. She was awarded the prize along with American activist Angela Davis, German communist and journalist Kurt Bachmann, Indian activist Krishna Menon, chairman of the Polish Peace Committee Halina Skibniewska and Vilma Espin, leader of the Cuban Women's Movement.[59] In awarding Freda her prize, the chairman of the committee Nikolai Blokhin said, 'her ebullient energy in the struggle for social and political equality of women in all countries, for the happiness of children, won her respect among progressive people of the whole world'. Even the Melbourne *Age* publicised Freda's win twice.[60] She had not expected the award:

> I would never have believed that I could have been considered for, let alone deserve, such a distinguished award. The only way I can reconcile myself to it is that I believe the award represents a tribute to my organisation.[61]
>
> I believe and hope that this award given to me, but in fact to all women who work for peace, will provide further impetus to this most decisive struggle of our day. Once aroused, women can be a mighty force for peace and progress. They are so direct, persistent, courageous and inventive in the methods they use.[62]

At first, I experienced a feeling of surprise, then I was seized by a feeling of pride in the honour given me. All the more so as this prize is associated with the name of Lenin, and has been awarded by the country that defeated fascism. I regard this high evaluation as a recognition of the work of all women of the world in maintaining peace on earth. And I am just one of them.[63]

Audrey McDonald was at Freda's award ceremony in Moscow.

The Soviet Women's Committee celebrated the occasion with a special dinner in her honour at one of the historic mansions in a tree-lined street in central Moscow. The Soviet Women's Committee was very proud of Freda as WIDF President and admired her ability and her directness, which helped give the WIDF its considerable international standing.[64]

The Soviet Women's Committee asked Audrey to organise a celebration for Freda back in Australia:

With her usual modesty, Freda said she hoped that the award given to her, and in fact to all women who worked for peace, would provide further impetus to the most vital struggle of the day peace and disarmament. She proposed that the best way to mark the prize would be to place an appeal in the newspaper. Ina (Heidtman) and I drew up the advertisement to which we got about 100 signatures of key identities in the unions and the peace and women's movement. Under the slogan, 'Peace on Earth for All Children – the Best Christmas Present for Children is World Peace', we raised sufficient money to insert the advert in *The Australian* just a few days before Christmas. For the UAW, it was a fitting conclusion to the International Year of the Child.[65]

On 9 November, the dinner to honour Freda's acceptance of the Lenin Peace Prize was held in Sydney. At the Moscow ceremony Freda had said, 'Man walked on the moon but millions of children have never held a book in their hand', and this quote was used extensively to promote the Sydney dinner. The attendance list is remarkable. It includes people from the Bulgarian and USSR consuls, the Australia–Bulgaria, Cuba, GDR and USSR Friendship Organisations (Betty

185

Bloch attended as one of the Australia–USSR Friendship Society), IYC government departments, and individuals including Lee and Pat Gorman, Rae Lewis, Stan Moran, Ann Symonds, Ina Heidtman, Daren McDonald, NSW MLCs, members of parliament, members of the Australian Peace Committee, including Ernie Boatswain its secretary, and leaders of the SPA including Bill Brown, Geoff Curthoys and Peter Symon its general secretary. Leaders of Australian trade unions including Pat Clancy from the BWIU, guests of the WFTU, and UAW leaders and members including Betty Mawdsley, Audrey, Lee, Ina, Paula Sharkey the NSW president, Barbara Curthoys, Hanna Middleton and Pat Tuohy; other women's organisations such as CARP, WILPF, the Women's Trade Union Commissions and the YWCA. It was a very big event and much preparation went into it. Sam Goldbloom, vice-president of the Congress for International Co-operation and Disarmament, travelled from Melbourne to give the main speech of the night. Freda wrote to Audrey,

> I was deeply moved and once again proud of the UAW's ability to put on such a warm but well organised night. Many people came to me and expressed their appreciation for what the UAW has done. While I have said it before, I do want to stress that I regard the award as honouring women of the UAW, as a national organisation of WIDF, for all they have done, some for thirty years, for peace.[66]

The World Conference for a Peaceful and Secure Future for All Children was another event in 1979. Freda chaired this Moscow conference of 700 people on 7–11 September, and opened the conference alongside President Mikhail Gorbachev. The meeting drew representatives from 135 international organisations.[67] Freda reminded guests that

> the Year of the Child is taking place in the middle of the UN Decade for Women. The problems of children can hardly be separated from women's problems. They are indivisible... I dream of the same conditions for my one-year-old grandchild Rory as Soviet children enjoy. In the USSR, I saw beautiful kindergartens and crèches, schools

where the children are being taught humanism and friendship. I saw that Soviet teenagers were absolutely confident that they would receive an education, a trade to their liking and a job.[68]

On another trip, Freda travelled to Western Sahara to have discussions with the National Union of Sahrawi Women. This group was created in 1974 through the Polisario Front, a Saharawi separatist group backed by Algeria. Freda recalls that trip:

We were hoping to hold the world congress in the International Year of the Child, and so they thought they'd hold it in Algeria. So I went to Algeria with this lass from France who came with me to interpret. But when we got there, they wanted recognition of the Polisario Front. The Polisario were the ones who wanted, who were struggling against the situation in Morocco in that time and wanted their right to independence of that part of the Sahara. That was supported by Algeria.

And so they said 'If you want to hold the congress in Algeria, you must go and visit them and see what the problem is.' So very early one morning they got us up at the crack of dawn – or before dawn cracked – put us on this tiny little plane and flew us into the Sahara. And this was the – of all the experiences, this was the most extraordinary experience of my life. We got out and then we get into this four-wheel drive and they drive us across the Sahara. And you're in the Sahara, it's just desert. There is nothing. And finally we come on this little camp around this water hole and I can remember sitting there. The whole thing was completely unbelievable. The heat was something you just cannot describe. Midday on the Sahara. And these little kids would arrive with little cans across the desert. Where did they come from? Just walking across the desert. They'd fill their billy up from the waterhole, they'd disappear back across the desert again. Now the girl with me said 'Freda, if I don't drink I'm going to die.' I said 'Look you can't drink. If you drink we'll both – we'll get sick. You can't.' And so we didn't drink all day. But that night we were in this huge tent and then they brought out tins of orange juice and we could have a drink. And the leaders of the Polisario arrived. It was like *The Desert Song*. They arrived on horseback in great, not white robes, but pale blue robes and sat there on the ground. We were all sitting on the ground. And spoke to me and told me about their struggle and what was happening in Morocco and how the King of Morocco was denying their freedom, etc. So it was really a quite extraordinary experience. And we did admit the Polisario Front. They became a member of the WIDF.[69]

In November, Freda travelled to Vietnam, where she opened the Mother and Child Research Centre in Hanoi. The UAW had contributed over $10,000 towards the WIDF's construction of this centre. At the opening ceremony, Freda said that 'the centre has become a symbol of unbreakable solidarity of women throughout the world with heroic Vietnam'.[70] Freda wrote

after the ceremony we walked up the steps and I cut the ribbon, it was a deeply moving movement...because one thought that, after all this time, the hospital is now open and the first patient will be admitted on 1 December 1979. But I would like to stress that we will need to continue our solidarity. There is still a great need for further equipment.[71]

Sylvia Harding, UAW National Executive member, was a very active UAW member on Vietnam, and was the UAW representative on the WIDF delegation to Vietnam and Kampuchea. Sylvia visited the hospital in 1984:

I was very pleased to visit the Hospital. The construction of this hospital was financed by the WIDF and many of (the UAW members) have contributed through this organisation. The hospital specialises in obstetrics, gynaecology and paediatrics. It cares for babies, mobilises and teaches women how to protect their health, and trains sisters and doctors. The Vietnam Women's Union pays much attention to the hospital which has received equipment from women in Japan and from Switzerland and West Germany.[72]

At 60 years of age in 1980, Freda's overseas trips continued but her health was starting to show the toll of all the travel. Coming home to Bondi, and breaks up at Copa, were increasingly welcome. Swimming was always important for her, and returning to the beaches of Sydney. The rips, tides and washes of Bondi's waves were a constant in Freda's politically turbulent world. Freda had been ill in hospital in Moscow earlier, with eye infections, and had come home to Bondi and to Copa to recover. On 15 March this year, Lee's second child Kilty was born, so Freda's desire to be at home increased. By 1980, Freda's role had changed in the UAW. She became honorary vice president, a position that she held for many years, but she was still on the National Executive.

Freda took at least four trips this year, however, and was working hard for the WIDF during this period. The first, in April, was to Berlin for the WIDF bureau; then later that month, to Warsaw, Budapest and Finland. She attended the international seminar on Women and Apartheid and, in Warsaw, the round table of women's organisations on Women and Disarmament organised by WIDF in preparation for the UN Women's Conference and the Forum. Freda was able to have discussions at the seminar with the Jamaican diplomat Lucille Mair, secretary-general for the UN World Conference, in Copenhagen.[73]

WIDF issues in 1980 included South Korea, Chile, South Africa, Palestine, and Uruguay. The 8 March 1980 was the 70th anniversary of IWD, and WIDF celebrated this. Brigitte Triems was one of the German representatives on WIDF, and was its secretary-general during the 1980s. She wrote that

for me, Freda was one of the most important persons in my life. I loved to travel with her and to have long and interesting discussions with her. She was a role model for me and I learnt a lot from her. I highly appreciated her modesty, her honesty and her political cleverness. Her contribution to the development of WIDF is indeed invaluable.[74]

In September, Freda travelled to Moscow and to Sofia in Bulgaria, for the World Parliament of the Peoples for Peace. This was a very large meeting, with 2,260 delegates from 137 countries, and was organised by the WPC.[75] Freda made subsequent trips to Europe for WPC duties. In October, she was at the UN Disarmament Week Conference, at the University of Sydney. Freda, as the WIDF representative, 'defended the USSR's position. She said it is a victim of US aggression. She also spoke about the USSR's peace proposals and of how the facts are distorted by the media. There is a rising protest in the world by doctors and scientists in general. She suggested an advertisement for Christmas – "Give peace to your loved ones".'[76]

In July, as leader of the WIDF delegation, Freda travelled to attend the NGO Forum in Copenhagen. The simultaneous forum was the 1980 World Conference on the United National Decade for Women. One of the important outcomes of this forum was the ratification, by 75 countries (including Australia), of the Convention on the Elimination of All Forms of Discrimination against Women (CEDAW). CEDAW was adopted in 1979 by the UN General Assembly, and ratified in 1981. This important convention has been characterised as 'one of the most widely ratified human rights treaties in history, yet many view it as a failure in terms of what it has achieved for women'.[77]

Leila Rupp writes of the gatherings throughout the UN Decade for Women,

> these international meetings brought together not only official government representatives but, more productively, auxiliary forums of non-governmental organisations. There debates about the impact of development policies, poverty, welfare systems, population policies, imperialism, and national liberation movements on women raised consciousness among women in the US and other industrialised nations. Women from the global South voiced criticism of the narrowly defined interpretation of gender interests often articulated by women from the affluent north.[78]

During 1981, Freda's travels continued. In February, she worked in Japan, and then in Moscow at the CPSU Congress. Working her way back through Europe, she broke her ankle in Vienna and had to travel with her ankle in plaster. Her mid-year travels took her to the US, where she was the keynote speaker at the second Women for Racial and Economic Equality (WREE) national conference at the University of Pittsburgh.[79] WREE was a WIDF-affiliated organisation, with the thawing of Cold War tensions in the US. Bettina Aptheker saw it as the CPUSA's 'counterpoint for the "bourgeois" radical feminists'.[80] It was based in New York, operating from 1975 to 1995, with Kay Camp one of their leaders.

World Congress of Women, Moscow

In September, Freda travelled to Moscow, and then to Prague for that year's World Congress of Women in October, which also marked the 40th anniversary of WIDF. Attending this Prague conference from the UAW were Freda, Audrey McDonald, and Beryl Miller from the Adelaide branch. Before the Congress, Freda had said,

> I have come to Prague with great enthusiasm and great hopes. It is an exciting and inspiring feeling to meet at the Congress with the delegates representing women from all over the world... I feel confident that the World Congress of Women will play a very important role in uniting women in their further struggle for world peace.[81]

In her keynote speech, Freda said,

> we are concerned about the destiny of our families and our children, the destiny of the coming generations. We are united by the hope that the efforts of people of good will are capable of safeguarding peace, the most valuable property of mankind.[82]

Interviewed on the international situation and the need to strengthen peace, Freda described the impression made on her by the 1981 Peace March from Copenhagen to Paris.[83] This event, organised by the Norwegian Women for Peace, Freda said, 'had introduced a qualitatively new element into the anti-war movement', and she took part in the Paris end of the event. The march had been supported by many other women through the international Women for Peace movement, which had been founded in Switzerland in 1976. The realisation of the dangers of nuclear stockpiling had impelled ordinary people to rise above 'narrow interests, political and religious prejudices and convictions' and to express their desire to live in peace. The struggle for peace was visibly growing in all countries, and women were much more actively involved in it than ever before. Virtually on the day the World Congress of Women opened in Prague, news arrived of a demonstration organised by the New Women's Organisation of Japan. Delegates from Tokyo brought petitions of protest against the threat being created by the arms race started by the imperialists. Speaking of the WIDF-sponsored congress, Freda said that delegates were unanimous in believing that only in conditions of peace could full equality and national liberation be achieved: 'The concept "peace", as the Soviet leader Leonid Brezhnev pointed out in his message of greetings to the Prague Congress, had indeed become all-embracing.' She looked forward to 'concrete steps towards disarmament, and consolidation of security, and confidence-building', and concluded, 'we shall move together with all who really want peace, whether they are Communists, Socialists, or Liberals, Catholics, Buddhists, Orthodox Christians or Muslims, civilian politicians, businessmen or generals – it is a fact that in the NATO countries some generals are urging disarmament. We shall act together.' According to some Yugoslav delegates, the impassioned congress included much dissension from the official line. The Yugoslavian delegate Dr Zora Tomic 'accused the organisers of the congress of suppressing public expressions of views not in conformity with the official Soviet line, especially with regard to détente and the situations in Afghanistan and Kampuchea'.[84] At this congress, which marked the 40th anniversary of WIDF, Freda was enthusiastically re-elected WIDF president.

Back home, at the Fourth SPA Congress in Sydney in October, there was much disunity, with Bill and Freda on the pro-Clancy, anti-Peter Symons faction. Bill was re-elected on to the CC. However, Bill 'made an impassioned speech stating he had been "set up".'[85] Freda did not stand for re-election to the SPA Elective: she was not there, but on her way to WIDF. Joyce Clarke defended Freda and all the work she had done. The congress put forth a resolution of support for Freda:

This Congress of the SPA expresses its deepest appreciation to Comrade Freda Brown – a foundation member of the SPA – for her untiring contribution to the international progressive movement, to the socialist cause and the cause of world peace. Few people in the world and only one other Australian has received the Lenin Peace Prize. Few Australians have received the international recognition attained by Comrade Freda and we congratulate her on her contribution and wish her well with her future work for the WIDF and here in Australia for women and for peace and progress of all mankind.[86]

On 22 October, there was a march in Sydney to highlight International Women's Peace Day of Action for Nuclear Disarmament. This event was inspired by the women of the Greenham Common protest in the UK and organised around the world, further inspiring women to form ongoing peace groups. Freda was there as one of the speakers, along with politicians Jenny George and Robert Tickner.

Through 1982, Freda's travel continued relentlessly, including to Moscow, Prague and Berlin. This year's overseas work for her commenced with the 11th Congress of the Democratic Women's League of Germany (DFD), in Berlin.[87] Freda had been attending these congresses since at least 1975. She wrote that

The DFD Congress was very good, high level discussion but also dealing in detail with the problems confronting women.[88]

I was very impressed with the Congress – the high political level, consciousness about peace, but concern with the problems of women. They have discussions with the supermarkets about distribution, the need to be polite and helpful to customers, they are seeking to save because of energy problems. They save food for pigs, waste paper, bottles etc., and arrange the collection and pick up points of greatest help to women. Childcare facilities cope for almost all children whose parents want them to go to kindy, the cost is very low, subsidised by the government. The women from farms and wives of artisans (self-employed) were very interesting in their devotion to the DFD, and a large number of religious women [also attended].[89]

During this time, Freda had more health problems, most pressingly a bad back; 'the long trip and then two days at Congress and then the cold damp weather doesn't help, but it really is a worry that I might be suddenly quite incapacitated; it's the worst it's been for a long time', she wrote.[90] Then, still in March, with her back injury, she flew from Europe to Havana and Nicaragua. From Berlin she wrote to Bill that 'I am dreading the long trip to Nicaragua, but I don't think I can escape it. Give Rory and Kilty a cuddle and kiss for me, I'm really missing you all so much, I always do, but when I'm tired and not feeling too well I get very homesick.'[91] She met women's groups in Havana, but this trip was not without problems:

> I will go to Havana by Interflug. They have a stop in Canada. Last week it was held up and searched on the excuse that they were carrying arms to Cuba for El Salvador. USA has now withdrawn all rights to Aeroflot to land, so now they have no planes going, it makes it very difficult as we must now go or our women must come via other lines and it's very costly.[92]

In Nicaragua, Freda worked at the capital, Managua, at a conference of Latin American women's organisations. She wrote that the conference 'has attracted social democrats and senators from the USA, and it has government support from Mexico'.[93] She described her time there as 'fantastic. I've never experienced anything like it, that feeling of determination. The people are terribly poor but there's a feeling of unity and that life is a positive thing, and that something can be achieved.'[94]

Back home in Sydney, she reported to the UAW and to SPA on the Latin American Conference she had attended in Cuba, and her trip to Nicaragua. An article that she had published in *The Australian* criticised the Australian media for not reporting on the work of the World Congresses of Women and the peace work of WIDF more broadly:

> how to stop this madness must be the concern of everyone, especially those owning and working in the mass media. How to lessen the tension in the world, how to get to know more about each other, how to build bridges between the women of other countries with other social systems should concern all.[95]

She also reported on the international preparations of world NGOs for the United Nations Second Special Session on Disarmament, following her trips to Geneva and New York. One of the achievements of this UN session was the establishment of the UN World Disarmament Campaign that sanctioned a new, expanded role for the UN in educating the public about disarmament issues and spawned an educational campaign that opened new avenues of participation and communication for NGOs and people throughout the world. While in the US, Freda attended the New York international WILPF Conference that was held before the Special Session on Disarmament there. 'There will be 250 participants with 150 from USA and 100 from other countries.'[96] It was a time of much action against nuclear weapons: WILPF's STAR Campaign to Stop the Arms Race brought a million signatures on a petition for disarmament to the UN Disarmament Conference.[97] According to WIDF, in the spring of 1982 women demonstrated for peace in Angola, Argentina, Australia, Belgium, Canada, Czechoslovakia, Finland, West Germany (800,000 citizens), East Germany (77,000 women), Great Britain (100,000), Greece, Italy, Japan (30,000 in Tokyo at Easter), Yemen, Mauritius, Mozambique (20,000 women), Nicaragua (100,000), Netherlands, New Zealand (20,000 women), Poland, Soviet Union, Sweden and the USA.[98]

Freda wrote about the expanding influence of WIDF, which was having more influence on the world stage through her leadership. 'We now have representation at UN in NY, UNESCO Paris, UNICEF Paris, and UN centres in Latin America and the Middle East, so our work in these areas is of added significance.'[99] Regarding these advances for her organisation, she noted,

We, WIDF, have had some extra-ordinary experiences; really, they should be written for future generations. In the last two years we have had three women from the Congo, they are really magnificent women, capable, very imposing. Each time we were informed they had two children, all came with six! We have a new Secretary from Lebanon; she arrived last week with an eight-month old baby. She is already six months pregnant, with a husband who has to be found work. Suzy from South Africa has a six-month old baby; she is going to Africa for us and so baby had to be minded at night and weekends.[100]

Freda wrote that 'there is great pressure on me to return [to Europe] in May for the Brussels Conference on Apartheid. It's a UN Congress and as I'm officially on the committee they will pay my fare.' That year, she also travelled to the war zones in Cambodia, Lebanon and Ireland: 'if I don't get shot in one place I should get bombed or mortared in the other', she joked to Bill.[101] Later, in September that year, Freda travelled to Sofia, Bulgaria, for a WIDF school for African women, and for an international writer's conference held there.

Massacre at Sabra and Shatila

As one of her most horrendous trips, Freda travelled to Beirut, to the Sabra and Shatila Palestine refugee camps after the 1982 slaughter. The massacre took place over two days in September, when the Israeli military allowed a Christian militia to attack the camps. An enquiry found that the then Israeli defence minister Ariel Sharon bore personal responsibility for the massacre. The Palestinian Women's Organisation hosted their visit, and took Freda and her WIDF colleagues through the camps. They saw the dynamited buildings, people with life-threatening injuries who still had not received medical attention, and children so traumatised they could not speak. Back in Berlin, and calling members of WIDF to action against the massacre, Freda wrote of this trip,

> I had a press conference today about the Damascus and Beirut visits. Both were traumatic, we saw the invasion on TV but to see in person hospitals with men in their early twenties without any legs, children blinded and in Beirut piles of rubble and rubbish, shells of flats with no windows, no doors, no side walls. You look up and on the fifth floor, people are living with no water, and no electricity. We talked to the refugees and displaced persons, we visited Sabra camp, and it is terrible, blocks of rubbish, just one tap, and people trying to clean up. We stayed in the Riviera Hotel, on the lovely waterfront, 800 rooms, only 2 inhabitable, we were in one and the WFTU delegation were

in the other. Streets have been shelled, blocks and blocks of buildings uninhabitable. Embassies and many UN buildings destroyed.

We were stopped every block for a check on papers and sometimes a search by soldiers. One nasty incident when we were stopped by Phalangists, we had to say we were visiting another town, as you were not permitted by them to go to Damascus. It was difficult to get to Beirut, as the main road is still dangerous, by air impossible and so we went by the mountain road, not a pleasant trip usually takes 1 to 1½ hours; we took 5. The Lebanese Communist Party arranged for us to get a visa and arranged our transport. We went over bombed bridges, roads that had been shelled and were cascading into valleys. We went to one of the hospitals established during a siege in a basement. Indian, Swedish and Soviet doctors are working with Lebanese doctors, young people joined civilian defence, they entertained children during long hours of bombing, carried the wounded when no fuel meant no ambulances, helped doctors operate and cared for children who had lost parents. Now they are working in gangs cleaning up the city. Soldiers were everywhere and blocking the city with tanks and searching for weapons. I fear it is really being used as further harassment on Palestinians and left-wing Lebanese.

Now I'm preparing reports for Warsaw and the WIDF Bureau, it's a lot of work. I was very ill in Damascus and that made the trip to Lebanon even more horrible. However, I just stopped eating and drinking the endless coffee with cardamom which they make a ritual you must join in. Much more but it must wait till I get home.[102]

By this time, 1982, Freda was spending an increasing amount of time working overseas, and some of her commitments in Australia needed to take a back seat; in September she resigned from SPA.[103] She later joined, for short periods, the newly formed Australian Marxist Forum, led by Pat Clancy, and then the Association for Communist Unity; however, her time working actively with an Australian political organisation was at an end with her resignation from SPA.

1983 and Freda's travels continued; now she was in her 64th year. In February and March, she was working at the WIDF headquarters in Berlin. Freda wrote to Lee from Berlin that, following Lee's news of a third pregnancy, 'everyone sends congratulations and are delighted

I'm to be a grandmum again!'[104] Next she worked in Prague for a WPC conference, the World Assembly for Peace and Life.[105]

Her work in the worlds of WIDF continued, and she became more well known for her tact and sensitivity to changing conditions. Lia Gorter, a Dutch women's organiser who worked with Freda in WIDF, recalled her to me as

> a warm-hearted, fantastic woman who was calm and reflective, and would rather think twice than respond spontaneously. She could bring unity to a pandemonium. But she was torn between her home situation and her obligations towards the women's movement.[106]

Next, Freda travelled to Vienna, working at the first session of the Commission on the Status of Women, Acting as the Preparatory Body for the World Conference to Review and Appraise the Achievements of the UN Decade for Women. Brigitte Kubisch from WIDF was there too. Freda wrote of events there, that the meeting was

> interesting, we (WIDF) were the first NGO to speak. America, Australia and other western countries obviously affected by world peace action are now saying 'Peace' must remain in the decade's slogan, but are still talking of depoliticising the Nairobi Conference. The Kenyan delegate and, officially, others all say 1985 will be in Nairobi, but unofficially, many express doubts.[107]

Next this year, Freda worked in Angola, in Luanda its capital, with members of the All-African Woman's Organisation (OWA).[108] Women of Angola had been attending WIDF congresses since 1963, soon after the establishment of the Pan-African Women's Organisation. The OWA and the Afro-Asian People's Solidarity Organisation were represented on the executive of the Preparatory Committee for International Women's Year, when that committee had been established in 1972. Forty years later in a remembrance service for the OWA, Freda was included amongst the 'icons of the African and International women's movement, which encouraged generations of women from around the world to seek new ways to advance the struggle for a better world'.[109]

While in the African continent, Freda also worked in Maputo in Mozambique, flying there from Angola. This trip stayed in her memories for a long time:

When I left Angola we went through a most hideous storm and we landed in Mozambique and we had been flying around and we were terribly late, hours and hours and hours late. But never mind, the women, literally hundreds of women were there on the tarmac as the plane came down. You could see them, and I didn't realise until we landed that they were there to meet me, this huge assembly of women in their national dress in Mozambique who at that time were terribly poor, appallingly poor.[110]

And how do they greet you? With a dance and a song. And I go to a meeting and so after the President introduces me, they get up and they don't talk about their problems, they sing about their problems. And they get up and dance, they do a dance. And that's how they explain what the problems are, these ordinary women in Mozambique. It was such an enriching experience for me.[111]

After Africa, Freda next worked in Mexico, where her back went out. She wrote to Lee that

it was terrible; on the final day [of a conference] I was unable to attend, it was as though I was paralysed. The trip back was a nightmare, I was in a lot of pain and the plane was delayed, from 6 p.m. to 3 a.m., then a 12-hour trip and I had to enter [East Berlin] through West Berlin. Then I went to the Berlin doctor. The electrical treatment seemed to help, but then they stretched me. I should have refused, but I didn't. It hurt and when I tried to get up it was terrible, I went through agony...needless to say it's got me worried.[112]

She wrote to Lee in that same letter that she was 'anxious to hear from you and wondering all day "is baby here yet?"' On 1 July, Freda's youngest grandchild Conor was born.

In this trip, she also worked in Prague, to present a WIDF Medal to Tsola Nincheva Dragoycheva, a member of the National Assembly of Bulgaria and another Lenin Peace Prize recipient who Freda described as 'an old Bolshevik'.[113] Dragoycheva was sentenced to death by fascists and saved by falling pregnant in jail. After Prague, Freda then worked at the International Labor Organisation's headquarters in Geneva at the International NGO Conference on Action against Apartheid and Racism.

That year Freda also worked in Cuba, and her reactions to this demonstrate the gulf that she was experiencing between her own views and those of younger, western second-wave feminists.

> I was very interested in how they handle sex education in Cuba, women's sensuality, and how the failure to understand this can result in women's unhappiness, family breakdown and economic drain on the state. They gave individual examples. It is really very interesting, and as they say, the Socialist countries must handle this and not leave it to the feminists.[114]

Freda wrote that 'WIDF has just been awarded the Simba Medal by the Academic Simba in Rome for our work for the promotion of women. I will go to Rome to receive it on 20 September, before that will go to Delhi probably 15 September to award our Eugene Cotton medal to Aruna (Asaf Ali) the President of the National Federation of Indian Women'.[115] Arriving in Delhi, Freda had forgotten 'the ubiquitous Indians squatting all along the hotel corridors, being saluted and called "Sir", the incredible slowness and inefficiency (e.g. at immigration) I'm sure they inherited from the British'.[116] Aruna Asaf Ali, another recipient of the Lenin Peace Prize, was a leading Indian activist, and a member of the Communist Party of India and then the Indian Congress Party, and a WIDF vice-president. In 1954, she had helped to form the National Federation of Indian Women, an organisation that Freda was close to for many years. While in India, Freda also worked with Indira Gandhi and Romesh Chandra, WPC president.

Later in 1983, Freda worked at peace meetings in Berlin and Moscow. Then to Prague for a WIDF Council meeting from 10–15 October, which Paula Sharkey and Audrey attended as UAW delegates. Still in October, she then travelled to Budapest for a WIDF Council meeting, where she said, the peace movement has taken on a breadth and militancy which a few years ago we could not have conceived. It can no longer be ignored. Though the Reagans and Thatchers may seek to denigrate it, they cannot ignore it…it is not the Soviet Union versus Reagan. It is the non-aligned movement, the great mass peace movement, the World Council of Churches [against nuclear deployment].[117]

This was also the time of the first Pine Gap protest, when around 800 women, including Lee who was one of the organisers, spent two weeks in central Australia at the gates of the Joint Defence Space Research Facility.[118] The ingenuity and passion of the protesters, the mass arrest and the Royal Inquiry that followed the Pine Gap action was to receive much publicity and raising of awareness of the dangers of nuclear weapons.

In 1984, along with Mirjam Tuominen of the Finnish Women's Democratic League, Freda received the Clara Zetkin Medal from the East German government, for her contribution to 'the struggle for the preservation of peace and the realisation of women's equality'.[119] Willi Stoph, chairman of the GDR Council of Ministers, presented Freda and Mirjam with their medals. Freda gave the money that accompanied the award to the WIDF solidarity fund.

A letter to Lee summarised some of her future work: 'next year will be busy not only Nairobi NGO forum and the Government Conference, but also the Youth Festival in Moscow and 75th Anniversary of IWD.' In a letter, 13 March 1984: 'Just back from hospital. Completed all tests, all OK and especially pleased she confirmed my eyes are good for my age and no pressure to wear glasses'. 16 March, from Berlin: 'The IWD celebrations in GDR are really most impressive. 1339 meetings, half a million women participation, 5 thousand spoke; they were mostly peace demonstrations.' When she was in Berlin, Trudy Solomon took Freda to visit the Jewish ceremony where Peter Bloch's ashes are; 'it will please Betty Bloch' back in Bondi Beach.

Back in Sydney in March, Freda's brother Leon had an operation; Freda wrote from Berlin, 'Dad said Leon had an operation and I'm wondering what for. I gather he's not much better. I hope when you get this he's not only better but out of hospital.'[120] Leon was a wharfie and a seaman during his working life, and lived in Canterbury. He participated in the School of Realist Art, and used to construct and paint the WWF's May Day floats in Sydney.[121] In May Leon died. 'May Day 1984 will carry a special tribute to the man who did so much to make May Day and other days of mass action, occasions of creative, militant declaration of working class policies and hopes.'[122] Later that month, Freda wrote to Lee that

I had thought that coming away I would not feel so upset about Leon's death, however, I find it still continually wells up in me and I feel it is impossible I will never see him again. Try to ring Rae every now and then: I think he too will be feeling the same, and to hear from you will help him.[123]

Freda spent her 65th birthday in Bulgaria.

I had a most wonderful birthday. At 6.30 a.m., I walked for an hour on the beach. At 7.30, the WIDF girls came with flowers at the school. They presented me with a crown of field flowers, gifts, a cake, and a huge birthday card with peace badges, and slogans. We sang 'We Shall Overcome'. It was very moving.[124]

She was in Bulgaria working at a peace school. In a letter to Lee, she wrote that

I would like us to give some attention to how we organise – how to be more effective – problems to fix – but others want heavy political discussion. It's a problem of combining the two and even a bigger problem of getting agreement on how to do it. Tolerance and flexibility are easy to say but not easy to carry out![125]

When she was in Poland, she also had a meeting with Prime Minister Wojciech Jaruzelski, who in 1981 had proclaimed martial law against Lech Walesa's Solidarity movement.

Freda was increasingly missing her family. Back in East Berlin in her flat, she wrote a letter to Bill: 'Last night I switched on the light and blew the fuse. I didn't know what to do. I thought I'd have to spend the night in darkness, but I finally got the housemaster to fix it. It was so easy; I think he thought I was a nong.' In the next sentence: 'Lots of work to do preparing reports for the Council, the meeting in Moscow and for *World Marxist Review*, wish you and Lee were here to consult with…missing the children so much, I keep wishing I had Conor here to cuddle and Rory and Kilt to talk to.'[126] In another letter to Rory, Kilty and Conor, 'the three most wonderful children in the world', from Berlin on 1 June (International Children's Day), Freda wrote.

> Every day I go for a long walk around the River Spree. Sometimes I feed the ducks and swans. What about when I come home, we do that long walk Kilt and I did last year from Bronte to Bondi, and then we might also do a long walk around Centennial Park. Walking is so good, first it's good exercise and makes you strong, but it's good because you have time to stop and see things which you can't see in cars and buses and trains. I loved to walk when I was a little girl; I went for long, long walks.

Back home in Australia, Freda attended the Fourth Women and Labour Conference in Brisbane, and gave a paper on Women's Anti-War Actions. She spoke of the 'innovative and leading role women are playing' in the world peace movement, detailing women's actions in Africa, Europe, Australia and elsewhere, and highlighting the internationalisation of the women's peace movement.

> The diversity of the forms of the women's movement is a factor that greatly facilitates the growth of that movement in its current anti-nuclear campaign. The principal condition of this growth remains the anti-war orientation of the movement, the striving to give it a mass character, to provide it with slogans containing a human message, and to help those who in principle support its aims to surmount passiveness and scepticism.[127]

Since 1981, women had protested against the use of nuclear weapons at the RAF's base at Greenham Common, and as part of the growing worldwide women's peace movement, the 1983 Women's

Peace Camp at the Pine Gap military base in the Northern Territory took their inspiration from the Greenham Common women and made waves locally. Freda made connections with women in Greenham Common organisations and with the Pine Gap activists, her daughter Lee amongst them, in her role as a leader of Women's Action Against Global Violence.[128]

That year, Gertrude Shope, head of the ANC Women's Section and National Executive, visited Australia and NZ at the invitation of the UAW, and Freda had another opportunity to work with her in Sydney. The New Zealand Friends of Labor group had sponsored Shope's tour, which Audrey McDonald organised. Audrey explained that 'As [WIDF] President, Freda often met women from South Africa, which facilitated the UAW quickly taking up new solidarity actions'.[129] Shope reported that she had 'her first good sleep in a year during her time in Australia'.[130]

The Association for Communist Unity (ACU) was formed on 23 February 1985 by Pat Clancy (Pat was deposed as SPA president), Bill and Freda, Tom and Audrey McDonald, Ray Clarke and Stan Sharkey, amongst others. Bill wrote that they established the ACU 'to help overcome the divisions that had arisen in the communist movement in Australia'.[131] Foremost of the ACU's aims was to 'advance the cause of scientific socialism in Australia, while participating in the struggles of the working class for social, political and economic reforms'.[132] Audrey writes that

soon after the ACU was formed it won international recognition, largely because a number of its leaders were well known within the international communist, trade union, peace and women's movements... ACU's basic aim was to work towards creating a united Marxist movement in Australia.[133]

Freda and Bill went to the March 1985 Broad Left Conference (initiated by the CPA and supported by the ACU and a long list of other organisations).[134]

In 1985 on International Women's Day, Fidel Castro awarded

Freda the Anna Betancourt Medal for her work in women's rights. Castro also awarded the medal to Ruth Neto of the Angolan Women's Organisation and others.[135] This was usually awarded to Cuban women who 'demonstrate revolutionary and internationalist merit and anti-imperialist fidelity or great merit in a field of work that contributes to the national interest'. Originally, this was the highest award of the Federation of Cuban Women, and was sanctioned as a state award in 1979.

Nairobi

In July 1985, Freda worked in Africa, at the UN World Conference on Women, in Nairobi, Kenya, to conclude the United Nations Decade for Women.[136] More than 2,000 women attended this congress. A UN document reads, 'The UN World Conference planned for 1985 will have the task of making a critical review and appraisal of progress achieved and obstacles encountered in attaining the goals and objectives of the UN Decade for Women: Equality, Development and Peace.'[137] Margaret Kenyatta, the head of the delegation of Kenya, was elected as the president of the conference. *FORUM 85*, a daily newspaper, was published throughout the conference. It included articles in English, French and Spanish.

Over 100 women from Australia attended the Nairobi conference, with an Australian government delegation of 18, led by Senator Pat Giles. The Australian federal government's Office of the Status of Women undertook much of the organising for both government and NGO delegations to the conference. Kathleen Taperell, the director of the Office of the Status of Women, corresponded with Audrey and the UAW about planning for Nairobi. There was a great Australian film festival at that conference; Jennifer Stott of the AFC went over and presented 17 films by Australian women. There was controversy; along with Israel and the USA, the Australian delegation abstained on a vote on apartheid. It was reported that the Australian government delegation was 'resoundingly booed twice' for their decision to abstain, along with Israel and the US.[138] This was common practice for the Australian government at the time, but was much maligned by Australian and other NGO delegates.[139]

The UAW was just one of the Australian women's organisations involved in the preparations and meetings. The UAW publicised it widely – as they did the Decade of Women. Angela Davis attended from the US, and Hortensia Allende from Chile. Audrey did not go from Sydney, but Merle Highet and others did, including UAW NSW reps Elma Matthews, Kristine Anderson and Betty Olle. In her report for the Victorian UAW Newsletter, Betty wrote,

> WIDF President Freda Brown spoke about the presentation of WIDF programs and workshops at the Forum and the need to make other delegates aware of the work of the Federation. The NSW UAW contingent is staying with the WIDF delegation, as their skills in typing etc. are much in demand. The Victorians are staying at a hostel near the University where most of the workshops are conducted so they can easily keep in touch with other members of the Australian delegation, which I understand numbers nearly 300. We all get together at 5.30 p.m. and now the official Conference has started we are getting daily briefings from our Government delegation. I presume the Australian press is providing some coverage, as there are several Australian women journalists here. Nairobi papers all carry daily reports, with one issuing a twenty-page supplement today on the conference.[140]

Lee travelled to Nairobi to work with Freda and the WIDF/UAW delegation. Lee said to me that she remembers the American delegates being very articulate and self-assured, compared with women from third world nations. In letters to Bill and Pat, Lee wrote,

> Being here with mum is wonderful – she does the most amazing job with the women and obviously has very wide respect and appreciation for her work. Living with the WIDF delegation is like a mini-Forum and the best part of it. Yesterday all 500 of us gathered together in the dining room – Mum spoke briefly under very difficult conditions because the acoustics were terrible. She then welcomed each delegation – it's hard to put in words the excitement of 45 minutes of clapping,

cheering, standing ovations to women from over 100 countries and the international organisation were welcomed. Mum did a brilliant job – a few words at the appropriate time made the welcome all the warmer and the applause all the more appreciative. The USA delegation were introduced as 'from the heart of the 'beast'; Ireland 'the country which has been fighting imperialism since its inception'; 'the fighting women from the PLO', and 'the country that has given so much – the USSR'. It was the USSR and the PLO that received standing ovations. The whole event moved many of us to tears. Coming from [Australia with our own] set of problems, the strength of the international movement was seen in a simple event, as this was so inspiring.

The Forum is a political hotbed – the Yanks have flown in two planeloads (paid for) of women, the Canadians one planeload. But Fidel has lent a helping hand – a Cuban plane arrived last night full of women from Latin America. Without this help, it would have been financially impossible for them to come.

The West has changed their tactics in their attempt to depoliticise the conference, having failed to stop discussion on peace and national liberation struggles, they are now flooding the program with cultural events and receptions in an attempt to dominate the Forum with non-political events. Also, there is great difficulty in finding out the program of events. This is why it is so good being with the WIDF delegation: they are very well organised and there are regular meetings to disseminate information.

[In discussions] the USA women were outstanding – their clarity and strength were very important to bring balance, particularly on the PLO issue. Although the Palestine women were very articulate and welcomed support from the women of Israel, the US women brought it back to a class struggle in a very non-sectarian way.[141]

I've just come from a press conference given by Angela Davis. She held it on the lawns and it attracted over 400 people. Listening to her must be one of the best assets for the international communist movement. She received a rousing reception – the final question to her was 'define feminism' – she gave a brilliant analysis – ending up by bringing in the nuclear war question and spelling out in very clear terms that it is the US that leads the arms race and the desire of Soviet people for peace. Her presentation was brilliant and I am sure she would have affected many there.[142]

1986 was the International Year of Peace (IWP). Tonia Shand was the IYP Secretariat (through the Department of Foreign Affairs) in Australia, and the WIDF held a world seminar – a peace school - in Sydney. Freda's travels continued unabated. At 67, her itinerary for that year is astounding:

4 Sept	Berlin
11 Sept	Dresden
16 Sept	Berlin[143]
19 Sept	Luanda
20–24 Sept	Paris
24–29 Sept	Berlin
29 Sept	Moscow
2–6 Oct	Tashkent[144]
7 Oct	Moscow
12–20 Oct	Copenhagen
20–24 Oct	Berlin
24–29 Oct	Geneva
29 Oct	Prague
1-6 Nov	Berlin
7–10 Nov	Athens
10–12 Nov	Berlin
12 Nov	Moscow
15 Nov	home

World Congress of Women, Moscow

The Moscow World Congress of Women in 1987 (which garnered SBS TV coverage – Freda organised a local fixer to work with the SBS team) attracted more than 2,250 delegates from 154 countries, all who have come, Freda said, to be 'joined and united by a desire for peace, justice and equality'.[146] Mikhail Gorbachev, general secretary of the Communist Party of the Soviet Union, opened the congress on 23 June. Elizabeth Evatt was amongst the Australia delegation. Lee went to this, also Debbie Knopman. Freda said in her opening speech that she expected frank discussion from delegates with differing political and religious views.[147]

The main obstacles to peace, justice and equality are the waste of money on the arms race and the ruthless exploitation of women in industry, as well as out-dated traditions and customs which still assign to women a subordinate role in society.[148]

Freda was moving away from the strict bureaucracy of earlier times: in one of her later speeches to the WIDF Bureau, Freda said that during preparations for this congress,

women had reservations, they featured they might be manipulated, pressured into voting when they had no mandate from their organisation or had personal doubts about being committed. After many consultations, and frankly after much agonising on our part, we decided to have no resolutions and no voting at Congress. It was one of the reasons that such a broad spectrum of women attended. It may not apply in future but for that moment in history it was a correct decision to have no documents so women felt quite free to say what they wished…the question inevitably comes – 'What did Congress achieve?' I find it rather politically naïve to raise such a question. No one Congress, no one meeting, one march can be said to accomplish great social advances. It is part of an ongoing process, it is part of organisations, education, mobilising forces, clarifying methods, finding ways through to confidence building, a willingness to work together, build bridges and maybe finding a way to improve organisational forms, as women sharing experiences.[149]

The congress awarded Freda with a small crystal ball representing the earth. There are photographs and film footage of Freda with Gorbachev. That congress, WIDF presented medals to Winnie Mandela, Doris Tichorio and the City of Moscow.

The theme of the congress was Towards 2000 – Without Nuclear Weapons. At the congress that year, Freda made a special homage to the Soviet war widows:

I told them I owed them a debt; it was their sacrifice which enabled me to become a mother and now a grandmother. I have seen war. In Vietnam, I saw little children deprived of their families. I saw the results of war in Lebanon and the Sahara. After the revolution in Nicaragua, I saw women receiving health care and education for themselves and their children for the first time in their lives.[150]

Canadian peace activist Ann Crosby attended the congress. She wrote,

In the Congress, ceremonies constantly reaffirmed women's natural role as peacemakers based on our function as mothers. This reached overkill proportions in the closing address by Robert Mugabe, the President of Zimbabwe and the Chairman of the non-aligned countries. He stated that whereas women are 'sensitive and human' because of their roles as mothers and nurturers, men are 'insensitive and inhuman'. Moreover, he added, because 'men are more abusive, more aggressive and belligerent…we need your hearts [women's] just as we need your wombs'. Many delegates felt that the boundaries of sexual stereotyping had been transgressed by this speech.[151]

During 1988, Freda's travels continued, she kept working in Moscow, Berlin, Prague for the World Peace Congress, et cetera. In March, she was in Paris. She wrote that the 'Paris visit was quite useful, we presented the medal to Marie-Claude Vaillant-Couturier [1912–1996, the first secretary of WIDF]. The function was at the Club Pernod on the Champs Elysees, many friends who had worked at WIDF came.'

In April, Freda worked in Stockholm with the 'President of the Social Democrats', as she called Anita Gradin, president of the Socialist International Women. They considered possibilities of further cooperation between the two international women's organisations. They also organised support for women in Central America and South Africa in the struggle for their peoples' national and social liberation, and the coming Third Special Session of the UN General Assembly on Disarmament.[152] While she was in Moscow that June, she got a chance to talk with Gorbachev again, and his wife Raisa.[153] She talked about some of the issues arising within WIDF at that time, with the end of the Cold War approaching:

Some aspects of work here, and I think in all international organisations, is difficult with the differences between socialist countries. We had a call from UFF France (the Union des Femmes Franchises) demanding we protest at what goes on in China, it was so difficult to get agreement, even on how we reply (phone, letter or cable), let alone what we say or don't say to them. However gradually they come to accept we must work in a new way, be more frank; but there is now another problem, because they don't want to interfere or appear to do so they tend to do nothing and hope things will solve themselves, which they don't do. This 'how to work' methods and forms and democratic procedures maybe need time to experience.[154]

Freda was concerned with the protests against Moscow beauty contests in this year, the first being Miss Moscow in June 1988.[155] She wrote,

> many women are angry at the holding of beauty contests in Moscow, it is worse than we realised, sponsored by YCL, supported by such bodies as the Writers Union, also by western cosmetic and clothing manufacturers. An interviewer in Federal Republic said, 'this is perestroika and glasnost at work', so I've written to Pravda about it. I rang the local Berlin office, I think it threw them into a tizz, so I'll just post it off direct... [T]here is a good article in the Australian *Guardian* by the New Zealander about the beauty competition, did you see it?... I had a discussion with the women in Moscow on the beauty competitions; they are against them but aren't doing enough. Many women here are horrified. It was initiated by the Moscow YCL and supported by 'cultural organisations' – writers, cinemas, television. There was an article in opposition in the *New York Times*.[156]

International Affairs published Freda's article 'Expectations and Concerns of the International Women's Movement', on the 70th anniversary of the Soviet revolution. She wrote about how 'the basic contradiction of women's roles as mothers and workers has been and is being reconciled, and to what extent is equality a reality'.[157] She described the achievements of the Moscow congress as 'part of an ongoing process'.

Another article was published in the *World Marxist Review*, where Freda wrote of the vital work of women in the peace and anti-nuclear movements in the preparations for the World Assembly for Peace and Life, held that year in Prague. 'A hallmark of the 1980s is the internationalisation of the women's movement, which is due to the global character of the threat of war.'[158]

On 23 November 1988, Freda appeared on SBS television in Australia, on the program *A Woman's Word*. Clare Dunn interviewed Freda Brown and Stella Cornelius about the 1988 Pine Gap protests, where women put their bodies on the line to try to keep Australia nuclear-free. Freda talked about disarmament.[159] Freda had participated in some of the six weeks of marches across Europe to stop disarmament. Freda and Stella had recently returned from international meetings on disarmament. She talks about the 1987 Women's Congress. Lee was at Pine Gap, and she took Conor when she was six months old; Freda told this story in the program.

Change in the air

By 1988, Bill's health was failing, and his memory. Talking about it, to his family and others close to him, he suggested to Freda that it wasn't just the effects of old age – he had Alzheimer's disease. Doctors confirmed his diagnosis in January 1989. Everything changed so quickly for Freda and Bill, then, living with his disease. Freda cared for Bill at home for four years.

Because of Bill's health, 1988, then, was the last year that Freda made trips overseas, to Berlin and Moscow, and to the WIDF Council meeting in Sofia. Throughout the next few years, she cancelled one after another of her commitments, retiring from her WIDF presidential role at the end of 1990 to care for Bill. It was a very easy decision for Freda to make, and she didn't miss the travel at all – Bill's health was her first priority. In her retirement, Freda had more time to devote to her own health as well as Bill's; she had recently begun regular yoga practice, and also became a vegetarian, and was still swimming regularly at Bondi Beach, as she had all her life. Soon, though, her own health was at issue: on 28 September 1990, she fell and cracked her ribs.

It was also in 1990 that the film *You Must Remember This: Inside Alzheimer's Disease* was completed, by director Helen Bowden and producer Susan MacKinnon through Vivid Pictures. The award-winning production, in the view of one reviewer 'exquisitely filmed',[160] features 'stories of five ordinary Australians with Alzheimer's' along with medical experts. Bill was one of those 'ordinary Australians', and he and Freda were filmed and interviewed for the production. This section of the production shows Freda and Bill at their beloved Bondi Beach and in their home, along with archival stills. Bill says that the disease 'turns your words upside down, it wrecks your capacity to talk and speak... I know it will eventually kill me.' Freda discusses the painful revelation, by both of them, of Bill's diagnosis, and what it means to them: 'A typewriter was almost part of Bill's physique...now he can't write. It's very painful, traumatic, to see.'

In October 1990, Audrey organised the UAW's Sydney tribute to Freda, who had retired as WIDF president. The incoming president, in 1991, was Fátima Ahmed Ibrahim, an experienced human rights activist and feminist of Sudan. The change of president officially happened at the 1991 Sheffield Congress. On leaving her post as president of WIDF, Freda said, 'History has many lessons and nothing is achieved without a struggle.'[161]

6

Never Retiring: 1991–2009

1990 was the first time for many years that Freda did not attend the World Congress of Women, which was in Sheffield, England, on 31 March–2 April 1991. Marie Muir, the UAW national president (1990–1993), attended from Australia. Jenny Prohaska was a Brisbane member of the UAW. She recalled Freda's work for the WIDF:

> Freda's now retired, but she did terrific work overseas and (in) some very difficult situations... I know she went about, here, there, and everywhere overseas, and it was a good organization... I think she was a bit lonely at times, I think she was in places where, you know, going into a hotel or something by herself in a strange country. She is a very good person and they've still got the WIDF Federation but with all the break up in the countries, the Communist countries and that, where the funding was given mainly, well that's going to have a big impact. But I think it'll keep going and I think it'll survive.[1]

Freda's life in 1991 was vastly different to her constant work and travelling of just a few years ago. Now she devoted her time and energies to the care of Bill. He had occasional respite stays in Strickland Villa, a nursing home at the Randwick hospital. She also attended Alzheimer's support meetings and other community meetings that supported the local population and the ageing population. Freda's health was starting to worsen too.

Later that year, a large group, organised by the UAW, gathered in Sydney to celebrate Freda's contribution to the women's movement. For this event, Audrey noted that her inspiring leadership assisted the organisation considerably in the years when it was not easy to work around progressive and forward-looking causes. Freda's contribution to the International movement for women, for peace and friendship has been dedicated and outstanding. She has been a great leader of the international women's movement and a great internationalist.

Freda enjoyed the celebration very much. She said, though, that although it was a joy to have Lee, her grandchildren and extended family present, 'I only regret Bill was unable to be present. I didn't mention him when I spoke because I would have wept and that would have been inappropriate for such a happy gathering; but he was as always in my heart, standing beside me as he has done for fifty years.'[2] She had always acknowledged Bill's unflagging support. To a Soviet magazine she had said that 'he is my first adviser and help. He shares my views and tries to help me in anything he can.'[3]

25 December 1991 marked the official dissolution of the Soviet Union, with President Gorbachev conceding power, after years of increasing chaos there and in Eastern Europe. It was fitting that Freda retired from her work with the Soviet world at the time of this most significant political development in world politics.

Bill died on 23 July 1992 at Phillip House, a nursing home at 321 Bronte Road, Waverley, after four years with Alzheimer's disease. His funeral was on 28 July 1992 at 10.40 at John Keeler Funeral home, 55 Enmore Road, Newtown, and he was cremated. Freda inserted a short notice in the *SMH*:

BROWN, Wilton John. July 23 1992, late of Bondi North. Beloved husband of Freda, father of Lee and grandfather of Rory, Kilty and Conor. Aged 75 years. Sadly missed.

Freda and her family scattered Bill's ashes at Bondi the next day. On 2 August, the family held a celebration of Bill's life at the Bondi Pavilion, where Lee gave a moving speech. The end of Freda and Bill's 50-year relationship affected Freda very much. She reflected that even through the difficult last year's with Alzheimer's disease coming between them, 'we were never silent. I can remember no matter what we faced, we'd walk up and down Bondi Beach solving the problems. Whatever happened we always, you know, what was happening overseas, we always had something to say to each other.'[4]

A couple of years after Bill's death, Freda recalled,

It was terrible to see [his] mind disintegrate, you know, it really was a very, very terrible period. So I don't know what to say about it. It was hard. It was difficult for the whole family. And it has affected my health so much that I feel, he's been dead two years now, even now it's very hard. For instance, in the last year [of Bill's life] I would never have slept more than two hours and very frequently I never slept at all. And that's one of the most terrible things that carers go through. Because he'd go to sleep quite early, but then he'd wake up. And all the time he'd come to you to be reassured, didn't he? He wanted to be reassured all the time, because obviously they don't know where they are. Suddenly they're not sure where they are, what's happened to them, it's really a terrible complaint. It's rather amusing I guess.

In the earlier stages [of his decline], we used to go out for trips and this day we went to the opera [house], 'Merry Widow' was on, and Bill liked that. And so he said 'I want to go to the toilet.' So in he goes to the toilet, and comes out – you can imagine the Opera House, he comes out and he's got his trousers folded over his arm, walks up to me in the middle of it and I said 'What's the matter, Bill?' He said 'Why, what's the problem? You said to go?' I said 'Bill, go back in there and put your trousers on.' He said 'Right-o, if you told me to do it, you told me to go in there and take them off, I've taken them off, now you're telling me – right-o if you tell me…' Because people said he was like that. Many of his qualities remained, didn't they? And so he'd always say to me 'Right-o if you say to do it, you're the boss. If you say I'll do it. But there are two sides to all questions and you want to realise that.' He'd often say that to me.

My valuable wrinkles

After Bill's death, Freda continued her activities with Alzheimer's disease support groups, as well as various seniors' organisations. In

1994, a Seniors Media Network Council was created (chaired by well-known Australian media identity Ita Buttrose), and Freda was on the eastern suburbs branch of it. The government's Seniors Media Network was set up to improve the image of older people in the media.[5] Freda said that during this period, after Bill's death,

> I've somehow migrated into this health business. For instance, every year the Premier puts on a forum. It's quite a good thing. It's on the United Nations Day for the Elderly, at the beginning of October. And it's in town at one of the big hotels. It's a very big gathering, I suppose about 700 or more. Well I'm on this committee to organise it, which I think is worthwhile, because there, older people get the opportunity to get up and put a point of view. And they have got through a number of their ideas to the government. So I think that's worthwhile. And then I'm on this help for older people group that I was at this morning.

The work that Freda was doing with these community groups, closer to home, helped in the transition after Bill's death. After she had recovered some of her inner peace, her smile returned – once again, after so many years, she had time to spend with her family, and this brought joy to her.

It was during 1994 that Anne Deveson published her book *Coming of Age*, a series of interviews with older prominent Australians. In her chapter, called 'Freda Brown: My Valuable Wrinkles', Freda said,

> I have my own personal campaign at the moment, and that is to change the image of 'old'. I get so sad when old people say, 'I'm not old'. I say, 'You are old, I'm old, and there is nothing wrong with being old.' In pre-literate society I doubt if people would have denied being old. Elders were respected for the value of their learning and knowledge. Today, people are afraid of being old, but you shouldn't be afraid. Look how much money is spent on the collagen or whatever they pump into you, so you won't have wrinkles. I say to my grandchildren, 'See my wrinkles, I've earned every one of them. And those grey hairs, I've earned every one of them. You haven't got them, have you? You haven't earned them yet; you've got to work hard before you'll have those very valuable wrinkles and grey hair!' That may sound a bit silly, but I just feel that you've got to get across the

idea that there is nothing to be ashamed of. All right, so you creak. And there are certain complaints that come with age. So, there were certain complaints that came with childhood. It's another period, and people need to see that. As far as I'm concerned, I don't know that I am any wiser; but I'm more tolerant, and I think that's important.

I do yoga twice a week. I swim every day. I walk. I'm also a vegetarian, and I don't drink. While I don't want people to give up the joys of youth, I do think you ought to prepare a bit for getting old. Just like you should save for being old, save your health as well. Enjoy yourself, but don't destroy your body.

Now I live my life from day to day. I don't plan very far ahead. I get pleasure from my daughter and my grandchildren, and out of simple things like swimming and walking. And I still work in some organisations.

...something we are doing here in the senior media network. It will be interesting to see how it goes. We go to schools and talk to the students. We suggest to the kids that they bring some photos of their grandparents or old friends – photos of when they were children, when they were adolescent, when they were working, or in the army or what you will, and now they are old. Then we will talk to the children about what it is like being old, and ask them to draw an old person, which the council has agreed to display.

I mentioned this Alzheimer's committee I am on, which has mostly professionals – doctors, social workers, etc. – and at times I have felt that they are patronising. I was there to represent the elderly, but I never felt I· was part of it. So I resigned. I had experience that was valuable, and I should have stayed and found the way to express it!

In 1994, Frank Heimans and Robin Hughes conducted a series of interviews with Freda for an episode of *Australian Biography*, when Freda was 75. It first screened on 15 November 1996.

That year a photographic exhibition was held at the Sydney Opera House. *Images of Our Elders* was presented in Seniors Week, and was organised through the Hammond Care Group. The lovely photo of Freda cross-legged on Bondi Beach was included in the exhibition. It was taken by Belinda Pratten, a photographer with the *Australian Financial Review*.

The lure of political protest never left Freda. In 1995, the NSW Roads and Traffic Authority (RTA) began plans to sell off land on Erskineville Road for high-rise development. This included the site of Freda's family home; the house itself was demolished in the 1960s, and the resulting open space was being used for community activity. The local community protested against the potential loss of open land in the inner-city suburb, and in support, the CFMEU placed a Green Ban on the site, prohibiting construction work. Because of this green ban and the radical protest of local residents, the RTA received no offers at the auction it held for the site.[6] Green Bans Park, opened in 1998, is now a testament to local action. Freda was involved, as her granddaughter Kilty recalls:

> In the 1990s and early 2000s Nana and Uncle Rae spent a lot of time together. Some of their favourite outings were to Erskineville where they would walk around the streets where they use to live and play. Another favourite was taking ferry trips up the Parramatta River and to Manly.
>
> On one of their visits to Erskineville we came across a street stall with people campaigning for a park on Erskineville Road. The locals told Nana and Uncle Rae that the following Saturday there was be a rally and they asked if Nana would like to come along and tell them what life was like when the Lewis family lived there. The Lewis family home by now had been demolished but the location was significant as this was part of the area that locals wanted to turn into a park.
>
> Any rate we turned up the following weekend. The rally was on and the MC asked Nana to speak. This was Nana as I imagine she was as a young woman. She gave a stirring, impassioned, fantastic speech. I remember some of the locals expressing amazement. They thought they had invited an old lady to chat with them and they got a fiery speaker who inspired the crowd.[7]

Egging on the young people

Even at the age of 78, Freda was still coming to political protests. A 1997 rally, at Sydney police headquarters, was against the arming of police and their murder of Roni Levi at Bondi Beach, was led by 17 year-old Kilty, Freda's granddaughter, who was then part of the Justice Action group. Freda said, 'I am absolutely appalled that such a thing could happen at Bondi. I am just concerned that there are too many guns in society. I don't want what happened in Tasmania happening here.'[8] A little later, Kilty's group, Justice Action, re-enacted the shooting of Levi. It broadcast within *Riots of Passage*, an ABC documentary program.[9] The documentary follows Kilty's work in the Justice Action group; in a few scenes, Lee and Freda support Kilty, at Bondi and at Sydney police headquarters. Later, Michael Egan described Lee and Freda 'egging on the young people' in the NSW parliament – which they clearly do not do in the film.[10]

In 1999, Lee became a Greens member in the Legislative Council of the New South Wales parliament. Freda was always very proud of Lee's achievements, each generation helping the next. Lee acknowledges that both her parents 'had considerable influence on the development of my overall political consciousness and my feminism in particular'.[11]

On IWD in 2004, Freda was awarded for her anti-apartheid work by the South African government in a ceremony in Johannesburg to mark the 10th anniversary of the end of apartheid.[12] Kilty travelled to South Africa with her brother Rory and her six-month-old son Jack to accept the honour on behalf of her Nana. At Pretoria they met Gertrude Shope, an ANC leader who had worked with Freda. The next day they went to Freedom Park for the celebrations. There, as the only white faces in the crowd, Kilty, Rory and Jack watched the South African president, Thabo Mbeki, open the park.

> Rory and I had a privilege to meet people who Nana told us about when she returned from her many trips. These people had inspired my life from afar when I was much younger. Now I was so proud to represent Nana in the company of these wonderful people.[13] Kilty said to me 'when I went to Africa, that's a long time since Nanna had been active', but many people remembered her with the esteem she was held. When we went to South Africa she didn't want us to go and she thought it was unnecessary that she'd be getting the award

and she was so worried the whole time we were gone because Nana worried a lot.

Senator Kerry Nettle noted the award in the Senate the next day.[14] Nettle recalled,

She also played a critical role in assisting many ANC women to travel from Africa to Europe, America and Australia to inform the world of the horrors perpetrated by the apartheid regime. In association with Gertrude Shope, former head of the ANC women's section, Freda arranged for South African women to participate in international women's conferences in Copenhagen, Mexico City, Nairobi and Moscow. The South African women who undertook this work did so at great personal risk. One of the women Freda worked with was Dulcie September, a former Cape Town teacher and ANC representative in Europe. In 1988 she was murdered in Paris. This was not an isolated incident. In just one year, 1985, 1,200 South Africans were killed for their opposition to the ruling regime and 6,000 were detained.

Kilty talked about Freda's last years:

Nana in her eighties was slowing down, but kept herself busy in her own way. She had her routine. She would often say she was pottering around. To me it was really old school. I learnt a lot about Nana and about growing old. Nana would go for walks, read the newspaper and books, do a bit of gardening. In the last few years, reading could frustrate her because her eyes were not so good.

Her great love was Bondi Beach and her family. She often walked to Bondi and in her later years, we would drive to the beach and walk along the sand or the promenade. Nana would have a swim and she was still catching waves into her mid-eighties. I didn't know Nana in her prime but at Bondi I could imagine Nana when she was younger. Nana had purpose and she was so engaging. We'd be walking along, deep in conversation and someone would recognise Nana and stop to talk. Often Nana did not remember the person but she was still so charming and interested in their lives and issues. Nana could make people feel special and even in her eighties she could still do that. Nana loved being in the water, she loved surfing, she loved looking out across Bondi Beach. She loved a simple life.

In 2008, Freda moved in to live with Lee and her partner Geoff. The following year, Freda fell at home, on 4 May, and she was in hospital for about three weeks, in St Vincent's Hospital. It was a very difficult three weeks. On 17 May 2009, Freda died.[15] She died a couple of weeks short of her 90th birthday, and the year before the 60th anniversary of the UAW, and the year before Australia's first female prime minister, Julia Gillard, took office. Her death certificate lists her 'usual occupation' as 'Political Activist'.

As they had done with Bill and Freda's mother Flo, Lee and the extended family put Freda's ashes into the Pacific Ocean at Bondi Beach. Lee and the family organised a celebration of Freda's life at Bondi Pavilion on 14 June. It was a big event; Kerry Nettle was the MC. Amongst the many people and organisations that sent their condolences was the Waverley Council.[16] The CPA's Central Committee described her as 'a woman of integrity, humanity and commitment, honest, dedicated and courageous', 'a true internationalist in words and deeds'.[17]

After Freda's death, Lee and the family received many letters of tribute from friends and colleagues in Australia and around the world. Newcastle CPA stalwart Vera Deacon remembered,

> I first heard Freda speak in Newcastle, not long after I joined the CPA, just short of my 17th birthday. I have never forgotten the power of her oratory, the passion of her conviction, the searing logic of her words. Her words became deeds.[18]

A world leader

Although hardly credited for her achievements during her life, Freda was a world leader in her field. She always put her actions in the service of her words. She had the courage of her convictions. Freda's story, like other activists, is clearly located in interpersonal networks. She connected herself into a very wide world, with friends, co-workers, and political and professional colleagues across the globe. She always fought for working-class aims, and for political and economic justice, especially for women and children. With her lifelong trait of the revolutionary burden of hope, she interpreted her own actions, decisions and choices in terms of being part of a collective identity rather than an individual one. In many instances, Freda's achievements, and her lifelong activism, were rendered invisible by her gender, and by her membership of the CPA. Although she is virtually unremembered outside her family, Freda played significant and consistent roles in a number of areas of public life.

Freda travelled from the bottom of society, with infections in her eyes and holes in her shoes in Erskineville, to the top, working alongside world leaders and charismatic political activists. She broke down a lot of barriers for women, that Australian capitalist society had constructed, walking right over them. She went from the stage of the New Theatre to the theatre of the world stage, the WIDF and the international women's and peace movements giving her many platforms to speak up against the injustices of the world. Behind Freda's personal story lies bigger ones, political and cultural: the flowering of alternative political ideas, the changes in colonial situations and the blossoming of globalisation; the changing nature of feminism, the sexual revolution, and the development of women's and children's rights.

Freda's ambitions were never repressed. She was incredibly fortunate in this, and it made her so different to many other Australian women of her age and class. She was never told that she was unable to achieve her aims; she also gave herself opportunities to do so many things that many other Australian women didn't get to experience. She was also incredibly resilient, always swimming against the tide of public opinion.

Her key value was fairness, across gender, class, nationality and culture. This value of Freda's, in particular her high ambitions and achievements to see fairness prevail, is why I admire her so highly. She never wanted fame, but she always wanted to fight for what she believed in.

Although she is virtually unremembered outside her family (apart from some virulent right-wing Australians' attacks on her daughter), Freda played significant and consistent roles in a number of areas of public life. Her entry in the *Who's Who of Australian Women* provides a quote from Freda: 'I believe in equal opportunity for women while recognising the difference from men. This can be only achieved in unity with men and eventually in a just society which I believe is Socialism.'[19] Lee wrote that 'Freda lived her life working for a just, peaceful and healthy world. Her passionate and committed approach was the essence of all her endeavours, and they were many.'[20]

In an interview, Anne Deveson asked Freda, 'How would you like to be remembered?' Freda responded,

> It doesn't matter much. You've lived your life; you have passed on. I've not made any enormous contribution to society. For a while, I hope Lee and my grandchildren will think about me with affection. But that doesn't matter, either. You come and go.

Afterword: the Path to Freda's Story – Biography, Memory and Fissures

In order to situate Freda's story, some explanation of my sources is necessary. I first 'met' Freda through watching her 1995 episode of the documentary series *Australian Biography* (SBS 1992–2007). Directed by Frank Heimans, the half-hour program aired on SBS TV in 2000 and then again in 2001, and has been screened in other countries.[1] Along with the edited television program, I obtained the transcripts of the two long interviews conducted for the production, a preliminary interview by Heimans and the on-screen interview by Robin Hughes. Freda Brown's life, as presented (chronologically) in the television program, relates her story through an uncontested representation of her memories, as told by her and her alone. Inevitably, it accords her an exceptional status in using this technique. And also inevitably, there are only a certain number of sub-topics that can be explored in such a short time: Heimans, the producer, 'had to leave out a whole lot of interesting stuff, as you have to when editing a 25-minute program from an interview lasting many hours'.[2] I was fascinated by this woman's achievements, and looked for more information. However, Freda had never found the time, or had the inclination, to write her memoirs, unlike other prominent Australian communists,[3] and although her political career is mentioned in some histories, no detailed biography exists. With the approval of Freda's daughter, Senator Lee Rhiannon, I decided to research Freda's life with a biography as one outcome. Starting with the *Australian Biography* interviews, I undertook the work of unearthing Freda's story in order to better understand this distinctive woman who stood apart from her times.

Throughout her adult life, Freda was used to speaking in public, and so the *Australian Biography* interview procedure was not a new phenomenon to her. She was also used to the narration of history, with her lifelong study of communism. Freda took on many of her achievements in the period before the second wave of feminism, before the concept that 'the personal is political'. When she did the interviews in 1994 and 1995, at the age of 75, the concept of political activity had changed dramatically. She grew up in an era when it was not the 'right thing' to talk about yourself, with modesty a valued personal characteristic and yet in her political work she invested political value in the 'housewife'. However, she'd lived through the second wave of feminism, the collapse of state communism and many other changes in politics and culture. And she undertook the interviews two years after Bill died.

Once I had decided to go ahead with a detailed study, I found many other sources alongside the *Australian Biography* interviews. Interviews with surviving family, friends and colleagues have been a great source for me, as well as existing oral histories and other, shorter published interviews with Freda. Most of these did not go into details about personal lives. Freda guarded her privacy, and was always careful to shield her personal and family life from the public sphere she often moved in. She never offered insights into her personal life in public at length, yet never hid the details if she was asked. She was a typical woman of her time, I believe, in creating a modest public persona. However, she never shunned the spotlight when it came to her causes. Another finding in studying all the interviews of Freda is the uniformity in how she framed pivotal events of her life. Throughout her longer interviews there was a consistency about her stories. Like her unwavering commitment to communism, her sense of her life seems to have been unchanging; there are few contradictions in the telling and retelling of Freda's stories, particularly by Freda herself.

In describing the production of her biography of another Australian activist, Jessie Street, Lenore Coltheart says, 'As in any political biography her work can only be explained in the context of contemporary national and international political events, but with the unofficial activist, the big-picture context tends to sever detailed connections within private lives.'[4] I was, at first, very excited to find that Lee had kept Freda's existing diaries and letters. Her diaries exist from 1967 to 1982, but they contain little personal information. She was not drawn to creative writing, and she gave no space at all to her emotional life in her diaries. They do demonstrate, however, the totality of how activism and family took up Freda's life. There are no detailed recollections of events, and no space for emotions. The archive of letters from Freda begin in 1967, and runs to 1988. These provided me with more detail into her travels and work, and some indication of how she saw the world and her place in it, along with rich evidence of her family life, and show how much she missed them when she was away. Within my research findings, they represent her most autobiographical moments.

Other literature and sources are, of course, vital. The papers of the CPA pointed to the wide range of Freda's work as a functionary, and include many of her speeches and reports. They indicate the close and generally supportive relationship that the Party had with the UAW in its early decades. At the 1971 split, when her husband Bill was expelled, Freda, along with a number of other pro-Moscow members, resigned to form the Socialist Party of Australia. The memoirs and memories of other party members of that era have also been sources for me, along with broader works focusing on the CPA.[5]

Much of Freda's political career was spent with the UAW and the history of this organisation has been vital.[6] The UAW archive in the Noel Butlin Archives Centre was also an important source. Firstly there is the great record-keeping of the women of the UAW, particularly Audrey McDonald, who has been an assiduous archivist and most generous with her papers and memories in interviews with me. And there are the records within the union's journals, the *UAW Newsheet* and *Our Women*. Freda wrote a regular column, and reported back on her work overseas. She was always keen to keep in touch with ordinary members, as some of my interviews show as well.

In order to write a biography of Freda that was able to encompass her later years of international work, I went looking for archives of WIDF. What I found, in what is ostensibly the main WIDF archive at the Institute of Social History in Amsterdam, was a wealth of printed programs and official documents, but no minutes of meetings or more personal papers. This is an issue that has been investigated by leading WIDF authority Francisca de Haan, who like me is concerned with the 'overwhelming silence' about the federation in most English-language scholarship about transnational women's movements.[7] I tried to gain access to, or even learn the whereabouts of, documents from the Cold War era, but like Francisca I came up against walls of silence: substantial parts of the WIDF archive either have been destroyed or are protected against researchers, due to censorship of communism in Europe and elsewhere.

Freda's file held by the Australian Security Intelligence Organisation (ASIO) comprises 38 volumes, tens of thousands of pages of documents, photographs, and film footage. Her ASIO file is one of the most extensive of all Australian communists; it opens in 1943 and runs until 1979. The ASIO director-general wrote to his London counterpart in 1964 that Freda 'has an extensive and adverse security record'.[8] Firstly there are the CPA, UAW and WIDF publications that provide criss-crossing references to those organisations. Then there are the surveillance records and photographs. Operatives spent a lot of time working alongside Freda in the UAW and the CPA; they went to her classes and attended meetings with her, including at her home. They made copies of her speeches, letters and notes, and intercepted her phone calls both at home and her offices. Many of her travel arrangements, flight bookings, visa applications are included. While many of the copied documents are reliable, of course I am aware of the issues with using ASIO reports as sources, and I have proceeded with caution in this area.[9]

By committing herself so totally to her political activism, Freda did not exactly become indifferent to her personal needs or subsume her personal life completely to her work. Her family were always important to her. But, like many communists of her era, she was dedicated to her causes. She did not crave an expensive lifestyle – and if she did, she never got it. She also never made any effort at any historical legacy, besides leaving her diaries and some photographs with her daughter Lee. Perhaps, for Freda, the political was, indeed, the personal in many cases. In writing on this subject, Bosch remarks that 'many women who played a visible role in the public arena in the period between, approximately, 1920 and 1980 – not just in politics, but equally in the academic world, government bodies, or education – erased, as much as possible, all traces of their personal lives to the detriment of their historical legacy'.[10]

The *Australian Biography* interviews are what revealed Freda as a person to me. She was used to speaking in public, and so this interview performance was not a new phenomenon to her. Until the time of those interviews, however, Freda never placed much importance in controlling how she was represented. And she certainly did not leave a singular written record of her life, or took much time, apart from when she was asked, to reflect on her life. In trying to understand how texts like these interviews operate within the sphere of biography, Roberta Micallef writes that 'people have to be understood as members of a variety of webs that sometimes overlap and at other times stand apart. Thus these life writings or first-person texts that are presented as non-fiction are replete with autobiographical traces.'[11] Freda was being interviewed about life events decades earlier, in a time when self-reflection was heightened. She was, presumably, also recalling her life and past injustices in order to compare them to the way things stood in 1994 – much improved in some ways, but with many battles still to be fought.

In the same year as the first *Australian Biography* interview, author and social commentator Anne Deveson interviewed Freda for her book

Coming of Age: Twenty-One Interviews about Growing Older.[12] The year after that, Freda's friend and colleague Barbara Curthoys interviewed her for an upcoming history of the Union of Australian Women. Up to this period, she had been interviewed briefly for newspaper and magazine stories. In 1976, Ruth Distler had interviewed Freda for the WIDF journal *Women of the Whole World*, upon her election to the WIDF presidency.[13] Compared with the 1990s interviews, the details of the stories she tells did not change over time.

'Through biographical narratives, the subject becomes known as someone who is constructed in and through interactions,' writes Kathleen Barry.[14] In my creation of Freda's biography, it has been crucial to understand how Freda crafted her activism through her networks. Like many other politically active women in Australia, she belonged to a number of different networks simultaneously, and these help to account for her activist successes. Her networks were by no means autonomous, cohesive or exclusively female. The importance of these was already quite evident in Freda's early criss-crossing activities with the New Theatre and the CPA through the 1930s, 40s and 50s; the addition of the UAW and, in particular, the WIDF helped to expand her work greatly, to build networks of international connections. It allowed her to tap into existing networks of women's, peace and left-wing organisations in every country through diverse sets of activities, friendships, and collaborations, as well as to build these up and help to establish new ones. The networks of people in these groups were at the core of Freda's activism throughout her life, and allowed and inspired her to mobilise other women to secure better human rights and living standards. They allowed her to connect to these women across borders as well as across areas of concern.[15]

Freda's life story draws on a rich web of stories of the development of women's political agency. Susan Ware, the biographer of American feminist Alice Paul, has noted that 'one of the hallmarks of recent feminist biography has been the foregrounding of the interplay between the personal and the political in constructing narratives of individual women's lives'.[16] As this afterword discusses, women speaking about their own lives is a very different act in the 1990s compared to the 1930s or 1950s. Freda's narration of her life through the *Australian Biography* interviews is partly a product of her present: an older woman, recently widowed, and with her retirement from the world stage, that has revealed previously forgotten memories along with often-retold stories. The request of the television production also undoubtedly prompted a celebration of experiences that may not previously have seemed significant.

Freda's story shows how the masculinist and right-wing tendencies of 20th-century Australian history (non-feminist) have worked to marginalise her and her achievements, to effectively disqualify her from historical memory. She was invisible for the most part of her life, because she was a communist, and because she was a woman. It is wrong to reduce Freda's 'historical invisibility' to the fact that she was a woman: she was definitely on the margins, fighting against the mainstream in most of her battles. Leonie Coltheart has written that 'tracing vectors of influence between people and through organisational networks is every bit as important in what might be called "non-government" political biography, as when the subject was officially a political actor'.[17] Freda's life can be seen as a reflection of some very big changes for Australian women over the course of the 20th century. For her, as was the case for many women, strong beliefs, friendship and networks were at the core of her activism.

Notes

1. Beginnings: 1919–1944

1. 'Greater Sydney: Suburban Mayors Not Enthusiastic'. *SMH*, 29 April 1920, p. 7.

2. Miriam Audet married Maurice Lewis at the Great Synagogue in Sydney on 1 November 1882. They had nine children. Miriam died on 2 August 1940 in Sydney.

3. 'Death of Harold Moore', *Maitland Daily Mercury*, 31 December 1904, p. 5.

4. Metropolitan Superintendent's Office, 'Application for Summons against Ben Lewis', NSW Police Records, 29 November 1918; 'Domain Orators Prosecuted', *SMH*, 19 July 1918, p. 5.

5. IWW Release and Defence Committee. Mr Windeyer's Great Indictment. Sydney, 1918. See also Ian Turner, *Sydney's Burning*. Vol. 33, Sydney, Alpha Books, 1969.

6. Interview with Frank Heimans. 5 December 1994.

7. 'A talk with Freda Brown', *Women of the Whole World*, no. 1, 1976, p. 48.

8. Interview with Robin Hughes, 3 February 1995.

9. Interview with Lisa Milner, 17 February 2011.

10. Interview with Frank Heimans, 5 December 1994; interview with Robin Hughes, 3 February 1995.

11. Interview with Robin Hughes, 3 February 1995.

12. Anne Deveson, 'My Valuable Wrinkles: Freda Brown' in *Coming of Age: Twenty-one interviews about growing older*, Newham, Victoria, Scribe Publications, 1994, p. 60.

13. *SMH*, 2 April 1923, p. 2.

14. Interview with Frank Heimans, 5 December 1994.

15. Grace Schwebel, interviewed by Sue Rosen, 16 July 1995. City of Sydney Oral History Program. http://cdn.sydneyoralhistories.com.au/wp-content/uploads/Schwebel-Grace-South-Sydney.pdf

16. Advertisement, *SMH*, 19 August 1932, p. 2.

17. Anne Deveson, op. cit., p. 61.

18. Interview with Robin Hughes, 3 February 1995.

19. Anne Deveson, op. cit., p. 72.

20. Interview with Frank Heimans, 5 December 1994.

21. For more on the importance of the work of extreme activists in order to achieve more modest aims, see Verity Burgmann, 'Syndicalist and Socialist Anti-Militarism 1911–1918: How the Labour Movement Beat Conscription' in *Fighting against War: Peace Activism in the Twentieth Century*, eds Phillip

Deery and Julie Kimber, ASSLH Conference Melbourne, Leftbank Press, 2015, pp. 55–78.

22. Jane-Anne Lee, 'Demonstrating her Character', *Newcastle Herald*, 14 October 1987, p. 4.

23. Vera Minaeva, 'Action is her Motto', *Soviet Women*, no. 4, April 1980, p. 8.

24. 'International Women's Day: Preparations in Sydney', *SMH*, 21 February 1936, p. 2. See also Joyce Stevens, *A History of International Women's Day in Words and Images*, Marrickville, IWD Press, 1985.

25. Phyllis Johnson, in Joyce Stevens, *Taking the revolution home: work among women in the Communist Party of Australia 1920–1945*, Spinifex Press, 1987, p. 198.

26. Jean Devanny, 'Wide Committee Organising Big Rally for International Women's Day', *Worker's Weekly*, 26 February 1936, p. 4.

27. Interview with Robin Hughes, 3 February 1995.

28. 'A talk with Freda Brown', *Women of the Whole World*, no. 1 1976, p. 48.

29. 'Labour Demonstration: Great Gathering and Procession', *SMH*, 6 June 1932, p. 8.

30. 'Desperate Fighting: Communists and Police', *SMH*, 20 June 1931, p. 13.

31. Interview with Robin Hughes, 3 February 1995.

32. 'Trinity Examinations', *SMH*, 6 May 1931, p. 9.

33. Correspondence with Linda

Radulovitch, Archivist, Sydney Girls High School, 2 April 2015.

34. 'Idealist with the Unions in her Blood', *SMH*, 12 February 1976, p. 17.

35. Phyllis Johnson. 'Our Freda Brown', letter, *Guardian*, no. 1417, 1 July 2009: 10.

36. 'Woman Sign Writer', *Daily Telegraph*, n.d.

37. Anne Deveson, op. cit., p. 61.

38. 'Anti-Nazi Play: Dramatic and Brutal', *SMH*, 2 July 1936, p. 17.

39. 'Banned Play: Man Fined £3', *SMH*, 1 September 1936, p. 9; see also Phillip Deery and Lisa Milner, 'Political Theatre and the State, Melbourne and Sydney, 1936–1953', *History Australia*, 12, 3, December 2015, pp. 113–136.

40. 'Move to Have Ban on Play Lifted', *SMH*, 5 August 1941, p. 6.

41. 'Ban on Play Lifted', *SMH*, 8 August 1941, p. 4.

42. Jean Devanny, letter to Miriam Hampson, MLMSS 6244 Box 232.

43. Anne Deveson, op. cit., p. 62.

44. Interview with Robin Hughes, 3 February 1995.

45. 'Drama of Spanish War', *SMH*, 29 January 1938, p. 6.

46. Colin Chambers, *The Story of Unity Theatre*, Lawrence and Wishart, 1989, p. 73.

47. 'Lion about Literature', *Columbia Daily Spectator* (UK), Volume LIX, no. 127, 29 April 1936, p. 2.

48. Colin Chambers, op. cit., p. 148.

49. 'Bury the Dead', *SMH*, 23 April 1937, p. 5; 'Music and Drama', *SMH*, 18 September 1937, p. 12.

50. 'New Theatre League', *SMH*, 23 April 1938, p. 7.

51. 'New Theatre League', *SMH*, 6 August 1938, p. 11.

52. 'New Theatre League', *SMH*, 24 September 1938, p. 6.

53. *McGraw-Hill Encyclopaedia of World Drama: An International Reference Work in 5 Volumes*, vol. 1, p. 20, New York, McGraw-Hill.

54. For a detailed analysis on this mobile theatre work, see Cathy Brigden and Lisa Milner, 'Radical Theatre Mobility, Unity Theatre, UK, and the New Theatre, Australia', *New Theatre Quarterly*, vol. 31, no. 4, 2015, pp. 328–342.

55. Elizabeth Kenworthy Teather, 'Voluntary organizations as agents in the becoming of place', *The Canadian Geographer*, vol. 41, no. 3, 1997, p. 231.

56. 'Trades Hall established at Wollongong', *Illawarra Mercury*, 20 September 1940, p. 9.

57. 'Lectures', *SMH*, 31 March 1943, p. 3.

58. This was on 20 October 1940.

59. FB ASIO file, Vol 1, 4905, p. 186. Ben Chifley established ASIO on 16 March 1949, and earlier intelligence was added to Freda's ASIO files.

60. FB ASIO file, vol. 5, p. 29.

61. *New Theatre*, New Theatre Constitution, 1936.

62. 'Music and Drama', *SMH*, 5 June 1937, p. 12.

63. Letter, 18 February 1941, NT files, Sydney. Jock Hector was to become a renowned war correspondent; he was in Darwin the week it was bombed in 1942, and was the only journalist to report on the events.

64. 'NTL Players at Jubilee Ball', *Tribune*, 3 May 1940, p. 4.

65. See Craig Johnston, 'The Leading War Party: Communists and World War Two', *Labour History*, no. 39, November 1980, pp. 62–77.

66. Beverly Symons, 'All-out for the people's war: Communist soldiers in the Australian army in the second world war', *Australian Historical Studies*, 26.105, 1995, p. 596.

67. Oriel Gray, *Exit Left: Memoirs of a Scarlet Woman,* Ringwood, Penguin, 1985, p. 35, 47.

68. Oriel Gray, op. cit., p. 51.

69. 'Nation-wide Drive by Police', *Burnie Advocate*, 17 June 1940, p. 5.

70. Interview with Robin Hughes, 3 February 1995.

71. Cited in Paul Herlinger, 'A New Direction for the New?' *Australasian Drama Studies*, 8 (April 1986), p. 102.

72. 'Communist Party Declared Illegal', *Launceston Examiner*, 17 June 1940, p. 1.

73. Interview with Robin Hughes, 3 February 1995.

74. W.M. Hughes, letter to Senator H.S. Fell, Minister of State for Information, 25 July 1941, NAA A467, SF42/149.

75. Freda Brown, letter to CPA, 31 May 1971.

76. Anne Deveson, op. cit., p. 62.

77. Interview with Robin Hughes, 3 February 1995.

78. Ibid.

79. Anne Deveson, op. cit., p. 62.

80. Interview with Robin Hughes, 3 February 1995.

81. Brian Fegan, 'Family history of the Fegans', MSS, p. 29. Cited in Andrew Moore, 'Red devils and white reaction: Jack Fegan and the Workers Defence Corps of the 1930s', *Journal of Australian Studies*, vol. 33, no. 2, 2009, p. 175.

82. 'Simon Bracegirdle', in Wendy Lowenstein, *Weevils in the Flour: an oral record of the 1930s depression in Australia*, Scribe, 1978, p. 199.

83. Fagan's screen credits include *The Overlanders, Eureka Stockade, Captain Thunderbolt, Sons of Matthew* and *Picnic at Hanging Rock*.

84. Interview with Robin Hughes, 3 February 1995.

85. See the work of Phil Griffiths and Joy Damousi, amongst others, in bringing to light the role of women in the CPA.

86. Beverley Symons, op. cit., p. 600.

87. Phil Griffiths, 'Women and the CPA', essay, 1998, n.p.

88. 'Bring Women to the Fore, Says City', *Party Builder*, September 1942, p. 2.

89. Richard Dixon, *A New Deal for Women*, CPA, Sydney 1944, p. 3.

90. 'Big Crowd Expected at ACP Town Hall Rally', *Tribune*, 2 July 1945, p. 7.

91. Betty Reilly, 'Winning the Women', *Communist Review*, May 1948, p. 209.

92. Ray Markey, *In case of oppression: the life and times of the Labor Council of New South Wales*, Sydney, Pluto Press Australia in association with the Lloyd Ross Forum, 1994, p. 294.

93. Freda Lewis, letter, 18 February 1941, New Theatre files, Sydney.

94. Dorothy Hewett, interview with Drusilla Modjeska, in *Writing lives: Conversations between women writers*, ed. Chamberlain, London, Virago Press, 1988, p. 93.

95. Bill's ASIO file, vol. 2, p. 112.

96. 'Action Speaks Louder'. play script, SLNSW, New Theatre archives, MLMSS 6244, box 136.

97. Tony Stephens, 'Rebel with plenty of causes', Freda Brown obituary, *SMH*, 27 May, 2009.

98. 'Mighty Drive for Brown in Coogee', *Tribune*, 17 April 1948, p. 1.

99. Bill's ASIO file, vol. 2, p. 104.

100. Lee Rhiannon, 'Memorial: Celebration of a Life', unpublished ms, 2 August 1992, p. 2.

101. Locksley Shaw, '"Let's Be Offensive" is All That and More', *Radio Times*, 21 August 1943, p. 8. Shaw was happy to review New Theatre productions amongst those of other Melbourne theatres.

102. No bylines were included for this paper. The editorial and main political articles were written by 'Liberty'. Responsibility was taken by H.D. Brett and P. Ree, of 300 King Street Melbourne.

103. *Tribune*, 16 October 1945, p. 8.

104. Bill's army number was NX202488. He had tried to enlist earlier, on 5 August 1940, but was rejected because of his political affiliation and the party's position on the war.

105. W.J. Brown, *The Communist Movement and Australia: An Historical Outline – 1890s to 1980s*, Sydney, Australian Labor Movement History Publications, 1986, p. 130.

106. Jim Cairns interview with Robin Hughes, 22 May 1998, available online at http://www.australianbiography.gov.au/subjects/cairns/interview4.html

107. Amirah Inglis, *The Hammer and the Sickle and the Washing Up: Memories of an Australian Woman Communist*, Melbourne, Hyland House, 1995, p. 140; Ian Turner, *Room for Manoeuvre: Writings on History, Politics, Ideas and Play*, Drummond Publishing, Richmond, 1982, p. 116.

108. Amirah Inglis, op. cit., p. 18.

109. Bill Brown, 'Soldier, Speak!' *Tribune*, 2 August 1945, p. 5.

2. Communism & the Union of Australian Women: 1945–1963

1. 'Miss Lewis to Speak Over 2CK', *The Cessnock Eagle and South Maitland Recorder*, 27 March 1945, p. 3.

2. See Lyn Finch, 'Could "Winnie the War Winner" organise women? Problems of CPA women during World War II', *Hecate*, 10, 1, 1984, pp. 7–27.

3. In Joyce Stevens, *Taking the revolution home: work among women in the Communist Party of Australia 1920–1945*, Spinifex Press, 1987, p. 194.

4. Phyllis Johnson, 'On Freda Brown', *Guardian*, 1 July 2009, p. 10.

5. Amirah Inglis, *The Hammer and the Sickle and the Washing Up: Memories of an Australian Woman Communist*. Melbourne, Hyland House, 1995, p. 16.

6. In Joyce Stevens, op. cit., p. 227.

7. Betty Reilly, 'Winning the Women', *Communist Review*, May 1948, p. 209.

8. Letter from Freda Brown to Sheet Metal Workers Union, 29 December 1943. NBAC E196, 3/15.

9. 'Mighty Drive for Brown in Coogee', *Tribune*, 17 April 1948, p.1.

10. Vera Deacon and Marilla North, 'Vera Deacon: A pen portrait part 1: 1926–1946', *Hecate*, 38, 1/2, 2013, p. 174.

11. *Tribune*, 12 February 1949.

12. 'Communist Election Policy Arouses People's Interest', *Tribune*, 30 November 1949, p. 1.

13. Interview with Frank Heimans, 5 December 1994.

14. 'Build Schools, Homes in Newtown', *Tribune*, 28 March 1947, p. 3.

15. Ibid.

16. 'Voice of the People', *Tribune*, 5 June 1948, p.6.

17. 'Report of Australian Party from August 1st to March 1936', 495–20–7, cited in David McKnight, 'The Comintern's Seventh Congress and the Australian Labor Party', *Journal of Contemporary History*, 32.3, 1997, p. 398.

18. Ernie Thornton, speech, CPA Central Committee Plenum 15–17 February 1946. CPA Papers, State Library of NSW, MLMSS 2389, Box 1.

19. Joy Damousi, *Women Come Rally: Socialism, Communism, and Gender in Australia, 1890–1955*, Oxford University Press, 1994, p. 142.

20. Freda Brown, 'Urgency of the Equal Pay Struggle', *Communist Review*, August 1949, pp. 242–243.

21. Jack Hughes was the person who was to ultimately change the line of party support for the war. Hughes writes, 'I had to deliver the speech in which the Party shifted from opposition to the war, into full support of it; support in every way, from subscribing to War Loans, to joining the forces, to increasing production in the factories, – everything in the war effort, no holds barred. Once you've decided, that's that. But immediate changes like that don't come easy to people. Delivering that speech was, without a doubt, the worst experience I've ever had. I've made a lot of speeches, addressed a lot of rowdy crowds, been toppled off the platform by the New Guard, been under attack at the Domain, and at street corners. But they were nothing, compared to the experience I had making that speech. It wasn't that anyone interjected, just that the meeting was suddenly so cold. I could feel the chill. I started to sweat. There was a swell of disbelief, almost hatred. And when I'd finished, this deadly silence.' Jack Hughes, cited in Nancy Wills, *Shades of Red: Personal and Political Recollections of a Communist to Mark the Occasion of Our Sixtieth Anniversary, 1920–1980*, Communist Arts Group, 1980.

22. 'Three Thousand Cheer ACP Speakers at Great Town Hall Rally', *Tribune*, 29 April, p. 1.

23. 'Digger in Japan Backs Freda Brown's Campaign', *Tribune*, 22 April 1947, p. 1.

24. 'Communists Select 76 Candidates – Open Biggest Election Drive', *Tribune*, 5 February 1949, p. 1.

25. 'Candidates Records', *Tribune*, 5 February 1949, p. 1

26. 'Housewives Demand Cheaper Food', *Tribune*, 3 December 1946, p. 1.

27. 'Communist Party Policy alone Points Path to Peace and Plenty', *Tribune*, 26 October 1949, p. 8.

28. 'Communists' Peace Call', *Tribune*, 9 November 1949, p. 8.

29. 'We Have Policy for Housewives', *Tribune*, 30 November 1949, p. 6.

30. Ian Syson, '"It's My Party and I'll Cry If I Want To": Recent Autobiographical Writings of

Australian Women Communists',
Hecate, 22.2, 1996, pp. 148–9.

31. 'What Women are Doing', *The West Australian*, 17 July 1944, page 3.

32. 'Freda Lewis in Cessnock', *The Cessnock Eagle and South Maitland Recorder*, 7 November 1944, p. 3.

33. 'Freda Lewis on Riverina Tour', *Tribune*, 22 February 1944, p.1; 'Freda Lewis Makes Fine Impression', *Tribune*, 13 March 1945, p.7; 'ACP Policy Backed in Country', *Tribune*, 20 March 1945, p. 7.

34. 'Freda Lewis Speaks at Graving Dock', *Tribune*, 7 August 1945, p. 3.

35. 'Riverina Welcomes Tour by Freda Lewis', *Tribune*, 1 March 1945, p. 8.

36. *Morwell Advertiser*, 18 October 1945, p. 7.

37. 'Freda Lewis Found Unity Demand in Countryside', *Tribune*, 7 September 1944, p. 6.

38. *Tribune*, 13 March 1945, p.

39. 'Freda Lewis Making Tour of Qld', *Tribune*, 5 March 1946, p. 6.

40. FB ASIO file, vol. 1 p. 96.

41. 'Communist May Speak from Boat', *Tribune*, 5 November 1947, p. 8.

42. 'Communist Speaker', *Tribune*, 22 November 1947, p. 1.

43. See 'Fantastic Upset at Communist Meeting', *Cowra Guardian*, 19 March 1948, p. 3.

44. 'Disruptors not Game to Debate', *Tribune*, 24 March 1948, p. 6.

45. NHA Constitution, NBAC Z236/Box 143

46. Barbara Curthoys and Audrey McDonald, *More Than a Hat and Glove Brigade: The Story of the Union of Australian Women*, Sydney, Bookpress, 1996, p. 4.

47. Zora Simic, 'Notes in Search of a Location for Between The Waves of Feminism', *Outskirts: Feminisms Along the Edge*, no. 5, 1999.

48. ASIO, vol. 1, p. 105.

49. Rhoda Bell, Provisional President, NHA, letter, 21 December 1948.

50. 'Police couldn't Gag Protest on Prices', *Tribune*, 19 November 1946, p. 3.

51. Cited in 'Bedlam Follows Sydney Police Clash with Reds', *Morning Bulletin* (Rockhampton), 16 November 1946, p. 1.

52. '556 Tribunes Sold in Successful Canvass at Newtown', *Tribune*, 1 April 1947, p.1.

53. Freda Brown, 'Urgency of the Equal Pay Struggle', *Communist Review*, August 1949, p. 243.

54. Robin Gollan, *Revolutionaries and Reformists*, Canberra, ANU Press, 1975, p. 255.

55. NAA ASIO file, A6122, 1592, p. 11.

56. This ban came into existence by the right wing of the ALP. Betty Reilly, 'Winning the Women', *Communist Review*, May 1948, p. 209.

57. 'The Labor Party: Mrs. Jessie Street Resigns', *Kalgooorlie Miner*, 18 January 1949, p. 3.

58. 'New Women's Organisation', *Tribune*, 19 July 1950, p. 6.

59. Interview with Barbara

Curthoys, 7 October 1994, Barbara Curthoys Collection, University of Newcastle.

60. Freda Brown, 'Women can Play Decisive Role in Changing World', *Tribune*, 30 August 1950, p. 4.

61. Audrey McDonald and Tom McDonald, *Intimate Union: Sharing a Revolutionary Life*, Sydney, Pluto Press, 1998, p. 49.

62. For more on one aspect of networking in Trades Hall, see Rosemary Webb: 'You could go to the Trades Hall and meet organisers: labour precincts and labour women in interwar Sydney', The Past is Before Us, Proceedings of the Ninth National Labour History Conference, The University of Sydney, 30 June–2 July, 2005.

63. Marilyn Lake, *Getting Equal: The history of Australian feminism*, Sydney, Allen & Unwin, 1999, p. 210.

64. Alice Hughes, interview with Teresa Collie, From Lunchroom to Boardroom: an Oral History Project for the Trades & Labor Council, 25 November 1991.

65. These organisations included the World Federation of Democratic Youth, the International Association of Democratic Lawyers, the International Organisation of Journalists, the International Union of Students, the World Federation of Scientific Workers and the World Federation of Teachers Associations.

66. WIDF's consultative status with the United Nation's Economic and Social Council was revoked between 1954 and 1967 on the back of such concerns at the UN.

67. 'Research Experiences: Francisca de Haan. UN History Project. http://unhistoryproject.org/research/research_experiences-haan.html

68. *Australian Communist*, March 1965, p. 39.

69. Lenore Coltheart, 'Citizens of the World: Jessie Street and International Feminism', *Hecate*, 31.1 2005, p. 192.

70. NAA A6122, 1450, p. 116.

71. NAA A6122, 1450, p. 51.

72. Betty Reilly, interviewed by Barbara Curthoys, 22 January 1994, cited in *More than a Hat and Glove Parade*, p. 7.

73. Heimanns interview.

74. Ibid.

75. Joy Damousi, '"Women – Keep Australia Free!" Women Voters and Activists in the 1951 Referendum Campaign', *Australian Historical Studies*, 44.1, 2013, p. 90.

76. John Murphy, *Imagining the fifties: private sentiment and political culture in Menzies' Australia*, Sydney, Pluto Press/UNSW Press, 2000, p. 101.

77. Cited by S.R. Price, letter to the editor, 'Gates Across Roads', *Narromine News and Trangie Advocate*, 19 December 1950, p. 1.

78. 'A Woman's Place', *SMH*, 12 March 1978, p. 79.

79. Audrey McDonald and Tom McDonald, op. cit., p. 118.

80. Heimans final interview.

81. Joy Damousi, op. cit., p. 90.
82. UAW, circular, 31/7/41, NSW UAW files.
83. Heimans final interview.
84. Caroline de Costa, 'A Bloody Business: A Short History of Placenta Praevia', *O&G Magazine* [The Royal Australian and New Zealand College of Obstetricians And Gynaecologists], vol. 8, no. 3 Spring 2006, pp. 36–38.
85. *Australian Biography* interview.
86. W.J. Brown, ed., *The Petrov Conspiracy Unmasked*, Current Books Distributors, 1956.
87. Heimans final interview.
88 ASIO file, vol. 1, p. 102.
89. http://www.wpc–in.org/about–wpc For more on the APC, see Ralph Summy, 'The Australian Peace Council and the Anti-Communist Milieu, 1949–1965', *Peace Movements and Political Cultures*, 1988, pp. 233–64.
90. Phillip Deery and Doug Jordan, 'Fellow Travelling in the Cold War: the Australian Peace Movement', *The Past is Before Us*, Australian Society for the Study of Labour History, 2005, p. 115.
91. John Sendy, *The Communist Party: History, Thoughts and Questions*, Melbourne, CPA History Group, 1979, pp. 27–28.
92. Rachael Calkin, Cracking the Stalinist crust – the impact of 1956 on the Communist Party of Australia, PhD dissertation, Victoria University, 2006, p. 75.
93. W.J. Brown, 'Positive Aspects of the Cult Exposure', *Communist Review*, August 1956, pp. 269–

272; W.J. Brown, '20th Congress Lessons on Criticism', *Communist Review*, September 1956, pp. 301–6.
94. Tom O'Lincoln, *Into the Mainstream: the Decline of Australian Communism*, Carlton, Red Rag Publications, 2009, p. 116.
95. W.J. Brown, '20th Congress Lessons on Criticism', *Communist Review*, September 1956, pp. 301–6.
96. Rachael Calkin, op. cit., p.18.
97. Bill's ASIO file, vol. 2, p. 93.
98. Bob Walsh, '1956, that "Secret Speech", and Reverberations in Sydney', *The Hummer*, vol. 3, no. 10, Winter 2003.
99. Heimans preliminary interview.
100. Freda Brown, Report to Central Committee, State Library of NSW, MLMSS5021, Box 1.
101. Freda Brown, 'Women and Farmers', *Tribune*, 26 September 1956, p. 9.
102. 'Women to Converge on Parliament', *Canberra Times*, 5 August 1958, p. 2.
103. Debbie Knopman, *History of UAW Eastern Suburbs Branch*, Sydney, 1995, p. 2.
104. Loma Thompson interview, 'Lunchroom to boardroom', Oral history project, 16 December 1991.
105. 'Premier Rejects Deputation's "Equal Pay" Claim', *SMH*, 10 May 1957, p. 3.
106. NAA A6122, 1447.
107. ASIO file, vol. 1, p. 8.
108. NAA, UAW ASIO file A6122, 1447, p. 16.

109. Freda Brown, 'Fifty Years in the March to Equality', *Communist Review*, March 1958, p. 118.

110. 'History Conference Breaks Through on Equal Pay', *Tribune*, 26 March 1958, p. 3.

111. Freda Brown, 'Women – a vital Social Force', *Tribune*, 9 April 1958, p. 9.

112. Freda Brown, 'Fifty Years on the March for Equality', *Our Women*, March 1958.

113. 'Freda Brown to Speak in Tasmania', *Tribune*, 7 September 1960, np.

114. 'This is Communism's Decade', *Guardian*, 11 February 1960.

115. This appeared on 11 August 1959.

116. Bill Brown's ASIO file, vol. 3, p. 25.

117. The poem was published in the *Tribune*, 4 February 1959.

118. Freda Brown, letter to Bill and Lee, 1 June 1969.

119. Freda Brown, 'Mrs Brown Goes to Moscow', *Our Women*, March–May 1961, p. 20.

120. 'Moscow's Media Benefits Impress Australian Patient', *Tribune*, 24 February 1960.

121. Bill Brown, 'Return from Tomorrow, *Tribune*, 19 January 1960.

122. Freda Brown, 'Mrs Brown Goes to Moscow', *Our Women*, March–May 1961, p. 21.

123. Bill's ASIO file, vol. 4, p. 48; *Official Year Book of the Commonwealth of Australia* No. 33, Australian Commonwealth Bureau of Census and Statistics.

124. NAA A6122, 4906, p. 94.

125. Freda Brown, 'Work Amongst Women', *Communist Review*, no. 236, August 1961, p. 341.

126. ASIO, vol. 2. p. 39.

127. NAA A6122/ 1449.

128. NAA A6122, 1450, p. 91.

129. NAA A6122/1451.

130. NAA A6122/1453.

131. NAA A6122, 1452.

132. Freda Brown, 'Color, Taste, Glamor in Soviet Fashions', *Tribune*, c. 1959.

133. Audrey McDonald and Tom McDonald, *Intimate Union: Sharing a Revolutionary Life*, Sydney, Pluto Press, 1998, p. 114.

134. Audrey McDonald, interview with Lisa Milner, 7 November 2012.

135. Audrey McDonald and Tom McDonald, op. cit., pp. 142–3.

136. 29 August. NAA A6122, 1453.

137. Barbara Curthoys interview.

138. Ibid.

139. Cheryl Griffin, A biography of Doris McRae, 1893–1988, PhD dissertation, University of Melbourne, 2005, pp. 251–252.

140. NAA A6122, vol. 5, p. 137.

141. For details of this visit see her ASIO file, vol. 4, p. 101.

142. UAW News Sheet, Perth, November 1962, p. 2.

143. Freda's fare was paid for by WIDF, while the CPA covered Bill's expenses.

144. 'Had Vodka with Mr. Khrushchev', *Melbourne Age*, 20 February 1963.

145. 'A Woman Says', *Tribune*, 28 January 1963.

146. 1000 Women Delegates from 80 Countries for Congress', *Guardian*, 21 February 1963. There is also a lovely photo of Freda and the Australian delegates in NBAC Z236/164. See a lovely article and photograph of Freda's visit on ASIO, vol. 4, p. 158. Her ASIO file, vol. 4, pp. 19, 20 has a great report that she gave to the Brisbane UAW on her return.

147. Freda Brown, 'We Say', *Our Women*, anniversary issue, 1963, p. 7.

148. Ibid.

149. Eugenie Cotton, *Pravda*, no. 68 (16389), 17 June 1963, p. 4.

150. The WIDF file in the UAW archives at NBAC (Box 6) provided a selection from delegate June Moore's letters, where she mentions Freda – see photo. Freda's ASIO file (vol. 4, p. 59) lists the whole contingent. There's a photo of her at this conference on p. 35 of Barbara Curthoys and Audrey McDonald, *More Than a Hat and Glove Brigade: The Story of the Union of Australian Women*, Sydney, Bookpress, 1996. There's also a film of this congress: on 12 June 1964 the Waverley UAW screened it at the Clarrie Martin Hall, Newland Street, Bondi Junction.

151. Freda Brown, 'We Say', *Our Women*, September–December, 1963, p. 8.

152. Freda Brown, Report on World Congress of Women to UAW National Committee members, branches, groups etc. NBAC Z236, Box 145, p. 4.

153. CCF Spry, letter to Secretary, Department of Immigration, 2 August 1963, NAA A1209, 1963:6602, p. 22.

154. See, for instance, Response by Central Committee to ECCI XIII Plenum, e.e. Circulars & Statements 1933–1941, CPA collection, Mitchell Library 5021 add-on 1936, Box 5; Isles of the Torres Strait, An Australian Responsibility, CPA, 1947; 18th National Congress, Communist Party of Australia, Draft: – Party Program, Agrarian Program, Constitution, for discussion, 18th Congress of the CPA, April 1958.

155. Freda ASIO file, vol. 4, p. 151.

156. See Yang Yun-Yu, 'The Struggle between two lines at the Moscow World Congress of Women', Foreign Languages Press, 1963.

157. Kapila Khandwala, letter to Freda Bill and Lee Brown, 11 January 1972, p. 3.

158. ASIO file, vol. 5, p. 126.

159. 'Women's Congress Ends with Anti-Chinese Roar', *Japan Times*, 1 July 1963.

160. Yang Yun-Yu, op. cit., 1963, pp. 20 and 60.

161. Freda Brown, letter to National Women's Federation of the People's Republic of China, 7 August 1963. NBAC Z236, Box 145, p. 14.

162. ASIO file, vol. 5, p. 66.

163. Freda Brown, Report on World Congress of Women to UAW National Committee members, branches, groups etc. NBAC Z236, Box 145, page 4.

164. Heimans interview.

165. Heimans final interview.

3. Branching Out: 1964–1969

1. Barbara Curthoys and Audrey McDonald, *More Than a Hat and Glove Brigade: The Story of the Union of Australian Women*, Sydney, Bookpress, 1996, p. 38.

2. For more about Freda's networking, see Rosemary Webb and Lisa Milner, 'Labour biography on screen: the case of Freda Brown', in Melanie Nolan (ed.), *Labour History and its People: Papers from the Twelfth National Labour History Conference*, Australian Society for the Study of Labour History, Canberra Branch, Canberra, 2011, pp. 191–203.

3. Elise Boulding, 'Feminist Inventions in the Art of Peacemaking: A Century Overview', *Peace & Change*, 20.4 1995, pp. 421–422.

4. Her speech is in her ASIO file, vol. 5, pp. 16ff.

5. Norman MacKenzie, *Women in Australia*, Melbourne, Cheshire, 1962, p. 161.

6. 'Equal Pay: Minister Stands Firm', *Canberra Times*, 9 April 1964, p. 3; 'Nation-Wide Stoppage Recommended: ACTU Equal Pay Conference', *Canberra Times*, 10 April 1964, p. 3.

7. *Dirty Secrets: Our ASIO Files*, Sydney, ed. Meredith Burgmann, Sydney, NewSouth Publishing, 2014, p. 63.

8. Ralph Summy, 'Militancy and the Australian peace movement, 1960–67', *Politics: the journal of the Australasian Political Studies Association*, 5.2 1970, p. 153.

9. ASIO file, vol. 5, p. 66.

10. See Ann Curthoys, *Freedom ride: a freedom rider remembers*, Sydney, Allen & Unwin, 2002.

11. Ann Curthoys provided excerpts from her Freedom Ride diary for publication in the UAW's journal *Our Women*, June–August 1965, p. 35.

12. CPA, Build the Party Campaign meeting, Melbourne, 12 March 1965. ASIO file, vol. 6, p. 88.

13. Bill's ASIO file, vol. 7, p. 14.

14. Freda Brown, 'We Say', *Our Women*, September–December 1964, p. 12.

15. ASIO file, vol. 6, p. 45.

16. Freda Brown, 'We Say', *Our Women*, September–December 1964, p. 12.

17. Personal interview, 7 November 2012.

18. Ibid.

19. Rowan Cahill, 'Joining the Dots: C/58/63', in *Dirty Secrets: Our ASIO Files*, ed. Meredith Burgmann, Sydney, NewSouth Publishing, 2014, p. 161.

20. Lee Rhiannon, Legislative Council, Walsh Bay Development (Special Provisions), Bill Hansard. 26 May 1999, extract. accessed online 2 August 2011, at http://www.parliament.nsw.gov.au/prod/parlment/members.nsf/0/ 32b725a7516e9802ca256 be2002535a5 /$FILE/ ATTK2SYV/Rhiannon.pdf

21. 'Three Held in Vietnam

Demonstration', *SMH*, 3 May 1965, p. 18. Mundey recalls this as the first time he was arrested in http://www.australianbiography.gov.au/subjects/mundey/interview4.html

22. Bill's ASIO file, vol. 8, p. 130.

23. Bill's ASIO file, vol. 8, p. 131.

24. Bill's ASIO file, vol. 7, p. 22.

25. See Esther Newill, 'American Voice', *Our Women*, June–August 1965, p. 29.

26. 'We Say', *Our Women*, March–May 1965, p. 12.

27. 'Island Prison Visit by Mrs Ambatielos', *Glasgow Herald*, 31 July 1963, p. 7. See also 'Two Ambassadors for a Democratic Greece', *Our Women*, June–August 1970, p. 30.

28. See Mick Tsounis, 'The Greek Left in Australia', *Australian Left Review*, March 1971, pp. 53–60; Con Allimonos, 'Greek Communist Activity in Melbourne: A Brief History', *Labour History*, 2004, pp. 137–155.

29. '20th Anniversary – WIDF', WA UAW Newsletter, August 1965.

30. 'We Say', *Our Women*, March–May 1965, p. 12.

31. UAW Newssheet for March 1965 relates her slide night in NBAC Z236/125.

32. 'The Veil is Being Lifted', *Australian*, 6 June 1965, p. 12.

33. UAW Newssheet, no. 8, Sept 1965, p. 5.

34. Herbert Roth, 'Moscow, Peking and N.Z. communists', *Politics*, 1969, vol. 4, no. 2, p. 181.

35. UAW Newssheet, October 1965, no. 9, p. 7.

36. NBAC UAW file, box 1.

37. 'Paris Communist Councillors Get Things Done', *Tribune*, 1 December 1965, p. 9.

38. NBAC UAW file, box 1.

39. Freda Brown, 'Catholics and Communists must Work for Peace', *Tribune*, 8 December 1965.

40. 'Paris Communist Councillors Get Things Done', *Tribune*, 1 December 1965, p. 9.

41. ASIO file, vol. 7, p. 20.

42. 'World Talks on Children', *The West Australian*, 17 November 1965, p. 27.

43. See Gisela Notz, 'Klara Marie Fassbinder (1890–1974) and Women's Peace Activities in the 1950s and 1960s', *Journal of Women's History*, 2001, 13, 3, pp. 98–122.

44. NAA ASIO file, vol. 8, p. 48.

45. UAW Newssheet, September 1966, no. 8, p. 7.

46. ASIO file, vol. 9, p. 82

47. See Roth, Herbert. 'Moscow, Peking and NZ communists', *Politics*, 4.2, 1969, p. 181.

48. NAA ASIO file, vol. 8, p. 27.

49. Minutes of National Executive, NSW State Executive and Trade Unions Women's Committee, 25 June 1966, NBAC Z236, box 151.

50. A photograph of the three WIDF delegates to Cuba accompanies Freda Brown, 'Island in the Sun', *Our Women*, October–December 1966, p. 9.

51. NAA ASIO file, vol. 9, p. 51.

52. Heimans final interview.

53. Freda Brown, 'Island in the Sun', *Our Women*, October–December 1966, pp. 8–9. Back in Australia, on 17 August she gave a UAW talk about her visit 'and her impressions on the life of women in Cuba today'.

54. NAA ASIO file, vol. 8, p. 14.

55. Freda Brown, letter to Robert Menzies, 10 August 1966, NAA ASIO file, vol. 8, p. 19.

56. Freda Brown, 'Voices of Women at the United Nations: Seminar on Disarmament', *Women of the Whole World*, NBAC Z236 Box 151 p. 47.

57. Her ASIO file, vol. 9 p. 86.

58. 'Holt punched, car attacked, at night rally', *SMH*, 24 November 1966, p. 1.

59. Freda Brown, 'Federal Election Results', UAW Newssheet, no. 11, December 1966, p. 2.

60. Adrienne Parr's notes on http://aso.gov.au/titles/tv/australian-visit/clip2/

61. 'New York and Sydney Crowds Protest against Vietnam War', *SMH*, 17 April 1967, p. 3; 'Orderly March Held over Vietnam War', *SMH*, 17 April 1967, p. 5.

62. Audrey McDonald and Tom McDonald, *Intimate Union: Sharing a Revolutionary Life*, Sydney, Pluto Press, 1998, p. 137.

63. Audrey McDonald and Tom McDonald, op. cit., p. 139.

64. Audrey McDonald and Tom McDonald, op. cit., pp. 136–137.

65. Alice Hughes, 'Women in Australian Society', 21st National Congress, CPA, State Library of NSW, MLMSS5021, Box 1.

66. 'Spock May Visit Australia', *Tribune*, 16 August 1967. p.5.

67. Freda Brown, 'A World Wide Protest CANNOT be Silenced', *Our Women*, September–December 1967, p. 25. Also see the report from this conference at http://www.thekingcenter.org/archive/document/reports-stockholm-world-conference-vietnam

68. See Melanie Ilic, 'Soviet women, cultural exchange and the Women's International Democratic Federation', in *Reassessing Cold War Europe*, eds Sari Autio-Sarasmo and Katalin Miklóssy, Milton Park, Routledge, 2011; Celia Donert, 'Whose Utopia? Gender, Ideology, and Human Rights at the World Congress of Women in East Berlin 1975', in *The Breakthrough: Human Rights in the 1970s*, eds Jan Eckel and Samuel Moyn, Philadelphia, Pennsylvania University of Pennsylvania Press, 2014.

69. See 'Soviet Propaganda Organisations: a Survey', Background Brief, Foreign and Commonwealth Office, UK Government, April 1989; 'California Committee on Un-American Activities, Report, 1948, pp. 228–232); P.G. Gittins, 'Communist Subversive Activities in Asia and the Pacific', *Australian Army Journal*, no. 140, January 1961, pp. 30–41.

70. Deborah Stienstra, *Women's*

movements and international organizations, New York, St Martin's Press, 1994, p. 87.

71. Freda Brown, 'Eugenie Cotton: Mother, Teacher, World Citizen', *Our Women*, September–December 1967, p. 24.

72. 'Letter from Freda', 21 June 1967, ASIO file, vol. 10, p. 40.

73. When Lee was later travelling in India, she stayed with Kapila at her house in Santa Cruz in Bombay in 1970 and 1971.

74. 'Their Voice can be Decisive', *Our Women*, March–May 1968, pp. 16–17.

75. Freda Brown, letter to Bill Brown, 20 October 1967.

76. NAA ASIO file, vol. 11, p. 17.

77. NAA ASIO file, vol. 13, p. 83.

78. Bill's ASIO file, vol. 14, p. 56. Also see Mark and Laurie Aaron's version of Bill's actions during October 1968, in Mark Aarons, *The Family File*, pp. 232–3.

79. Jon Puccini, 'More than an Abstract Principle: Reimagining rights in the CPA, 1956–1971', *Journal of Australian Studies*, 39, 2, 2015, p .213.

80. W.J. Brown, 'Party Organisation and Methods of Leadership', *Communist Review*, 282 (July 1965), pp. 195–96.

81. Freda Brown, letter to the Soviet Women's Committee, 26 August 1968, cited in Barbara Curthoys and Audrey McDonald, *More Than a Hat and Glove Brigade: The Story of the Union of Australian Women*, Sydney, Bookpress, 1996, p. 99.

82. UAW National Minutes 1968, NBAC Z236/163.

83. NAA ASIO file, vol. 11, p. 26.

84. NAA ASIO file, vol. 12, p. 99.

85. Lee Rhiannon, '"Old Sisters", and a New Future', in *Taking a Stand: Women in Politics and Society*, ed. Jocelynne A. Scutt, Melbourne, Artemis, 1994, p. 97.

86. NAA ASIO file, vol. 12, p. 48.

87. Audrey McDonald and Tom McDonald, *Intimate Union: Sharing a Revolutionary Life*, Sydney, Pluto Press, 1998, p. 146–7. For another reference to the 'Lady Anglers', see John Percy, *A History of the Democratic Socialist Party and Resistance*, Volume 1, Chippendale, Resistance Books, 2005, p. 196.

88. NAA ASIO file, vol. 13, p. 22.

89. Audrey McDonald and Tom McDonald, op. cit., p. 143.

90. Max Ogden, 'Union Education for Social Change', *Australian Left Review*, February–March 1970, p. 67.

91. Bill's ASIO file, vol. 15, p. 9.

92. John Percy, op. cit., p. 196.

93. See Freda's ASIO file, volumes 12–16, on her work in the Vietnam moratorium campaign.

94. Pat Clancy, 'The Case for Equal Pay', *Tribune*, 19 February 1969, p. 5.

95. 'Atlas Club Audience Calls for End to Greek Repression', *Tribune*, 9 March 1969, p. 4; see also NAA ASIO file, vol. 12, p. 70.

96. NAA ASIO file, vol. 13, p. 15.

97. Freda Brown, letter to Deanna Levin, WIDF Berlin, 9 May 1969.

in Jean McLean's ASIO file, vol. 2, p. 162.

98. Bettina Aptheker, *Intimate politics: how I grew up Red, fought for free speech, and became a feminist rebel*, Emeryville, Seal Press, 2006, p. 298.

99. Ibid.

100. Bettina Aptheker, personal communication with the author, 30 October 2014.

101. Bettina Aptheker, op. cit.

102. Freda Brown, letters to Bill and Lee Brown, 17, 20 and 25 June 1969.

103. Freda Brown, letter to Bill and Lee Brown, 25 June 1969.

104. 'Bombshell Jean is back from N. Viet', *SMH*, 11 July 1969.

105. 'A Visit to Hanoi', *Our Women*, September–December 1969, p. 26.

106. Ibid.

107. 'Australian women visit Hanoi', *SMH*, 10 July 1969, p. 3.

108. 'Supplies to North Viet', *Daily Telegraph*, 13 July 1969.

109. 'Troops have "no right" to be in Vietnam: UAW Leader', *Tribune*, 16 July 1969.

110. NAA ASIO File, vol. 14, p 84.

111. NAA ASIO file, vol. 13, p. 40.

112. NAA ASIO file, vol. 13, p. 44.

113. Coverage includes the *Tribune*, 16 July 1969, p. 1, 'A Pineapple of Death'; there' is a photo on the front page of Freda and Jean with a 'pineapple' anti-personnel bomb. Also see 'DRV Taking No Risk on Bombing, says woman visitor', *Tribune*, 30 July 1969 (a copy is in Jean's ASIO file, vol. 2, p. 128–

129, along with other publicity from this trip).

114. Circular to UAW National Committee Members and State Branches, August 1969. NBAC Z236, 163. See also 'Hanoi Makes Trinkets out of US Planes', *Australian*, 12 July 1969.

115. NAA ASIO file, vol. 13, p. 80.

116. Circular to National Committee Members and State Branches, September 1969,. NBAC Z236, 163.

117. NAA ASIO file, vol. 13, p. 47. 'NSW Woman flying money to Hanoi', *WA Daily News*, 5 September 1969.

118. Freda's report on this conference, which she presented to the CPA National Executive on 20 October 1969, is in her ASIO file, vol. 14, p. 119.

119. Read Freda's account of this trip in her article 'North Korea: Eastern Outpost of Socialism', in an unknown newspaper.

120. Freda Brown, 'The Pen, the Camera and the Microphone our Weapons', Sydney Scans, p. 190.

121. Tom Heenan. 'From Traveller to Traitor: *The Life of Wilfred Burchett*, Carlton, Melbourne University Press, 2006, p. 259.

122. Benjamin Young, '"Our Common Struggle against Our Common Enemy": North Korea and the American Radical Left', North Korea International Documentation Project, e-dossier 14, p. 2, online at http://www.wilsoncenter.org/sites/default/files/NKIDP_eDossier_14_North_

Korea_and_the_American_
Radical_Left.pdf

123. 'View from a Typewriter',
National Road Traveller
(Indiana), 24 June 1970, p. 2,
http://www.newspapers.com/
newspage/33417112/

124. UAW News Sheet, December
1969, p. 6.

4. Living in the Seventies: 1970–1974

1. Freda Brown, 'Combatting
Illiteracy', *Our Women*, June–
August 1970, p. 29.

2. Ibid.

3. Circular to States and National
Committee Members of the UAW.
April 1970. See also 'Women's
Group Plans N. Vietnam
Hospital', *West Australian*, 24
February 1970, p. 21.

4. 'Vietnam', no. 2, 1971, NBAC
UAW files, box Z236/6, p. 4.

5. Wendy Bacon, 'A Bacon Family
Affair', *Dirty Secrets: Our ASIO
Files*, ed. Meredith Burgmann,
Sydney, New South Publishing,
2014, p. 258.

6. NAA ASIO file, vol. 14, p. 32.

7. NAA ASIO file, vol. 15. p. 93.

8. NAA ASIO file, vol. 15. p. 101.

9. Fred Wells, 'A third Communist
Party', *Nation*, 11 July 1970, p. 7.
See also NAA ASIO file, vol. 15,
p. 88.

10. in particular, see the *Australian
Financial Review*'s series of articles
throughout March to May.

11. Her report is in her ASIO file,
vol. 15, pp. 55–56.

12. See Greg Mallory's article, 'The

Communist Party of Australia,
1967–1975, and the circumstances
surrounding the formation of the
Socialist Party of Australia, *The
Hummer* 3.7, 2001, pp. 15–33.
See also 'Rebels Likely to Split Red
Party', *SMH*, 18 July 1970.

13. Including Edgar Ross – see 'An
autobiographical sketch'. See the
papers of the 22nd CPA National
Congress, State Library of NSW,
MLMSS 5021, Box 2.

14. Freda Brown, speech, 22nd
National CPA Congress, State
Library of NSW, MLMSS 5021,
Box 2. See also another, slightly
different, version of Freda's speech
as reported in her ASIO file, vol.
15, pp. 56–56.

15. Freda Brown, letter to Carole
Rooke, ASIO file, vol. 15, p. 79.

16. NAA ASIO file, vol. 15, p. 24.

17. NAA ASIO file, vol. 15, p. 18.

18. Marilyn Lake, *Getting Equal:
The history of Australian feminism*,
Sydney, Allen & Unwin, 1999,
p. 7.

19. Minutes, UAW meeting,
Adelaide, 10 May 1970. NAA
ASIO file, vol. 15. p. 96.

20. Margaret Penson, Scarlet
Moons: The Australian Women's
Liberation Movement and the
Communist Party of Australia,
1965–1975, dissertation,
Macquarie University, 1975, pp.
vii and 150.

21. Audrey McDonald and Tom
McDonald, *Intimate Union:
Sharing a Revolutionary Life*,
Sydney, Pluto Press, 1998, pp.
138–9.

22. For more on the planning and effects of the 1970 Moratoriums, see Nick Irving, '"Couldn't we actually try and do this in Australia?": Reading the Vietnam Moratorium in its Global Context', *Fighting against War: Peace Activism in the Twentieth Century*, ed. Phillip Deery and Julie Kimber, ASSLH Conference Melbourne Leftbank Press, 2015, pp. 268–290.

23. John McLeay, speech, House of Reps, Parliamentary Debates, 7 May 1970, p. 1.

24. NBAC Z236/Box 151.

25. 'A Visit to Space City', *Our Women*, March–May 1971, p. 31.

26. Lee Rhiannon, 'Did I meet Hillary Bray on a Russian cruise ship?' 6 February 2012, http://leerhiannon.greensmps.org.au/content/blog/did–i–meet–hillary–bray–russian–cruise–ship

27. http://www.realestate.com.au/property–house–nsw–north+bondi–111715323

28. Heimanns interview.

29. 'CPA Resignations', *Tribune*, 9 June 1971, p. 11.

30. See Greg Mallory, 'The Communist Party of Australia, 1967–1975, and the circumstances surrounding the formation of the Socialist Party of Australia' (edited version of a paper presented to the Brisbane Labour History Association Conference), *The Hummer*, vol. 3, no. 7, Summer 2002, pp. 15–33.

31. 'Seven Hour Sitting in Aarons Case', *Tribune*, 10 March 1971, p. 2. See also NAA ASIO file, vol. 16, p. 48.

32. Bill Brown, letter to CPA CC, 19 December 1970. Papers of Eva and Ted Bacon, UQFL 241, University of Queensland.

33. 'Laurie Aarons Replies to Bill Brown – "for a United, Revolutionary Party"', *Tribune*, 31 March 1971, p. 7.

34. W.J. Brown, *What Happened to the Communist Party of Australia? Policies of the CPA Leadership on Trial*, Socialist Unity Committee, 1971.

35. 'Two Top Women Reds Quit', *SMH*, 020671, p. 2.

36. 'Eight Go from Party', *Tribune*, 14 July 1971, p. 11.

37. NAA ASIO file, vol .17, p. 27.

38. Audrey McDonald and Tom McDonald, op. cit., p. 143.

39. Lee Rhiannon, speech, celebration of Freda's life in 2009.

40. Robin Hughes, Heimans interview.

41. Heimans final interview.

42. Ibid.

43. Kapila Khandwala, letter to Bill and Lee Brown, 8 November 1971, p. 3.

44. Kapila Khandwala, letter to Freda Bill and Lee Brown, 24 June 1971, p. 2.

45. Freda Brown, Report on Visit to Calcutta Refugee Camps and Mukti Bahini Camps, pp. 28–30 1971. See her statement at UAW Scan NBAC Z236 Box 146 p. 22.

46. Kapila Khandwala, letter to Freda Bill and Lee Brown, 20 October 1971, p. 2

47. Kapila Khandwala, letter to Bill and Lee Brown, 15 December 1971, p. 1. Letters from Kapila to the Browns on the developments in Bangladesh, and other topics, continue through to 1977.

48. For more on the split, see Greg Mallory, op. cit.

49. See W. Higgins, 'Reconstructing Australian Communism', *Socialist Register*, 1974, pp. 151–88; Rowan Cahill, 'Security Intelligence and Left Intellectuals: Australia, 1970', *International Gramsci Journal*, 1(1), 2008; Mark Aarons, 'Comment: the Greens and Fundamentalism', *Monthly*, May 2011.

50. Socialist Party of Australia, 'Introducing the Socialist Party of Australia', p. 2. Mitchell Library Communist Party of Australia Collection, MLMSS 5021/58.

51. Ibid.

52. Freda's diary notes that the decision to open the party's bookshop was made on 15 March 1971.

53. Gisele Mesnage, personal communication to the author, 13 February 2014.

54. NAA ASIO file, vol. 22, p. 108.

55. NAA ASIO file, vol. 22, p. 14.

56. Freda and Barbara were critical of Jack McPhillips.

57. NAA ASIO file, vol. 23, p. 66.

58. Freda Brown, letter to Lee Brown, 6 December 1972, p. 1.

59. Janey Stone, 'The radical history of International Women's Day', https://redflag.org.au/article/radical-history-international-women%E2%80%99s-day

60. Barbara Curthoys and Audrey McDonald, *More Than a Hat and Glove Brigade: The Story of the Union of Australian Women*, Sydney, Bookpress, 1996, p. 159.

61. Senator Clyde Cameron, letter to UAW, 18 September 1973. NBAC Z236/Box 87.

62. NBAC Z236/Box 89, p. 26.

63. Gough Whitlam, speech to the inaugural meeting of the National Advisory Committee for IWY, Canberra, 11 September 1974, recorded in Australian Foreign Affairs Record, vol. 45, no. 9, 1974, p. 602.

64. NAA ASIO file, vol. 21, p. 127.

65. Audrey McDonald and Tom McDonald, op. cit., p. 157–8.

66. Romesh Chandra was the President of the International Committee of Solidarity with Cyprus; it was an offshoot of the WPC.

67. Evgenai Kiranova, 'Friends of Bulgaria – Freda Brown – The Bulgarians are Happy People', *Patriotism*, n.d., p. 181.

68. Hilkka Pietilä and Jeanne Vickers, *Making women matter: the role of the United Nations*, London, Zed Books, 1990, p. 73.

69. Hilkka Pietilä, 'Engendering the Global Agenda: A Success Story of Women and the United Nations', Geneva: UN Non-Governmental Liaison Service 13 2002, p. 20.

70. 'Nixon – It's Peace with Honour', *SMH*, 25 January 1973, p. 1.

71. Freda Brown, letter to Lee Brown, 10 January 1973, p. 1.

72. Freda Brown, letter to Lee Brown, 24 January 1973, p. 1.

73. Freda Brown, letter to Lee Brown, 19 May 1975, p. 2.

74. Minutes, The Committee to Plan for 1975, 29 March 1973. NBAC Z236/Box 87, p.36.

75. 'Women ask for Holiday', *Advertiser* (Adelaide), 7 March 1974.

76. Freda Brown, 'How Women of World Marched Into History', *The Modern Unionist*, January–March 1973, pp. 33–34.

77. NAA ASIO file, vol. 25, p. 37.

78. 'Castro accepts invite for Cuban Unions to Come Here', *The Modern Unionist*, April–June 1973, p. 63.

79. 'Freda found Fidel incredibly charming', *Illawarra Mercury*, 28 June 1973; 'Fidel and Freda in Cuba: friendly exchange of Views'. *SMH*, date unknown, 1973.

80. Hortensia de Allende, et al., Plaintiffs, Appellees, v. George P. Shultz, Secretary of State, et al., Defendants, Appellants., 845 F.2d 1111 (1st Cir. 1988), accessed online 7 Feb 2014 at http://federal-circuits.vlex.com/vid/hortensia-allende-george-shultz-secretary-37206878

81. At this time, the World Peace Councillors were elected for each country; and communist Bill Gollan was responsible for Australia.

82. WIDF, 'International Day of Solidarity with the Chilean People, 4 November 1973'. NBAC UAW deposit Z236 Box 6.

83. WIDF, 'Extraordinary Meeting of the WIDF in Solidary with Chile, Berlin, 12–13 October 1973'. NBAC UAW deposit Z236 Box 6.

84. E.G. Whitlam, Hansard, House of Representatives, question, Foreign Intelligence Services in Australia, 4 May 1977.

85. 'Books: noted, received', *Politics*, vol. 8, no. 2, 1973, p. 414.

86. Malcolm Long had interviewed them.

87. NAA ASIO file, vol. 25, p. 17.

88. letter from Audrey McDonald UAW to Elizabeth Reid, Convenor, National Advisory Committee on IWY, 20 September 1974. NBAC Z236/Box 87.

89. This met from 14 January to 1 February.

90. Freda Brown, 'UN Women's Commission in Action', *Women of the Whole World*, 1974, pp 2–3.

91. Freda Brown, 'A Tale of Two Cities', *The Socialist*, April 1974.

92. 'News from the National Committee', UAW News Sheet, March 1974, p. 2.

93. Freda Brown, letter to Bill and Lee Brown, 14 November 1976, p. 1

94. Freda Brown, letter to Lee and Bill, 16 June 1988.

95. 'News from the National Committee', UAW News Sheet, March 1974, p. 2.

96. Letter to Valentina Titova, 13 March 1974.

97. Jadwiga E. Pieper Mooney, 'Fighting fascism and forging new

political activism: the Women's International Democratic Federation (WIDF) in the cold war', in *De-Centering Cold War History: Local and Global Change*, ed. Jadwiga E. Pieper Mooney, Fabio Lanza, London, Routledge, 2012, p. 65.

98. In 1987 John Benson was vice–president of this committee; Ernie Boatswain was secretary.

99. Freda Brown, 'Unity, Co-operation and Action', *Women of the Whole World*, special number, 1975, pp. 8–11.

100. Freda Brown, 'Closing Statement', Report from the Working Group to Establish an International Preparatory Committee for the World Congress for International Women's Year, 1974, p. 5.

101. See Pirkko Kotila, 'Hertta Kuusinen – The "Red Lady of Finland"', *Science & Society*, vol. 70, no. 1, Biography Meets History: Communist Party Lives in International Perspective, January 2006, pp. 46–73.

5. A President on the Move: 1975–1990

1. Freda Brown, UAW, letter to UN Secretary-General, 23 February 1972.

2. UNAA, minutes, UNAA IWY Committee meetingm 6 June 1975: 7. NBAC Z236/Box 7. I have scans on the UAW's presentations of that organisation's preparation and activities for IWY.

3. Marilyn Lake, *Getting equal: the history of Australian feminism*, St Leonards, Allen & Unwin, 1999, p. 255.

4. WIDF, 'Documents and Information, WIDF Council Meeting, Warsaw 20–23 May 1974, p. 3. NBAC Z236/Box 6.

5. UN, Newsletter on the Status of Women, no. 46, June 1974, p. 16. NBAC UAW Deposit, Z236/Box 7.

6. Freda Brown, 'Listen to the Women for a Change: Fifty World Feminists on Equality, Development, Peace', compiled by Kay Camp, Switzerland, WILPF, 1975, p. 10.

7. Cited in UN, Newsletter on the Status of Women, no. 46, June 1974: ii. NBAC UAW Deposit, Z236/ Box 7.

8. Elise Boulding, 'Feminist Inventions in the Art of Peacemaking: A Century Overview', *Peace & Change*, 20.4 1995, p. 424.

9. See Judith P. Zinsser, 'From Mexico to Copenhagen to Nairobi: The United Nations Decade for Women, 1975–1985', *Journal of World History*, 13.1 (2002), pp. 139–168.

10. Freda Brown, letter to Lee Brown, 15 May 1975, p. 3.

11. Freda Brown, letter to Bill and Lee Brown, 18 June 1975, p. 1.

12. Elizabeth Reid, quoted in Ian Hicks, 'Tiny Steps to Liberation', *SMH* 17 August 1975, p. 7.

13. 'Eva Bacon reports on Mexico IWY Meetings', *Tribune*, 19 August 1975.

14. Freda Brown, letter to Bill and Lee Brown, 18 June 1975, p. 1.

15. 'Equal Rights Yet to Come', *Age*, 23 October 1975, p. 10.

16. Ibid.

17. Raluca Maria Popa, 'Translating Cold War Equality Between Women and Men across Cold War Divides: Women Activists from Hungary and Romania and the Creation of International Women's Year', in Shana Penn and Jill Massino, eds, *Gender politics and everyday life in state socialist Eastern and Central Europe*, Palgrave Macmillan, 2009, p. 68.

18. US State Department, 'World Congress of Women in Berlin'. 31 October 1975, http://www.wikileaks.org/plusd/cables/1975BERLIN06642_b.html

19. Freda Brown, UAW National Circular, December 1975, p. 2.

20. Freda Brown, in *Listen to the women for a change: a sixtieth anniversary publication of the Women's International League for Peace and Freedom*, ed. Kay Camp, Genève, WILPF, 1981, pp. 10–11.

21. Heimans final interview.

22. Freda Brown, interview with Barbara Curthoys.

23. Email from Sylvie Jan to the author, 23 April 2012.

24. P. Toms, report. NBAC UAW Z235 box 145.

25. Audrey McDonald and Tom McDonald, *Intimate Union: Sharing a Revolutionary Life*, Sydney, Pluto Press, 1998, pp. 167–8.

26. Francisca de Haan, 'The Women's International Democratic Federation (WIDF): History, Main Agenda, and Contributions, 1945–1991', in Women and Social Movements (WASI) Online Archive, edited by Thomas Dublin and Kathryn Kish Sklar, http://alexanderstreet.com/products/women-and-social-movements-international

27. Cited in Paul Cates, 'Concerning Your Children: The International Year of the Child', *The Projector*, vol. 7, no. 10, October 1978, p. 4.

28. Carolyn Stephenson, 'Feminism, Pacifism, Nationalism, and the United Nations Decade for Women', *Women's Studies International Forum*, 5, 3/4 1982, p. 287.

29. Helen McCarthy, 'The Diplomatic History of Global Women's Rights: The British Foreign Office and International Women's Year, 1975', *Journal of Contemporary History*, first published on 27 April 2015, p. 2.

30. UAW National Circular of January/February 1976. NBAC X236 163.

31. Freda Brown, letter to Lee Brown, 20 February 1976, p. 1.

32. Ibid.; Freda Brown, letter to Bill Brown, 13 March 1976, p. 1.

33. Freda Brown, letter to Bill Brown, 27 April 1976, p. 1.

34. Freda Brown, letter to Lee Brown, 27 February 1976, p. 1.

35. Freda Brown, letter to Bill Brown, 13 March 1976, p. 1.

36. Freda Brown, letter to Lee Brown, 4 October 1976, p. 1.

37. Freda Brown, letter to Bill and Lee Brown, 2 May 1976, p. 1.

38. Freda Brown, letter to Bill Brown, 12 May 1976, p. 1.

39. 'A talk with Freda Brown', *Women of the Whole World*, no. 1 1976, pp. 48–49.

40. Freda Brown, letter to Lee Brown, 27 February 1976, p. 1.

41. WIDF, press release, 'Visit to Angola by Freda Brown', *News In Brief*, no. 7, 1976, p. 1.

42. Freda Brown, letter to Bill Brown, 28 April 1976, p. 1.

43. Freda Brown, letter to Lee Brown, 27 February 1976, p. 1.

44. Freda Brown, letter to Bill Brown, 22 March 1976, p. 1.

45. 'Presentation of Award', *Soviet Woman*, no. 8, 1976.

46. Minutes, UAW National Executive, 11 August 1976. NBAC, UAW papers, Z236, 163.

47. Freda Brown, letter to Delegates of UAW National Conference, 26 August 1976. NBAC Z236, box 151.

48. 'National News', UAW Newsletter, January/February 1977, p. 2.

49. Freda Brown, letter to Bill and Lee Brown, 20 October 1976, p. 1.

50. Clive Rose, *Campaigns Against Western Defence*, Palgrave Macmillan UK, 1986, p. 276.

51. Cited by Irene Slovak, in The Battle for the Rights of the Family: A Report on the International Year of the Child and the International Women's Year, The Angelus Online, May 1979, http://

www.angelusonline.org/index.php?section=articles&subsection=show_article&article_id=223

52. UAW, NBAC Z236/Box 146.

53. *Mike Walsh Show*, 28 March 1978, episode 8040. Also see 'The Dirty Tricks Game', *Australian*, 23 August 1978, p. 7. In this article, reprinted from *US News and World Report*, WIDF is included in 'The Spider Web of Communist Fronts'.

54. 'Our Freda keeps the UN on its toes', *Australian*, 8 March 1978.

55. Sue Molloy and Margaret O'Sullivan, 'A Woman's Place', *Sun Herald*, 12 March 1979, p. 79.

56. Freda Brown, interviewed by Natalya Sarafanova, 7 September 1979. APN press release.

57. Cited by Alex S.G. Maaliw in *1979 International Year of the Child: From Local to Global – The Two Year Campaign for the Welfare of Children*, Manila, Unicef, 2005, p. 6.

58. Alex S.G. Maaliw, op. cit., p. 159.

59. 'Freda Brown awarded Lenin Peace Prize', *The Socialist*, 9 May 1979.

60. 'NSW Lenin Prize', *Age*, 2 May 1979.

61. 'Prize Big Shock to Writer', *Age*, 3 May 1979, p. 4.

62. 'Freda Brown presented with Lenin Peace Prize', *The Socialist*, 26 September 1979.

63. Freda Brown, interviewed by Natalya Sarafanova, 7 September 1979. APN press release.

64. Audrey McDonald and Tom

McDonald, *Intimate Union: Sharing a Revolutionary Life*, Sydney, Pluto Press, 1998, p. 248.

65. Audrey McDonald and Tom McDonald, op. cit., p. 7.

66. NBAC Z236 box 74.

67. The Australian delegation was Anne Gorman, NSW state government director of the IYC secretariat; Keith Suter from the University of Sydney, who was the NSW divisional president, international coordinator of the People's World Assembly; Rob Dobson, executive member of the National Youth Council; and Audrey McDonald, who was the leader of the delegation, the UAW national secretary, member of NSW Women's Advisory Council, NSWIYC Steering Committee and vice-president of the Australian Peace Committee, and a world councillor of WIDF.

68. Freda Brown, interviewed by Natalya Sarafanova, 7 September 1979. APN press release.

69. Heimans final interview.

70. 'Mother–Child Centre Opens in Hanoi at WIDF initiative', *The Socialist*, 5 Dec 1979.

71. Press release. NBAC UAW Z236 box 94.

72. Sylvia Harding, UAW Report on peace, development and happiness for women and children in South East Asia seminar in Hanoi Seminar, 14–15 January 1984', p. 7. NBAC [Z236/38].

73. 'Report, Planning Committee, NGO Activities at the World Conference of the UN Decade for Women', p. 1; http://pdf.usaid. gov/pdf_docs/PNAAX560.pdf

74. Brigitte Triems, email to Lee Rhiannon, 25 May 2009.

75. Vladimir Bukovsky, *The peace movement and the Soviet Union*, Coalition for Peace through security, 1982, p. 33.

76. ASIO file, vol. 32, p. 22.

77. Lisa Pruitt and Marta Vanegas, 'CEDAW and Rural Development: Empowering Women with Law from the Top Down, Activism from the Bottom Up', *Baltimore Law Review*, 41, 2012, p. 263.

78. Leila J. Rupp, 'From Rosie the riveter to the global assembly line: American women on the world stage', *Magazine of History*, vol. 18, no. 4, 2004, p. 55.

79. 'Equality Parley', *Pittsburgh Press*, 3 July 1981, p. 7.

80. Bettina Aptheker, *Intimate politics: how I grew up Red, fought for free speech, and became a feminist rebel*, Emeryville, Seal Press, 2006, p. 298.

81. 'They said before the Congress', UAW press release. NBAC Z236/ Box 89.

82. 'World Congress of Women – a new stage in the struggle', *The Socialist*, 21 October 1981.

83. *World Marxist Review*, no. 12, December 1981. This march was from 22 June to 6 August (Hiroshima Day).

84. Zdenko Antic, 'Yugoslavs Accuse Prague of Distorting World Congress of Women', Radio Free Europe Background Report/305, 3

November 1981, in ASIO file, vol. 32, p. 57.

85. ASIO file, vol. 32, p. 40.

86. 'A Tribute', *The Socialist*, 21 October 1981.

87. Ilse Thiele of WIDF was at this conference; see League Executive Report to the 11th DFD Congress Berlin 1982, Bulletin 1, pp. 7ff.

88. Freda Brown, letter to Lee Brown, 6 March 1982, p. 1.

89. Freda Brown, letter to Lee Brown, 9 March 1982, p. 1.

90. Freda Brown, letter to Lee Brown, 13 March 1982, p. 1.

91. Freda Brown, letter to Bill Brown, 3 March 1982, p. 1.

92. Freda Brown, letter to Lee Brown, 4 October 1976, p. 1.

93. Freda Brown, letter to Lee Brown, 9 March 1982, p. 1.

94. Jane Cadzow, 'How Nicaragua interferes with the Housework', *Australian*, 13 April 1982, p. 3.

95. Freda Brown, 'Building Bridges Between Women', *Australian*, 19 May 1982, p. 8.

96. Freda Brown, letter to Lee Brown, 9 March 1982, p. 1.

97. It was at this WILPF conference that Alva Myrdal, member of WILPF Sweden, was awarded the Nobel Peace Prize for her work with the UN for disarmament.

98. 'Women for Peace', http://www.san.beck.org/GPJ28–WomenforPeace.html

99. Freda Brown, letter to Lee Brown, 9 March 1982, p. 1.

100. Freda Brown, letter to Lee Brown, 13 March 1982, p. 1.

101. Freda Brown, letter to Bill Brown, 12 April 1982, p. 1.

102. Freda Brown, letter to Lee Brown, 10 October 1982, p. 1.

103. ASIO file, vol. 33, p. 15. Also see vol. 34, p. 54.

104. Freda Brown, letter to Lee O'Gorman, 14 February 1983, p. 1.

105. This conference was controversial in that E.P. Thompson, British left historian and one of the founders of END (European Nuclear Disarmament), boycotted it.

106. Lia Gorter, interview with Lisa Milner, 18 September 2012.

107. Freda Brown, letter to Lee O'Gorman, 27 February 1983.

108. Freda had been coming to Africa since 1975; see her speech in the 'Documents of the Afro-Asian Symposium on Social Development of Women', Alexandria, 8–10 March 1975: published on the Occasion of the International Women's Year 1975, pp. 23–48.

109. 'OMA remembers women that represented Angola in international forums', Angola Agency Press, 13 March 2012, http://www.portalangop.co.ao/angola/pt_pt/noticias/sociedade/2012/2/11/OMA-relembramulheres-que-representaram-angolanas-foruns-internacionais,3db969c5-b4b6-41e6-8995-aa216b1c6476.html

110. Freda Brown, interview with Barbara Curthoys, 5 October 1995.

111. Freda Brown, Frank Heimans final interview.

112. Freda Brown, letter to Lee O'Gorman, 13 June 1983.

113. Ibid.

114. Freda Brown, letter to Lee O'Gorman, 14 June 1983.

115. Ibid.

116. Freda Brown, letter to Bill Brown, 15 September 1983.

117. Freda Brown, opening address, Council Meeting of WIDF, 11–14 October 1983.

118. Freda writes about this in 'Women's Anti-War Actions', Fourth Women and Labour Conference: papers, Brisbane, 1984, St Lucia, Organising Committee of the Fourth Women and Labour Conference, 1984, pp. 36–40.

119. 'Freda Brown awarded Clara Zetkin Medal', *Survey*, May 1984, p. 7.

120. Freda Brown, letter to Lee O'Gorman, 10 March 1984.

121. See Lisa Milner, *Fighting Films*, Sydney, Pluto, 2003.

122. Memorial speech from Leon's funeral, 1984.

123. Freda Brown, letter to Lee O'Gorman, 24 May 1984.

124. Freda Brown, letter to Bill Brown, 10 June 1984.

125. Freda Brown, letter to Lee O'Gorman, 8 June 1984.

126. Freda Brown, letter to Bill Brown, 26 September 1983.

127. Freda Brown, 'Women's Anti-War Actions'.

128. See 'Suellen Murray, 'Taking the toys from the boys: Feminism and Australian women's peace activism in the 1980s', *Australian Feminist Studies*, 25.63, 2010, pp. 3–15.

129. Audrey McDonald and Tom McDonald, op. cit., p. 263.

130. Cited in Peter Limb, 'The anti–apartheid movements in Australia and Aotearoa/New Zealand', *The Road to Democracy in South Africa*, 3, 2008, p. 951.

131. Bill Brown, *The Communist Movement and Australia: An Historical Outline, 1890s to 1980s*, Australian Labor Movement History Publications, 1986, p. 257.

132. 'The Association for Communist Unity', *People's Cause*, vol. 2, December 1988, p. 7.

133. Audrey McDonald and Tom McDonald, op. cit., p. 253. The ACU published a journal called *People's Cause* from 1987 to 1993, as well as a theoretical journal *Socialism Today* from 1987 to 1989.

134. Audrey McDonald and Tom McDonald, op. cit., p. 253.

135. 'OMA Secretary General Honoured', *Luanda Jornal De Angola*, 12 March 1985, p. 1.

136. Nelya Ramazanova, 'Forty Years Working for Peace', an interview with Freda Brown, *Forum*, 85, p. 2.

137. UN, questionnaire, NBAC Z236/Box 86.

138. Helen Thomas, 'Australia Abstains in Apartheid Vote at UN Women's Conference', *SMH*, 29 July 1985, p. 6. NBAC Z235/Box 85, p. 3.

139. Jane Sullivan, 'Old Male

Rituals as Women Flex Muscles', *Age*, 13 July 1985, p. 13.

140. Betty Olle, a Report on the UN 'End of Decade' Women's Forum held in Nairobi, Kenya, July 1985. NBAC Z236/Box 84.

141. Lee O'Gorman, letter to Bill Brown and Pat O'Gorman, 15 July 1985.

142. Lee O'Gorman, letter to Bill Brown and Pat O'Gorman, 17 July 1985.

143. Letter of 17 September 1986: 'Yesterday went to WFTU Congress, must say I was impressed by Ernie [Boatswain], he spoke well, seems to be handling the 23-member delegation well, and organised a very good meeting of the delegates of Pacific countries for us to speak about the World Congress.'

144. The Tashkent meeting on 2–6 October 1986 was a regional seminar for women's organisation in Asian and Pacific countries. The topic was Women and Development; Women's Contribution to the Maintenance of Peace' WIDF was there, UNESCO, Janet Mundie, Joan Ross from UAW etc.

145. Lia Gorter, interview with Lisa Milner, 18 September 2012.

146. 'For Peace and Happiness on Earth', *Pravda*, 24 June 1987, p. 1.

147. William Eaton, 'Soviet Women: More Rights – and Toil', *Los Angeles Times*, 24 June 1987.

148. 'Gorbachev Says Women Have Greater Rights', *Los Angeles Times*, 24 June 1987, p. a19.

149. Freda Brown, 'Expectations and Realisations', speech ms, Moscow, November 1987.

150. Cited by Leslie Stevenson, 'Peach Peeler Turned Peace Seeker', *SMH*, July 22, 1987.

151. Ann Crosby, 'Women from 184 Nations Meet in Moscow', *Peace Magazine*, October–November 1987, p. 8.

152. NBAC Z326/95.

153. Yvonne Preston, 'Freda Steals the Limelight', *SMH*, 6 June 1988, p. 8.

154. Freda Brown, letter to Lee O'Gorman, 12 June 1988.

155. See Melanie Ilic, 'Soviet Beauty Contests', in Katalin Miklóssy and Ilic Melanie, eds, *Competition in Socialist Society*, Routledge, 2014, p. 162.

156. Freda was referring to 'Eye of the Beholder', *New York Times*, 26 June 1988.

157. Freda Brown, 'Expectations and Concerns of the International Women's Movement', *International Affairs*, vol. 2, issue 34, 1988, pp. 105–108.

158. Freda Brown. 'Towards the World Assembly for Peace and Life: The Noble Mission of All Women', *World Marxist Review*, no. 26, 1988, pp. 23–27.

159. In 1973, Stella Cornelius had initiated a Peace and Conflict Resolution Program for the UN Association of Australia.

160. Carole-Lynn LeNavenec, 'You Must Remember This: Inside Alzheimer's disease', review, *The Gerontologist*, vol. 38, no. 2, 1998, p. 397.

161. Cited by Ada Donnoa, in 'WIDF', AWMR-Italia Associazione Donne della Regione Mediterranea http://awmr-donneregionemediterranea-italia. blogspot.com.au/p/fdim-widf.html

6. Never Retiring: 1991–2009

1. Jenny Prohaska, interview with Therese Collie, Lunchroom to Boardroom Oral History Project about women in the Labor movement, 21 November 1991.
2. 'Tribute to Freda', *UAW Ink*, December 1991, p. 10.
3. 'The Dream of Freda Brown', Soviet Woman, n.d.
4. Heimans final interview.
5. NSW government funding for this organisation did not continue after 1995.
6. See CFMEU, 'Green Bans'. https://activefolklore.files. wordpress.com/2011/02/ greenbansapril2005.pdf
7. Kilty O'Gorman, personal communication, 2 July 2015.
8. Kate Minogue, 'Trigger unhappy – Hand over your guns – this is a protest', *Daily Telegraph*, 10 July 1997, p. 4.
9. *Riots of Passage* was televised on ABC television at 8 p.m. on Tuesday 30 March 2000.
10. Michael Egan, speaking on the Police Service Disarmament Campaign, NSW Parliament, 1 June 2000, http://www. parliament.nsw.gov.au/prod/ parlment/hansart.nsf/V3Key/ LC20000601009. Another parliamentary criticism was from

Elaine Nile on 30 May: see http:// www.parliament.nsw.gov.au/prod/ parlment/hansart.nsf/V3Key/ LC20000530036
11. Lee Rhiannon, '"Old Sisters", and a New Future', in *Taking a Stand: Women in Politics and Society*, ed. Jocelynne A. Scutt, Melbourne, Artemis, 1994, p. 96.
12. 'Honours for brave Freda', *Northern Territory News*, 14 March 2004, p. 2; 'Veteran Activist Honoured', *Illawarra Mercury*, 6 March 2004, p. 12.
13. Kilty Gorman, 'Freedom wasn't Free', unpublished ms.
14. Kerry Nettle, Senate, Tuesday, 9 March 2004, pp. 21147–9.
15. Tony Stephens, 'Rebel with Plenty of Causes', *SMH*, 27 May 2009.
16. Minutes of the Waverley Council Meeting, Waverley Council Chambers, 19 May 2009.
17. 'Tribute to Comrade Freda Brown', *Guardian*, issue 1415, 17 June 2009.
18. Vera Deacon, letter to Lee Rhiannon, 27 May 2009.
19. Freda Brown entry, *Who's Who of Australian Women*, compiled by Andrea Lofthouse, Methuen, p. 87.
20. Lee Rhiannon, 'Freda Brown (Lewis) 1919–2009', *OWN Matters: Newsletter of the Older Women's Network NSW*, vol. 6, no. 7, August 2009, p. 16.

Afterword

1. For a discussion on this television program and biography, see

Rosemary Webb and Lisa Milner, 'Labour biography on screen: the case of Freda Brown', in Melanie Nolan, ed., *Labour History and its People: Papers from the Twelfth National Labour History Conference, Australian Society for the Study of Labour History*, Canberra Branch, Canberra, 2011, pp. 191–203.

2. Frank Heimans, personal communication with Lisa Milner, 12 May 2011.

3. See Peter Beilharz, 'Elegies of Australian communism', *Australian Historical Studies*, vol. 23, 1989, p. 293.

4. Lenore Coltheart, 'Jessie Street and the New Political Biography', in Nethercote, John, Tracey Arklay, and John Wanna, eds., *Australian Political Lives: Chronicling political careers and administrative histories.* ANU E Press, 2006, p. 79.

5. See, for instance, Joyce Stevens, *Taking the Revolution Home: Work among Women in the Communist Party of Australia 1920–1945*, Melbourne, Sybylla Feminist Press, 1987; Peter Beilharz, 'Elegies of Australian communism', *Australian Historical Studies*, 23.92, 1989, pp. 293–306; Carole Ferrier, 'Constructing and deconstructing Jean Devanny', *Australian Feminist Studies*, 7.16, 1992, pp. 144–157; Joy Damousi, *Women Come Rally: Socialism, Communism, and Gender in Australia, 1890–1955*, Oxford, Oxford University Press, 1994; Ian Syson, '"It's my party and I'll cry if I want to": Recent autobiographical writings of Australian women communists', *Hecate*, 22.2, 1996, p: 144; Stuart Macintyre, *The Reds: the Communist Party of Australia from origins to illegality.* St Leonards, Allen & Unwin, 1999.

6. Barbara Curthoys and Audrey McDonald, *More Than a Hat and Glove Brigade: The Story of the Union of Australian Women*, Sydney, Bookpress, 1996.

7. Francisca De Haan, 'Continuing Cold War paradigms in western historiography of transnational women's organisations: The case of the Women's International Democratic Federation (WIDF)', *Women's History Review*, 19.4, 2010, p. 548. See also Francisca De Haan, 'The Women's International Democratic Federation (WIDF): History, main agenda, and contributions, 1945–1991', in T. Dublin and K.K. Sklar, eds, Women and Social Movements (WASI) (Online Archive), 2013, available at: http://alexanderstreet.com/products/women-and-socialmovements-international

8. ASIO file, CRS A6119, B/3/5, p. 29.

9. For discussions on this topic see Fiona Capp, *Writers Defiled: Security Surveillance of Australian Authors and Intellectuals, 1920–1960*, South Yarra, McPhee Gribble, 1993; Michelle Arrow, *Upstaged: Australian Women Dramatists in the Limelight at Last*, Sydney, Currency Press, 2002;

and Meredith Burgmann, *Dirty Secrets: Our ASIO Files*, Sydney, NewSouth, 2014.

10. Mineke Bosch, 'Gender and the Personal in Political Biography: Observations from a Dutch Perspective', *Journal of Women's History*, 21.4, 2009, p. 28.

11. Roberta Micallef, 'Identities in Motion: Reading Two Ottoman Travel Narratives as Life Writing', *Journal of Women's History*, vol. 25, no. 2, Summer 2013, p. 104.

12. Anne Deveson, 'My Valuable Wrinkles: Freda Brown', in *Coming of Age: Twenty-one interviews about growing older*, Newham, Scribe, 1994.

13. Ruth Distler, 'A Talk with Freda Brown', *Women of the Whole World*, no. 1, 1976, pp. 48–49.

14. Kathleen Barry, 'The new historical syntheses: women's biography', *Journal of Women's History*, vol. 1, no. 3, 1990, p. 76.

15. For more on transnational feminist networks, see, for instance, Ann Taylor Allen, Anne Cova, and June Purvis, 'International Feminisms', *Women's History Review*, 19.4, 2010, pp. 493–501; Valentine M. Moghadam, *Globalizing Women: Transnational Feminist Networks*, Baltimore, Johns Hopkins University Press, 2005; Aili Mari Tripp, 'The evolution of transnational feminisms', in M.M. Ferree, A.M. Tripp, eds., *Global Feminism: Transnational Women's Activism, Organizing, and Human Rights*, New York, New York University Press, 2006, pp. 51–75.

16. Susan Ware, 'The Book I Couldn't Write: Alice Paul and the Challenge of Feminist Biography', *Journal of Women's History*, 24.2, 2012, p. 20.

17. Lenore Coltheart, 'Jessie Street and the New Political Biography', in *Australian Political Lives: Chronicling political careers and administrative histories*, ed. Tracey Arklay, John Nethercote and John Wanna, Canberra, ANU EPress, 2006, available online at http://press.anu.edu.au/anzsog/auspol/mobile_devices/ch12.html

Acknowledgements

Lee Rhiannon
Rae Lewis
Kilty O'Gorman
Rory O'Gorman
Geoff Curthoys & Anne Curthoys
Audrey & Tom McDonald
Heather Goodall & Devleena Ghosh
Frank Heimans
Robin Hughes
Carrolline Rhodes
Gill Chapman
Rebecca Albury
Lyn Collingwood
Francisca de Haan
Karen Bindoff

Southern Cross University
State Library of NSW
National Library of Australia
Noel Butlin Archives Centre,
   Australian National University
Victoria University, Melbourne
National Archives of Australia
National Film and Sound Archive
Jessie Street National Women's
   Library
The New Theatre, Sydney
The Search Foundation
Nambucca Valley Writers Group
Bodleian Library, University of Oxford
International Institute of Social
   History, Amsterdam, Netherlands
Peoples History Museum,
   Manchester
Sydney Girls High School